Cooperative Learning

Cooperative Learning

Integrating Theory and Practice

Robyn M. Gillies
The University of Queensland

SAGE Publications
Los Angeles • London • New Delhi • Singapore

For information:

Sage Publications, Inc.
2455 Teller Road
Thousand Oaks, California 91320
E-mail: order@sagepub.com

Sage Publications Ltd.
1 Oliver's Yard
55 City Road
London EC1Y 1SP
United Kingdom

Sage Publications India Pvt Ltd
B 1/I 1 Mohan Cooperative Industrial Area
Mathura Road, New Delhi 110 044
India

Sage Publications Asia-Pacific Pte Ltd
33 Pekin Street #02-01
Far East Square
Singapore 048763

Printed in the United States of America

Library of Congress Cataloging-in-Publication Data

Gillies, Robyn M., 1949–
Cooperative learning : integrating theory and practice / Robyn M. Gillies.
    p. cm.
Includes bibliographical references and index.
ISBN-13: 978-1-4129-4047-4 (cloth)
ISBN-13: 978-1-4129-4048-1 (pbk.)
    1. Group work in education. I. Title.

LB1032.G55 2007
371.39'5—dc22

2006035649

This book is printed on acid-free paper.

07   08   09   10   10   9   8   7   6   5   4   3   2   1

Acquisitions Editor:	Diane McDaniel
Editorial Assistant:	Ashley Plummer
Production Editor:	Libby Larson
Copy Editor:	Kristin Bergstad
Typesetter:	C&M Digitals (P) Ltd.
Proofreader:	Word Wise Webb
Indexer:	Jeanne Busemeyer
Cover Designer:	Janet Foulger
Marketing Manager:	Nichole Angress

Contents

Acknowledgments | xiii

1. **Cooperative Learning in Schools** | 1

Introduction and Learning Objectives | 1
Case Study 1.1: The Case of Tom | 2
Introducing Cooperative Learning | 4
  Group Task | 6
  Grouping Practices | 6
  Promoting Student Discourse | 7
  Cooperative Learning Pedagogy in the
    Classroom: Teacher's Role | 9
  Effective or Expert Teachers | 9
The Impact of Mandatory Testing on
  Cooperative Learning | 11
  Specific Requirements of the No Child Left
    Behind (NCLB) Act of 2001 | 12
  Why Test? | 12
  What Happened? | 13
  Teachers' Perceptions of Mandatory Testing | 14
  The Case Against Testing | 15
  Is Mandated Testing Working? | 16
The Potential to Transform Schools: Using
  Cooperative Learning Pedagogy | 17
Case Study 1.2: Transforming a School:
  A Principal's Story | 17
  Schoolwide Cooperative Learning | 19

Teachers' Reported Satisfaction With
Cooperative Learning   20
A Comprehensive School Reform Model   22
Structure and Content: Overview of the
Chapters That Follow   23
Chapter Summary   25
Activities   26
Suggestions for Further Reading   27

2. **Key Components in Establishing
Successful Cooperative Groups**   **29**

Introduction and Learning Objectives   29
*Case Study 2.1: An Example of Cooperative
Learning in a First-Grade Classroom*   30
Cooperative Learning   33
Positive Interdependence   33
Types of Interdependence   34
Practical Activity: Ways of
Structuring Positive Interdependence   35
Promotive Interaction   36
Practical Activity: Ways of Promoting Interaction   37
Individual Accountability   39
Practical Activity: Ways of Ensuring
Individual Accountability   39
Interpersonal and Small-Group Skills   41
Practical Activity: Ways of Ensuring That Children
Learn These Interpersonal and Small-Group Skills   42
Group Processing   43
Practical Activity: Ideas for Group Processing   45
How Long Should Students Work in
Cooperative Groups?   47
Bringing It All Together: Understanding the Research   48
Low-Ability Children   49
Affective Development   49
What Is Cooperative Learning?   50
The Role of the Teacher in Establishing Cooperative Learning 51
Chapter Summary   58
Activities   58
Suggestions for Further Reading   59

3. **Teachers' Discourse to**
    Promote Student Thinking and Learning   61

    Introduction and Learning Objectives   61
    Case Study 3.1: Teacher's Dialogue With a
    Small Group of Students   62
    Teachers' Discourse During Whole-Class,
        Small-Group, and Cooperative Learning   63
            Whole-Class Versus Cooperative Learning   63
            Small-Group Versus Cooperative Learning   64
            Communication Skills and Cooperative Learning   65
            Types of Mediated Learning   66
            Pedagogical Practices That Promote Thinking   68
    Case Study 3.2: An Exchange Between a
    Teacher and One of the Small Groups in
    Her Fifth-Grade Class   69
    Case Study 3.3: A Discussion Among
    Students in a Small Group   71
    Case Study 3.4: An Exchange Between an
    Eleventh-Grade Teacher and a Small Group of Students   73
    Case Study 3.5: A Group Discussion
    Among Eleventh-Grade Students   76
            Other Ways of Challenging Students' Thinking
                and Facilitating Interactions   77
    Creating the Learning Environment   78
    Practical Activity: Ways of Creating a Cooperative Learning
        Environment   79
    Bringing It All Together: Understanding the Research   82
    Chapter Summary   87
    Activities   87
    Suggestions for Further Reading   89

4. **Strategies to Promote Student Discourse**   91

    Introduction and Learning Objectives   91
    Strategies for Helping Students to Dialogue Together   93
        Reciprocal Teaching   93
    Case Study 4.1: An Example of the Four
    Reciprocal Teaching Strategies   94

Practical Activity: Ways of Teaching Reciprocal
Teaching Strategies to Students to
Enhance Students' Discourse and Develop a
Greater Understanding of a Passage of Text   97
Practical Activity: Ideas for Establishing Audience Roles During
the Report-Back Stage of Each Small Group's Presentation   100
Collaborative Strategic Reading   101
Practical Activity: Ways of Introducing CSR to
Students to Enhance Their Understanding of Text   103
Scripted Cooperation   105
Guided Reciprocal Peer Questioning   108
ASK to THINK-TEL WHY Strategy   110
Case Study 4.2: Example of Fifth-Grade
Students Dialoguing Together Using the
ASK to THINK-TEL WHY Questioning Strategies   111
Self-Regulated Strategy Development   113
Bringing It All Together: Understanding the Research   115
Chapter Summary   118
Activities   118
Suggestions for Further Reading   120

5. **Group Composition**   **121**

Introduction and Learning Objectives   121
Harnessing the Power of the Group: Productive Small Groups   122
Case Study 5.1: Students' Perceptions of
Mixed-Ability Groupings in Their Classroom   122
Ability Groupings   124
Catering for Students With Diverse Needs   125
Practical Activity: Ideas for Establishing Mixed-Ability Groups 126
Gender Groupings   127
Teachers' Perspectives on Grouping Students   129
Friendship Groupings   130
Practical Activity: Ideas for Establishing Friendship Groups   132
Status   134
Case Study 5.2: Enhancing Mandy's
Low Status in Her Group   134
Multiple Intelligences   137
Interest Groupings   138
Surveying Students' Interests   140
Computer Technology Groupings   140

Promoting Student Talk 144
Case Study 5.3: Preparing a PowerPoint
Presentation on Nicotine 145
Practical Activity: Ideas for Establishing Computer Groupings 148
Bringing It All Together: Understanding the Research 150
Chapter Summary 152
Activities 153
Suggestions for Further Reading 154

6. Assessing Small-Group Learning 155

Introduction and Learning Objectives 155
Case Study 6.1: Teachers' Reports on How
They Assess Small-Group Learning 156
Formative Assessment 158
Curriculum-Based Assessments 158
Peer Assessment 160
Computer-Supported Peer Assessment 161
Practical Activity: Conducting Formative
Assessments of Small-Group Learning 164
Summative Assessment 171
Criterion-Referenced Assessments 172
Authentic Assessments 173
Using Authentic Assessments in Different Contexts 174
Case Studies 175
Portfolios 176
Exhibitions of Performance 177
Problem-Based Inquiries 177
Problem-Based Learning Using Formative and Summative
Assessments 178
Key Points on Summative Assessments and
Their Purposes 179
Practical Activity: Conducting Summative
Assessments of Small-Group Learning 180
Bringing It All Together: Understanding the Research 187
Chapter Summary 191
Activities 191
Suggestions for Further Reading 192

7. Teachers' Responsibilities in Establishing Cooperative Learning 193

Introduction and Learning Objectives 193

Case Study 7.1: A High School Teacher's Experience With
  Cooperative Learning   195
    Creating a Cooperative Learning Environment   198
    Student-Centered Learning   199
    Negotiate Expectations for Small-Group Behaviors   201
    Developing Communication Skills for Group Discussion   202
    Specific Metacognitive Skills That Promote Discourse   204
    The Teacher's Role in Promoting Mediated Learning   206
    Developing Appropriate Helping Behaviors   208
    Choosing Tasks for Small-Group Discussions   211
    Monitoring Students' Progress and Evaluating Outcomes   212
  Case Study 7.2: Developing Criteria for
  Assessing Group Outcomes in Sixth Grade   213
  Chapter Summary   216
  Activities   216
  Suggestions for Further Reading   217

8. **Future Developments in Using Small Groups**   219

  Introduction and Learning Objectives   219
    Comprehensive School Reform (CSR)   221
  Case Study 8.1: Two Middle School Teachers' Experiences
  With a Comprehensive School Reform Program   224
    The Implications of CSR Programs for
      Democratic and Learner-Centered Teaching Practices   228
    Student Participation in Negotiating Opportunities
      for Learning   229
  Practical Activity: Helping Schools Establish Positive Learning
    Environments   230
    The Impact of Computer Technology on
      Small-Group Learning   232
    The Implications for Designing Classrooms of the Future   235
    The Importance of Teamwork and Communication   240
  Chapter Summary   241
  Activities   242
  Suggestions for Further Reading   242
  Classrooms of the Future Web Sites   243

Glossary   245

References   253

Index   267

About the Author   273

Acknowledgments

I would like to thank the reviewers whose feedback helped me shape this book so that it will best serve the needs of students and instructors:

Cynthia L. Gissy, West Virginia University at Parkersburg

Brian A. T. Husby, Nebraska Wesleyan University

Lynn Lindow, Augsburg College

Susan Carol Losh, Florida State University

Nancy L. Markowitz, San José State University

Linda Kuzan Metzke, Lyndon State College

Jacqueline A. Norris, The College of New Jersey

Jan Riggsbee, Duke University

Jan E. Waggoner, Southern Illinois University at Carbondale

Janet Whitley, Tarleton State University

CHAPTER 1

Cooperative Learning in Schools

INTRODUCTION AND LEARNING OBJECTIVES

Cooperative learning involves students working together in small groups to accomplish shared goals. It is widely recognized as a teaching strategy that promotes socialization and learning among students from kindergarten through college and across different subject areas (Cohen, 1994). Cooperative learning has been used successfully to promote reading and writing achievements among middle school students (Stevens, 2003), understanding in high school science classes (Foley & O'Donnell, 2002), and problem solving in mathematics (Sahlberg & Berry, 2002), to name just a few. It has been shown to enhance student's willingness to work cooperatively and productively with others with diverse learning and adjustment needs (McMaster & Fuchs, 2002) and to enhance intergroup relations with those from culturally and ethnically different backgrounds (Slavin & Cooper, 1999). It has also been used successfully as a teaching strategy to help students learn to manage conflict (Stevahn, Johnson, Johnson, Green, & Laginski, 1997) and to help students identified as bullies to learn appropriate interpersonal skills (Cowie & Berdondini, 2001).

The major benefits of cooperative learning that teachers have identified for students with special needs include improved self-esteem, a safe learning environment, and better classroom success rates and products (Jenkins, Antil, Wayne, & Vadasy, 2003). In fact, it has been argued that cooperative learning experiences are crucial to preventing and alleviating many of the social problems related to children, adolescents, and young adults (Johnson, Johnson, & Stanne, 2000). There is no doubt that the benefits attributed to cooperative learning are widespread and numerous. Moreover, it is the apparent success of this approach to learning that led Slavin (1999) to propose that it is one of the greatest educational innovations of recent times.

There is no doubt that when students work cooperatively together, they learn to listen to what others have to say and how they say it, share ideas and perspectives, give and receive help, seek ways of resolving difficulties, and actively work to construct new understandings and learning. The result is that cooperative learning creates a group ethos where students realize that members will work to help and support their endeavors, and it is the sense of group cohesion that develops that enhances students' motivation to achieve both their own and the group's goals (Johnson & R. Johnson, 2003).

The purpose of this chapter is to provide an overview of the social and academic benefits widely attributed to cooperative learning and how it can be used to promote effective learning in students from K–12. Understanding these benefits is particularly important given the scrutiny schools receive as a consequence of the No Child Left Behind Act of 2001 (*Executive Summary*, 2004) and its emphasis on ensuring that all students, including those who are disadvantaged, achieve academic proficiency. Given these expectations, teachers need to feel confident that if they implement cooperative learning in their classrooms, students will achieve not only the social but also the academic outcomes attributed to this pedagogical practice.

When You Have Finished This Chapter You Will Know:

- The academic and social benefits that accrue to students K–12 from cooperative learning
- Key aspects of successful cooperation
- Practices that promote quality teaching and learning
- The effect the demands of the No Child Left Behind (NCLB) Act of 2001 has on different pedagogical practices in schools, particularly cooperative learning
- The potential that cooperative learning provides for transforming schools

Case Study 1.1

The Case of Tom

Tom is in his second year of high school and appears to have adjusted well to his school routine; however, this was not the case when he first arrived. The continual movement from class to class and from building to building was initially very stressful for Tom, who had difficulties reading his school timetable and understanding the school map that showed where the buildings were located. Tom had an intellectual disability, and although he could participate in most activities, he had difficulties organizing his routines, such as locating the books he needed for each class and understanding instructions. It was not long before his teachers realized that unless they acted, he would always be late for lessons and, unfortunately, the butt of peer ridicule and jokes.

Helping Tom by providing him with some additional guidance and prompts to avoid making his difficulties obvious was their first step. This included ensuring that Tom was linked with a "buddy" who accepted responsibility for helping him to arrive at his class on time. Although only one student volunteered for this task initially, it was not long before other students in Tom's home room accepted responsibility for helping him to organize his routines and arrive promptly for his lessons.

Tom was very sociable and well liked by his peers because of his easy-going mannerisms, so his teachers' second step was to ensure that he was included in different cooperative learning groups that they established in their classes. This enabled Tom to work in small supportive groups where he could take risks with his learning that he would find too intimidating in a larger class. His peers encouraged his participation and ensured, like others in his group, that he undertook specific roles. These included helping organize resources, act as the media manager for a PowerPoint presentation of a group's work, present his ideas on a topic through different media, and work with his peers to bring the project or activity they were working on to fruition.

The opportunity to make meaningful contributions enhanced Tom's self-confidence and increased his status among his peers as they realized he was able to make worthwhile contributions to his group. Tom is now enjoying school, and although his learning difficulties are still apparent, he is well liked and he has strong support from his peers, who willingly include him in their classroom activities.

Tom's case is not unique. Many other similar cases have been reported that provide evidence of the success of cooperative learning as a pedagogical practice that promotes socialization among students and motivation to learn. In Tom's case, this was particularly important because if his teachers had not established cooperative learning in their classes, Tom's peers would never have realized that he was able to make many positive contributions to the groups in which he worked. Through contact with Tom, his peers not only realized his worth as a contributor but also were able to get to know him as a person. They discovered his easygoing personality, which helped them to realize that he was very sociable and that they enjoyed working with him.

Tom was successfully included in his groups because his teachers had made the effort to ensure that they established their cooperative learning groups carefully. Tom worked in different groups in different classes, which ensured he had opportunities to work with a number of different students, and it also enabled him to try out new skills and seek help from others in a supportive small-group environment.

INTRODUCING COOPERATIVE LEARNING

Research indicates that if students are to reap the benefits widely attributed to cooperative learning, then groups need to be established so that

■ *Positive interdependence exists among group members.* This involves all members working together to complete the group's goal. Johnson, Johnson, and Holubec (1990) maintain that when positive interdependence is established, students will understand that each member's contributions are indispensable, with each member having a unique contribution to make to help the group achieve its goal. In effect, students learn that "they sink or swim together" (p. 11) and that they must complete their assigned work if the group is to attain its goal. In Tom's case, he was assigned different but complementary tasks that he had to achieve, such as using multimedia to present an aspect of his group's task. This work, in turn, was augmented by the contributions of others and together represented the group's total efforts or the group's goal. The group receives recognition for having attained their group goal when students present a group report or product to the class or demonstrate that the group goal has been attained by showing how the various contributions by members come together as a total whole.

■ *Promotive interaction is encouraged.* This involves students' working in small groups where they can see each other so they can engage in face-to-face discussions about the group's task. When this occurs, students understand that they must actively encourage each other's equal participation in the discussions. It provides opportunities to develop personal rapport that encourages students to be more willing to reach out to others, listen to what they have to say, and actively work to include others' ideas in the group discussions. These personal relationships and the synergy that they can create occur only when students work in close contact with each other, giving them the capacity to read both the verbal and nonverbal body language that are critical to building these personal connections. In Tom's case, his peers learned about his personal attributes only when they had the opportunity to work with him in their small groups.

■ *Individual accountability is required.* This involves students' understanding that they will be held accountable for their individual contributions to the group, that free-loading will not be tolerated, and that everyone must contribute. Students like to receive recognition from their peers for their contributions, and this occurs only when they carry their share of the workload. When they do contribute and receive acknowledgment for their efforts, their sense of self-efficacy is enhanced and they are motivated to continue to work for the group's success. Tom was widely accepted by the members of the different groups in which he worked because he was perceived as being a "worker" or someone who was prepared to shoulder his fair share of the load. This appealed to his peers—when debriefing sessions followed the group activities, other students would often remark on how they appreciated the effort he put into "doing his share."

■ *Interpersonal and small-group skills are employed.* Students need to be taught how to communicate effectively with each other so they know how to express their ideas, acknowledge the contributions of others, deal with disagreements, and manage conflicts. In addition, they need to know how to share resources fairly, take turns, and engage in democratic decision making. These are not easy skills to master, particularly when many students still work in classes where they are rarely given opportunities to interact with their peers and are expected to be passive recipients of the teaching that occurs. Tom's teachers spent time discussing the importance of these skills for successful group work with their classes, which undoubtedly helped Tom and his classmates understand what they were expected to do and how they were expected to behave. One of the most common reasons for students to be excluded by their groups is inappropriate interpersonal or small-group behaviors. Helping students realize the importance of using appropriate social skills helps to ensure that this will not happen to them.

■ *Group processing is practiced.* This is a type of formative assessment that involves students' reflecting on how they are managing the processes of learning, including what they may still need to do to accomplish their goal. It involves students asking such metacognitive questions as: *How are we doing? Is there anything else that we should be doing? What could we do differently?* In addition, group processing encourages students to reflect on the role of group members to determine if there are any decisions they need to make to streamline the group's functioning and enhance how members contribute to the group. Johnson, Johnson, and Holubec (1990) maintain that when groups learn to engage in such processing, it enables them to validate students' contributions and focus on maintaining positive working relationships and provides opportunities to celebrate the success of the group.

When groups have been established so the above five key components of cooperative learning are evident, the groups are generally referred to as being *structured*, whereas when these components are not evident or have been only partially implemented, the groups are regarded as being *unstructured* (Gillies & Ashman, 1998). This distinction is very important because research has consistently shown that students who work in structured cooperative groups work more productively and attain higher learning outcomes than students who work in unstructured groups (Johnson & Johnson, 2002).

Group Task

The type of task assigned to the group is also very important for determining how group members interact and work together. For example, Cohen (1994) argued that when the procedure for completing the task is fairly straightforward so that students are only required to exchange information, request assistance, or provide an explanation, such as occurs when students work on well-structured mathematical tasks, there is little need to discuss how to proceed as a group or negotiate problem scenarios. Cohen referred to this type of task as one that promotes low-level cooperation among students because students need to engage in only minimal interactions with each other as they work on solving the problem.

In contrast, when students work on tasks that are open and discovery based and where there are no clear answers, they must discuss how to proceed as well as the substantive content of the task if they are to resolve the problem at hand. Cohen refers to this type of task as one that promotes high-level cooperation because interaction is vital to productivity. Interestingly, Cohen has consistently found that the frequency of task-related student interactions is related to learning gains on tests of computational and mathematical concepts and applications as well as content-referenced tests in both mathematics and science. In short, students learn from task-related talk.

Grouping Practices

Teachers often make personal judgments about how well students will work together when they are deciding how to group students for cooperative learning. While this may be appropriate for individual classroom situations, the research is quite informative about the types of grouping practices that appear to be effective. In a meta-analysis (an analysis of the findings of a number of smaller studies) of grouping arrangements within classes, Lou et al. (1996) were able to provide some insight into how to group students for cooperative learning.

The dilemma of how to construct groups so that there is a mix of students of different abilities is one that regularly confronts teachers. There is no doubt that students benefit from working with others, as the research on such grouping practices as *reciprocal teaching* (Palincsar, 1999), *peer tutoring* (Topping, 2005), and cooperative learning (Gillies, 2003b) demonstrates, but there is concern as to whether these benefits apply to all students regardless of ability and whether certain ability compositions are likely to be of greater benefit than others.

Certainly, there is evidence that low-ability students benefit from being included in mixed-ability groups because they are able to take advantage of the additional insights and often the extra tuition their more able peers provide. In contrast, high-ability students appear to perform equally well in either mixed- or same-ability groups. The group composition appears to have no effect on their ability to achieve. On the other hand, there is some evidence that medium-ability students appear to learn better when they work with students of similar ability, possibly because they are not the bystanders they appear to be in mixed-ability groups where high- and low-ability students often work together in a tutor–tutee relationship.

The size of the group is another issue that teachers express concerns about: *Is there an ideal size? Are groups of between six and eight students too large? How can I manage smaller groups in my class?* While these are genuine concerns for practicing teachers, there is evidence that when groups are too large, students can "disappear" or get lost among members. It can be very difficult to have a genuine group discussion among eight members. Furthermore, when groups are too large, it is often difficult for members to work in close proximity to each other (face-to-face interaction is a key element of successful cooperative learning) so they can hear and see what is being discussed. Lou et al. (1996) reported that the optimal size for learning was three or four students per group, while groups of between six and ten members did no better than students who worked in whole classes who were not grouped for learning.

Promoting Student Discourse

Cooperative learning provides students with ways of interacting together so they learn to listen to what others have to say and how they say it, challenge their own perspectives, and develop new or alternative positions or arguments that are logical and that others will accept as valid. When students interact with others in this way, they learn to develop their ability to use language as a tool for thinking and reasoning and, in so doing, learn to construct new understandings and learning (Mercer, Wegerif, & Dawes, 1999).

Although cooperative learning provides opportunities for students to think and reason together, research indicates that unless students are helped to dialogue together, they only infrequently give rich and detailed help to each other or engage in cognitively sophisticated talk (Meloth & Deering, 1999). In fact, Chinn, O'Donnell, and Jinks (2000) found that students used higher-level discourse only when they were required to discuss reasons for their conclusions. In effect, both Meloth and Deering and Chinn et al. argue that students must be explicitly taught the skills needed to dialogue together if they are to learn to use these skills to enrich their discourse and enhance their learning.

A number of peer-mediated strategies have been developed to teach students how to dialogue together, seek information, clarify understandings, and ask questions that promote higher-level complex thinking and learning. Among these strategies is *reciprocal teaching* (Brown & Palincsar, 1988), designed to help students generate questions to assist their comprehension of written text. Also included is *scripted cooperation,* a strategy that involves alternatively acting as the listener or the recaller as students take turns recounting information they have been researching together (O'Donnell, 1999). Each student acts as a check on the other as they are forced not only to focus on what they have learned but also on each other's understanding and interpretation of what they have learned, a process that enhances students' understanding of text, challenges their cognitive and metacognitive processing, and facilitates learning.

Collaborative strategic reading (CSR) is another approach to helping students dialogue together to enhance their comprehension of text (Vaughn, Klingner, & Bryant, 2001). It involves students' learning to generate questions designed to help them predict what the text is about, identify words or concepts they don't understand, recognize the main idea, and reflect on the key questions a good teacher may ask about what they have just read. During CSR, students work in small, mixed-ability groups (2–4 students) to collaboratively implement the strategies with the text they are reading.

Finally, two other approaches to helping students dialogue together and to ask cognitive and metacognitive questions are *guided reciprocal peer questioning* (King, 1990) and the ASK to THINK-TEL WHY® strategy (King, 1997). Guided reciprocal peer questioning is designed to enhance students' comprehension of lecture material, whereas the ASK to THINK-TEL WHY strategy is employed to assist students to ask different types of questions that promote higher-level complex thinking. Both strategies were initially designed for students working in pairs; however, they have both been employed successfully with students working in groups of three or four.

The research on the five different peer-mediated strategies (outlined above) indicates that they have all been highly successful at helping students to dialogue together to promote thinking and learning among students with diverse learning needs. Their success, however, depends on the extent to which teachers implement these approaches as a way of helping students interact together and think cognitively and metacognitively about the issues under discussion.

Cooperative Learning Pedagogy in the Classroom: Teacher's Role

Teachers play a critical role in establishing cooperative learning pedagogy in their classrooms. Included in this is responsibility for ensuring that the groups are well structured so students will cooperate and promote each other's learning and that the group task is relevant and open and discovery-based, requiring students to dialogue together. Students are more likely to cooperate when they believe the task is interesting and relevant to their learning and that all group members understand how they are to operate and contribute. While the phrase "the guide on the side" has often been used to refer to the facilitating role teachers play during cooperative learning, experienced teachers know that the success of this initiative, to a large part, depends on the preparation they have undertaken before implementing this approach in their classes. Teaching students to learn how to operate in groups is hard work, and it is not achieved without a great deal of forethought and planning.

Success also depends on how teachers dialogue with their students to help motivate their interests, promote student-to-student interaction, and model how to interact with each other in socially appropriate ways. Simultaneously, teachers need to be able to challenge students' thinking and scaffold their learning, necessary skills to help students construct new ways of thinking and learning. In fact, teachers who implement cooperative learning effectively demonstrate many of the characteristics attributed to effective or expert teachers described in the literature.

Effective or Expert Teachers

Taylor, Pressely, and Pearson (2000), in a review of a number of studies on how and why some schools across the United States are attaining greater-than-expected reading achievement with students who are at risk of failure, identified the characteristics commonly shared by effective teachers. They noted that effective teachers, in contrast to less effective teachers, had higher student engagement; provided more small-group instruction; had a preferred teaching style of coaching or facilitating as opposed to telling students what to do; and asked more higher-level comprehension questions, or questions designed to encourage students to think. Furthermore, the more teachers emphasized higher-order meaning making as opposed to lower-order skills, the more effective was their instruction. Taylor et al. (2000). also reported that achievement was higher when reading and writing tasks were integrated, students had opportunities to discuss what they were reading, deep understanding of text was emphasized, skills were embedded within the task as opposed to being taught as isolated skills to be mastered, and students were expected to use these skills to self-regulate their learning.

Varrella (2000) reports on the characteristics of expert science teachers who were identified from their participation in the Iowa Scope, Sequence, and Coordination (SS&C) Project. These teachers were regarded as experts because they were identified as having a high level of expertise in constructivist teaching, which they demonstrated through observations on their teaching style, interviews, and personal written reflections on their teaching practice and on the nature of the relationship between the teacher and the learner. Overwhelmingly, these teachers had a philosophy of working with students as opposed to telling them what to do, and they believed that learning needed to be student-centered and focused on experiences that enabled students to construct meaning from them. Learning needed to be challenging, and students needed to be provided with opportunities to interact with each other to ask questions and seek help. Furthermore, these teachers demonstrated efficient use of higher-order questioning strategies, used wait time effectively to promote student reflection on questions, and used a variety of assessments including contextual assessment to gauge students' understanding of subject matter and concepts.

In a study of 30 exemplary fourth-grade teachers, Allington, Johnson, and Day (2002) identified five focal elements that these teachers had in common and that together accounted for the superior educational gains the children in these teachers' classes achieved. These focal elements included: *the nature of classroom talk, the curriculum materials, the nature of instruction, the nature of students' work,* and *the nature of evaluation.* However, while all these elements were important for students' overall achievement, the authors noted that it was the nature and complexity of classroom talk that created the deepest impression. Teachers demonstrated courteous, supportive, and productive talk in their interactions with their students. Talk between teachers and students was friendly and personalized, with teachers using these conversations to learn more about their students. The authors noted that even the instructional talk was often conversational as teachers probed students' understandings, offered tentative suggestions, and encouraged their continued exploration of a problem. Furthermore, teachers encouraged students to think about how they selected topics, located information, and solved problems, and they encouraged students to share those thoughts with their peers.

Allington et al. (2002) also found that expert teachers chose curriculum materials that were multisourced and designed to challenge students' interest and learning. They used other sources of information as well as the text book for students to use as resources. Also, their instruction was more conversational than didactic as they moved around the room encouraging students to teach each other as they worked collaboratively. In fact, collaborative, meaningful problem-solving work dominated the school day, and working together was valued and viewed as developing important learning skills, including self-responsibility and independence. Group tasks were integrated across different subjects and often lasted for a week or more, ensuring that the topic was substantive and involved a clear commitment from students to complete. Finally, evaluations were personalized and students were provided with rubrics to help them understand and think about the feedback they received (see Chapter 6 for a discussion on constructing rubrics for evaluation).

In summary, effective or expert teachers have a number of pedagogical practices in common. These practices include the following:

- Recognizing that students need to work on complex and interesting tasks
- Using a variety of sources to stimulate students' interests
- Modeling the types of talk they want students to use
- Encouraging students to dialogue together
- Creating opportunities for students to collaborate and problem-solve around tasks
- Promoting higher-order thinking
- Ensuring learning is student-centered
- Encouraging students to accept responsibility for their own learning
- Providing students with explicit feedback on their progress

Given that many of the above *pedagogical practices* are used by teachers who implement cooperative learning in their classrooms, questions naturally arise as to how these practices are accommodated when teachers are required to respond to demands from mandatory testing.

THE IMPACT OF MANDATORY TESTING ON COOPERATIVE LEARNING

In January 2002, President George W. Bush signed into law the No Child Left Behind (NCLB) Act, which is designed to ensure that no child is trapped in a failing school by linking *high-stakes testing* with strict improvement policies in schools whose students have traditionally not done well. The Act includes

- Increased accountability for states, school districts, and schools to ensure all groups of students reach proficiency within 12 years
- Greater choice for parents of students who attend schools that fail to meet state standards
- More flexibility for states and local education authorities in the use of federal funding
- A stronger emphasis on reading, particularly for younger children (*Executive Summary*, 2004)

While this is certainly a commendable piece of legislation, and the Act received bipartisan support from Congress when it was introduced, the consequence is that teachers often express concerns about the pressure they are under to ensure students meet required proficiency levels on mandatory standardized tests and the effect this has on what they can teach and the pedagogical practices they can employ.

Specific Requirements of the No Child Left Behind (NCLB) Act of 2001

With the enactment of the NCLB Act, the accountability provisions of this federal law now govern Title 1 schools and non–Title 1 schools in all states. The accountability provisions are intended to close the achievement gaps between able and less-able students, minority and nonminority students, and disadvantaged students and their more advantaged peers (Kim & Sunderman, 2005).

Schools must now meet adequate yearly progress (AYP) requirements for improving school performance and the academic achievements of different minority and disadvantaged groups of students within schools. Moreover, the NCLB Act requires that states must provide information on how they intend to close the achievement gap and ensure that all students, including those who are disadvantaged, meet required proficiency levels.

Under the NCLB Act, schools are required to meet specific standards in reading and mathematics with these standards being uniformly applied to all subgroups within a school. Performance is measured in terms of annual measurable objectives (AMOs), which indicate the percentage of students who must meet the required standards in reading and mathematics. States are required to measure students' progress yearly in Grades 3–8.

Why Test?

Flagging student progress in science, mathematics, and reading provided the impetus for the NCLB Act. Different public reports on students' progress across the nation indicated schools were not producing students with the knowledge and skills required in science and mathematics that would enable the United States to provide global economic leadership and homeland security in the 21st century. The National Assessment of Educational Progress (2000, as cited in *The Facts About . . . Math Achievement [Math Achievement]*, 2004, and *The Facts About . . . Science Achievement [Science Achievement]*, 2004) in science and mathematics indicated that only 25% of fourth and eighth graders were performing at proficiency or above proficiency levels while 82% of 12th graders performed below proficiency level in science (*Math Achievement*, 2004; *Science Achievement*, 2004). Moreover, an examination of the National Assessment of Educational Progress (2001, cited in *Science Achievement*, 2004) results in science indicated that the longer students stayed in the current system, the worse they performed (*Science Achievement*, 2004). Similar results were obtained for reading, with only 32% of fourth graders performing at or above the proficient achievement level (Questions and Answers on NCLB—Reading, 2003). In short, students were not performing well enough.

What Happened?

Schools scrambled to put in place curricula, programs, and strategies that would ensure that the required proficiency targets for students and disadvantaged groups within schools and districts were met. They also spent time and money on either developing or accessing testing material that would enable them to prepare students for the proposed mandatory testing. In some schools, this meant teachers spent large proportions of classroom time in test preparation activities covering those parts of the curriculum that they knew were to be tested. Although mandatory testing had existed in many states for some years, few had the high-stakes mandatory sanctions attached to tests that the implementation of the NCLB Act now had.

The NCLB Act required that if schools failed to meet adequate yearly progress (AYP) for 2 years, they could be subjected to a series of sanctions, including allowing parents to transfer their children to other public schools; requiring that schools develop an improvement plan; and mandating that schools spend 10% of their allocated funds on teacher professional development. After 3 years, schools can be required to provide students with additional supplemental services such as tutoring, while after 4 years, they must take corrective action that may include replacing the school staff, adopting new curriculum, or extending the school day. Finally, after 5 years, schools that continue to fail to meet AYP standards can face takeover by the state or a contracted private educational firm (Peterson, 2005).

The concern with the AYP reports is that not only must schools reach specific performance standards in reading and mathematics, but they must ensure that all minority groups within their schools also meet the required proficiency standards if they are to be regarded as having satisfied the AYP proficiency requirements. It is these very demanding requirements that many teachers express concern about, believing that the requirements are placing undue pressure on them to meet targeted goals and adversely affecting how they teach and what they teach.

Teachers' Perceptions of Mandatory Testing

In an effort to discover how teachers were reacting to mandatory testing, Hoffman, Assaf, and Paris (2001) conducted a survey among Texas reading teachers to find out how the Texas Assessment of Academic Skills (TAAS), a state-based criterion-referenced mandatory test that focuses on the areas of reading, writing, and mathematics, was affecting their teaching and students' learning. The survey found that many teachers reported spending nearly 8 to 10 hours a week preparing students to take the test. This included activities such as demonstrating how to answer the test correctly, providing tips on how to take the test, reviewing and teaching topics that will be on the test, and using practice tests to prime students. Moreover, many respondents noted that when they planned their curriculum, they emphasized the areas that will be tested on the TAAS while those aspects of the curriculum that were not tested were not taught or were de-emphasized, so students often did not have the benefits of a full curriculum.

Students also seemed to be affected by the TAAS, with teachers reporting that many experienced headaches and stomachaches, while a surprising number were anxious, irritable, and aggressive. If students are not well or experience stress or anxiety during assessment, their results are likely to be adversely affected, further affecting the validity of the results obtained (Hoffman et al., 2001).

In a national survey of teachers' perceptions of the impact of state testing programs conducted by the National Board on Educational Testing and Public Policy (Pedulla et al., 2003), Abrams, Pedulla, and Madaus (2003) found that the majority of teachers were positive about their state's content standards or framework, with 58% of all respondents indicating that their state-mandated test is based on a curriculum that all teachers should follow. Moreover, nearly 55% of all teachers reported that if they teach to the state standards, students will do well on the state test. However, when the responses are divided between high-stakes states (i.e., those states where sanctions apply to test results) and low-stakes states (i.e., no known consequences attached to test results), the survey found that state tests have a differential effect on what curriculum content is taught and how students are assessed.

In high-stakes states, 43% of teachers reported spending greatly increased time on instruction, whereas only 17% of teachers in low-stakes states reported doing so. Moreover, 25% of teachers in high-stakes states reported spending less time on instruction in nontested areas (vs. 9% in low-stakes states), 51% reported creating classroom tests in the same format as state-mandated tests (vs. 29% in low-stakes states), and 44% reported spending more than 30 hours per year preparing students specifically for the state test (vs. 10 hours in low-stakes states).

State-mandated tests also had a high impact on teacher and student motivation and morale, with 80% of respondents in high-stakes states reporting that students were under intense pressure to perform well in the state test. Other issues of concern expressed by the majority of teachers in both the high- and low-stakes states included the inappropriate use of test results to award school accreditation, evaluate teachers and administrators, and award teachers and administrators financial bonuses. The issue that Abrams et al. (2003) found most disconcerting, however, was the substantial proportion of teachers from both high- and low-stakes states who indicated that state-mandated testing had led them to teach in ways that contradicted notions of good educational practice.

In summary, the NCLB Act has

- Mandated accountability requirements that schools must meet
- Imposed uniform proficiency standards in reading and mathematics across all groups, including disadvantaged groups
- Led to teachers' spending inordinate amounts of time preparing students for standardized testing
- Subjected schools to a series of sanctions if they fail to meet adequate yearly progress standards
- Resulted in students' not having the benefit of a full curriculum because teachers focus on the aspects to be tested

The Case Against Testing

The National Center for Fair & Open Testing (NCFOT) (2005) argues that while states maintain that state-mandated testing must be based on state content and performance standards, measure higher-order thinking, provide useful diagnostic information, and be valid and reliable, there are limits to what can be achieved by these tests. For example, much of the content in state standards is not assessed; state standardized tests offer few opportunities for student to display the attributes of higher-order thinking, mainly because most questions involve multiple-choice answers; most standardized tests are summative assessments and are not designed to provide diagnostic information; and relying solely on the scores of students on one test is likely to lead to incorrect inferences about their competencies. In contrast, the NCFOT proposes that well-designed classroom assessments can provide richer and more consistent information that enhances validity and provides more meaningful information on students' progress toward required standards.

Alfie Kohn (2000), in his article "Burnt at the High Stakes" (2000), argues that the problem with standardized tests is that they fail to assess the skills and dispositions that matter most. For example, "reading comprehension exams usually consist of a concentration of separate questions about short passages on unrelated topics that call on students to ferret out right answers rather than engage in thoughtful interpretation" (p. 317). Similarly, science tests often focus on vocabulary, test very boring material, and fail to judge the capacity of students to think. Given that most of the standardized testing is done in multiple-choice formats, students have few opportunities to demonstrate higher-order thinking or complex problem-solving skills. Furthermore, even when students are able to respond to open-ended questions, their responses are often scored on the basis of how many facts they have recalled rather than on their capacity to think. Kohn argues that teachers need to be able to teach in ways that promote creative and critical thinking in their students to help them become fully engaged in the process of learning.

Is Mandated Testing Working?

This is a question teachers often ask as they seek answers as to whether state-mandated testing is helping to raise students' performances. While it is still too early to be able to determine how successful or otherwise such testing has been, there are some trends that appear to be emerging that cannot be discarded. The National Center for Education Statistics (2005) has published national trends in reading and mathematics for students at 9, 13, and 17 years of age.

The national trends in reading, expressed in percentiles, indicate that for 9-year-olds, the score at the 50th percentile (the median) was higher in 2004 than in any other assessment period (records have been kept since 1971), and scores at the 10th (i.e., lowest 10% of scores), 25th (i.e., lowest 25% of scores), and 75th percentile were significantly higher than in 1999 (the last assessment period). Essentially, this means that students' reading test scores at the 10th, 25th, and 75th percentiles have improved. However, for 13-year-olds and 17-year-olds there were no significant differences in the scores between 1999 and 2004.

The national trends in mathematics, expressed in percentiles, show that for 9-year-olds, the scores at the 10th, 25th, 50th, 75th, and 90th percentile were higher than they were for any other assessment period since records commenced in 1978. For 13-year-olds, the scores were higher at all percentile points since 1978 except for the 10th percentile, where the score in 2004 did not differ significantly from that of 1999. For 17-year-olds, however, there were no significant differences between 1999 and 2004 for any of the percentile scores. Effectively, mathematics scores for 9-year-olds and 13-year-olds have generally improved, while for 17-year-olds there is no change.

In short, the trends in standardized testing for reading and mathematics are generally positive for younger children, but the trends for older students are mixed and in some cases changes have not occurred. Although some of the trends outlined above indicate that positive changes appear to be emerging, caution needs to be exercised in interpreting these results, because these tests tend to report global scores that have been based on the assessment of specific content areas rather than wider curriculum areas and experiences. Furthermore, while they assess knowledge, they often fail to provide opportunities for effective testing of students' higher-order thinking and problem-solving skills— skills that are critical if students are to learn to think critically and creatively and act responsibly as autonomous learners.

THE POTENTIAL TO TRANSFORM SCHOOLS: USING COOPERATIVE LEARNING PEDAGOGY

Case Study 1.2

Transforming a School: A Principal's Story

Jim was the principal of a large high school located in a low socioeconomic inner-city area known for high rates of drug abuse, crime, and poverty. More than a third of the students attending his school were from single-parent families that were on welfare and the remainder were from homes where one or both parents worked in blue-collar industries or were self-employed. Because of the high rates of poverty, the mixture of students with diverse learning and adjustment needs, and the generally poor performances of students on different state tests, the school had been designated in the lowest 10% of schools in the state. In addition, the school had a reputation as a tough school to teach in because students were difficult to manage and parents could often be abusive and threatening to staff.

I'll never forget my impressions of this school when I visited it for the first time. It was break time and the students were out on the grounds, sitting under trees or standing together in small groups chatting and laughing. There wasn't the harsh criticism or swearing or abusive language that I thought I might hear. In short, there was no sign of the TOUGH school I thought I would be visiting.

As I wandered across the school grounds and up to the administrative building, I could see that the grounds were well kept, trees and plants were thriving, the buildings were free of graffiti, rubbish was in the bins, and there were no signs of vandalism. As I walked through the buildings, I could see that students' bags were in their lockers or otherwise put away and classrooms were generally tidy and well maintained. Those students who chose to stay in their classrooms to finish projects or read worked quietly so there was none of the mayhem and chaos I had expected to see.

I was so surprised by what I had seen, I asked the principal (I was visiting the school on a totally unrelated matter) what had happened to bring about such an amazing transformation, given that the school was located in a high crime area with a seedy reputation.

Jim's response was that he and his teachers worked together to put in place small changes that they believed they would be able to manage. "First, we worked on making the curriculum more relevant to the students so they did a lot of practical work with background knowledge and skills embedded into it. . . . Next, we changed our assessments so they were criterion-referenced and kids knew exactly what was needed to demonstrate specific standards. We took away the fear of failure, and if a kid was not meeting adequate standards, we used the term *developing*. The students responded well to this because it gave them a chance to see that we were not out to fail them but to help them understand how to attain the required standard, be it developing, developed, or well developed.

"Following that, we looked at our own professional development and made sure we had experiences that would help us learn how we could improve and change how we taught. What skills did we need to have to be able to work with these students? This is when we did some inservice on cooperative learning. Most of us had thought that we could just pop students into groups and that was cooperative learning, so we were quite surprised to find out how structured it needs to be and how systematically it must be introduced.

"Many of the teachers have commented on how well the students responded to the group activities . . . they accept more responsibility for their work, help each other, and are more motivated. It even helps to set a nice tone for how they interact with each other in the classroom.

"We also found that when we worked in groups with students, it made our teaching more personal and friendly. The students seemed to like the attention and the contact, and we found that we tended to be less directive and more facilitative in the way we encouraged students. I think they responded well to that.

"There is no doubt that cooperative learning played a big part in helping to bring about the changes you've seen. It's been like a total package. We had to do lots of things at the school level and with the teachers to get it working, but we've got them in place now. We still get 'hiccups,' but that's natural and we deal with those situations when they occur."

In Case Study 1.2, Jim recounts the changes his school made to the following:

- the curriculum to make it more relevant to students' needs
- the assessment so students learned what the criteria were for success
- the professional development program to help teachers learn new ideas and strategies that they could use to change how they taught

Jim's school dealt with these issues one step at a time so they could look at how they were managing each of the changes before introducing the next. These ideas on how to bring about change are very consistent with the approach adopted in a number of studies where schoolwide interventions have been implemented with success.

Schoolwide Cooperative Learning

One such intervention, reported by Stevens and Slavin (1995), involved a 2-year study that used cooperation as the overarching philosophy to change school and classroom organization and instructional processes. The study was conducted in five elementary schools and involved more than 1,000 students from Grades 2–6. The two schools that formed the treatment condition agreed to adopt the cooperative elementary school model, which included the following elements:

1. Cooperative learning was used widely in classes.
2. Students with learning disabilities were included in regular classes.
3. Teachers agreed to observe and coach each other as they introduced innovative ideas in their teaching.
4. Teachers worked together to plan and discuss their curriculum.
5. Principal and teachers agreed to collaborate on school planning and decision making.
6. Parents were encouraged to be active participants in school planning and activities.

The three comparison schools did not implement the cooperative elementary school model but continued using their regular teaching methods and curriculum.

Cooperative learning was phased in over the first year of the project through a series of professional development activities so that it was used by all teachers in the treatment schools in a variety of curriculum areas. Teachers were given feedback by the research staff on implementation to improve the quality of their instruction and maintain fidelity with the basic tenets of this approach to learning. Teachers observed each other's lessons and provided feedback to one another as they began using cooperative learning.

By the end of the second year of the intervention, the results showed that the students in the schools where cooperative learning had been widely implemented made significant gains in reading vocabulary, reading comprehension, language expression, and mathematics computation that their peers in the comparison schools did not make. Interestingly, students in the cooperative elementary schools listed significantly more friends than their peers in the comparison schools.

Gifted children (i.e., children in the top 10% of the standardized assessment pretests) in the cooperative elementary schools outperformed gifted children in the comparison schools on reading vocabulary, reading comprehension, language expression, and mathematics computation. Moreover, they listed significantly more friends than their peers in the comparison schools.

The results with learning disabled (LD) children nearly mirrored the results obtained for gifted children, with LD children in the cooperative elementary schools obtaining significantly better results in reading vocabulary, reading comprehension, language expression, mathematics computation, and mathematics application than LD children in the comparison schools. Similarly, these children also listed more friends than their peers in the comparison schools.

Although many components contributed to the outcomes obtained, Stevens and Slavin (1995) argue that when cooperative learning is the primary mode of instruction and when it is integrated with effective instruction in reading, language arts, and mathematics and with changes in school organization and with peer coaching, it is effective in producing higher student achievements for all, including students with learning disabilities and gifted children. Moreover, all students in the treatment schools listed significantly more friends than their peers in the comparison schools, indicating that there were better peer relations in the cooperative elementary schools.

Teachers' Reported Satisfaction With Cooperative Learning

Shachar (1997) reports on a study that assessed teachers' satisfaction and dissatisfaction with their work as a consequence of their participation in a schoolwide intervention project designed to provide teachers with the concepts and skills needed to implement cooperative learning pedagogy in their classrooms. The project was aimed at implementing long-term change in the way teachers taught and how they interacted with each other, and involved extensive inservice training in cooperative learning and opportunities to practice new strategies and ideas in a supportive school environment. Teachers from nine junior high schools in Israel participated in the project, which was implemented over a 3-year period.

Shachar (1997) notes that schools in Israel are characterized by wide diversity in their student populations, with students differing in the pace in which they are able to absorb and work through academic material, their personal abilities and talents, their motivations to succeed, and the meaning and emotional responses different subject matter arouses in them. Moreover, Shachar proposes that because these differences are highly correlated with students' ethnicity or socioeconomic status, teachers aim to reduce the disparities between academic achievement and students' background variables, promote positive peer relationships, improve intergroup relations, and create conditions that promote students' learning.

In order to ascertain teachers' sense of satisfaction or dissatisfaction with their teaching as a consequence of their participation in the schoolwide intervention project, questionnaires were administered pre- and postintervention. The results showed that teachers believed that there had been significant improvements in teachers' relationships with each other and that there was more collaborative lesson planning. This, in part, may have occurred because the project placed great emphasis on developing practices of cooperative planning in small teams of teachers, a practice that had not occurred in these schools before. Teachers also believed that teacher–principal relations had improved as a consequence of the project, which had encouraged principals to support teachers in their efforts to implement cooperative learning. Teachers noted, however, that their ability to reach and motivate all students had declined and that the large gaps in social status and levels of motivation between students had increased.

Shachar (1997) proposed that some of the dissatisfaction teachers expressed about students' progress may be the result of the changes in classroom organization and instruction during cooperative learning. When cooperative learning is implemented so students work in small groups and learning is student-centered, teachers may not have as clear an understanding of the progress students are making as they would have in more traditional classrooms where teachers interact directly with students as they work on teacher-initiated activities. Furthermore, Shachar noted that teachers often find it more difficult to determine the criteria for success for all students when they work in groups, and this creates a more ambiguous situation in terms of student assessment. This may lower teachers' sense of satisfaction from their work and account for some of the dissatisfaction they expressed.

A Comprehensive School Reform Model

Another schoolwide intervention that has been implemented with success is the *Success for All* comprehensive approach to reading reform that is based on the cooperative elementary school model, outlined above (Stevens & Slavin, 1995), but is supported and supplemented by other components such as one-on-one tutoring for young children experiencing difficulties in reading, an extensive family support program, and a full-time facilitator who works with teachers to improve the quality of implementation of the model (Slavin, 1999).

Slavin (1999) argues that the Success for All approach has been resoundingly successful, with many studies indicating that schools that adopted this schoolwide approach to reform outperformed matched control schools in reading. Moreover, recently released results of a national randomized field trial indicate that students in the Success for All schools outperformed students in control schools on their word attack test score results for the first year of the trial (Borman & Slavin, 2005). The authors maintain that this finding is consistent with previous patterns in Success for All studies where the strongest first-year effects of the program are in the word attack domain. In succeeding years, the phonetic and structural analysis skills tapped by the word attack skills help children to develop their comprehension and reading skills. In fact, Borman and Slavin maintain that the effects in comprehension and reading become more pronounced after 2 or more years of participation in the Success for All program.

The following summarizes the key findings on schoolwide cooperative learning interventions discussed above:

- All interventions were long term and lasted 2 to 3 years
- Positive outcomes were often not evident until the second year of the intervention
- Whole-school commitment to the intervention was needed by staff and principal
- Cooperative learning needed to be embedded in the majority of school subjects
- Professional development needed to be provided to teachers to help them understand the background theory, principles, and skills of cooperative learning

- Teachers needed to be supported by their principal and peers as they implemented this new instructional approach
- Implementing cooperative learning in classrooms is demanding because it requires careful planning, and student progress may not be readily evident
- Cooperative learning may need to be augmented by other specific teaching strategies
- When cooperative learning is implemented systematically, it contributes to greater achievements for all students, including gifted children and those with learning disabilities

Structure and Content: Overview of the Chapters That Follow

The preceding information provides a broad introduction to the collection of chapters, including an overview of the social and academic benefits attributed to cooperative learning and the requirements for establishing cooperative groups to promote student discourse and learning, including the different student-mediated strategies that are used to help students dialogue together. It also included a discussion of the No Child Left Behind (NCLB) Act, the consequences of high-stakes testing states and schools, and a review of the national trends in science and mathematics standardized testing since records were first kept. The benefits of schoolwide interventions in cooperative learning are presented and discussed in the context of such interventions being long term and requiring full staff commitment to implement the strategies espoused.

The following chapter focuses on the key components in establishing successful cooperative groups, including how to establish positive interdependence in groups so students will strive to achieve both their goal and the group's goal, promotive interaction to encourage and facilitate each other's efforts, and individual accountability so students accept responsibility for completing their task while ensuring others complete theirs. Considerable attention is also devoted in that chapter to the interpersonal and small-group skills needed to work effectively together, including examples of how to teach these skills to students and the importance of group processing as a way of helping group members to monitor their progress.

Chapter 3 discusses the key role teachers' discourse plays in promoting student thinking and learning in the cooperative classroom. The different types of discourses teachers engage in when they teach in cooperative classrooms as opposed to traditional classrooms or classrooms where students work in small groups are discussed. The importance of teaching teachers specific communication skills to help them engage in mediated-learning interactions with their students is emphasized, along with specific strategies for promoting these dialogues.

Strategies to promote student discourse are presented in Chapter 4. A number of specific dialoguing scripts that can enhance students' interactions in small groups is presented along with the background research that validates their use. Included in this chapter are such dialoguing scripts as *reciprocal teaching, scripted cooperation, collaborative strategic reading, guided reciprocal peer questioning,* and the *ASK to THINK-TEL WHY* strategy. The chapter is replete with specific ideas on how these dialoguing scripts can be taught to students to enhance student-to-student interaction, problem solving, and reasoning during small-group learning.

Chapter 5 outlines the research on group composition and its effects on students' discourse and learning during cooperative learning. Particular attention is given to discussing the advantages and disadvantages of same- and mixed-ability groupings and the implications for students with learning disabilities and students who are second language learners. Gender groupings are also discussed, as are teachers' perspectives on grouping students—what works and what strategies teachers need to use to ensure that group members work productively together. Friendship groupings, interest groupings, and computer technology groupings are discussed as well as how to enhance the status of low-status students to ensure their inclusion. Once again, a range of strategies for grouping students is presented and discussed.

Teachers often struggle with how to assess students' learning in small groups because of the nature of group work and the need to disentangle the individual's contribution from that of the group's. Chapter 6 examines the different types of formative and summative assessments that teachers use to assess students' progress and demonstrates how both these types of assessments can be used successfully to inform the teaching and learning process, including curriculum-based assessments, peer assessments, and computer-supported peer assessments. Students learn more when these assessments are criterion referenced because they are designed to help students understand what they must do to succeed. The chapter also presents a range of examples of rubrics that can be developed to make the assessment criteria and process explicit.

Chapter 7 deals with the responsibilities teachers need to accept when they introduce cooperative learning into their classrooms. This includes establishing a supportive milieu or environment that is inclusive of all students whether they be students with learning difficulties or learning disabilities, second language learners, or students from culturally or ethnically diverse backgrounds. In setting the scene, teachers need to ensure that they set expectations for students for small-group behaviors, they teach students the interpersonal and small-group skills that facilitate group discussion, and they help students to understand the importance of providing explanations or elaborated help to others. Teachers also need to ensure that they take time to teach those scripts to students that promote helping discourses such as reciprocal teaching, scripted cooperation, or the ASK to THINK-TEL WHY strategy. In addition, teachers have responsibilities to ensure that they develop strategies for monitoring students' progress and assessing their achievements.

The final chapter focuses on future developments in using small groups in schools. The adoption of the principles of democratic schooling and child-centered learning means teachers can no longer expect children to act as receptacles of knowledge. Rather, students will be encouraged to be active in the construction of their own learning experiences, with teachers ensuring that they have opportunities for this to occur throughout the school day. Students, along with their parents and teachers, will be actively involved in negotiating their curriculum, with mutually agreed-upon goals. Opportunities will be provided for students to use technology to facilitate access to a more flexible curriculum so knowledge, ideas, and resources not available in the immediate classroom can be included in students' learning experiences. This means that students are more likely to work in small teams throughout the school day as they negotiate different tasks and seek different solutions to problems at hand. Consequently, a great deal of emphasis will be placed on the importance of establishing cohesive teams where members have well-developed communication skills.

CHAPTER SUMMARY

The research on cooperative learning in schools suggests

- There are academic and social benefits to working in cooperative groups.
- Groups need to be structured if students are to work cooperatively together.
- Group tasks will determine how students interact together, with well-structured tasks requiring little interaction while ill-structured tasks, or ones that are open and discovery-based, require students to interact if they are to resolve the problem at hand.
- Groups can be constructed in different ways, but teachers need to be mindful of the effects groups have on students' interactions and learning.
- There are scripts that students can be encouraged to use to promote dialoguing.
- Expert or effective teachers have a number of common pedagogical practices.
- The No Child Left Behind (NCLB) Act has mandated accountability provisions for ensuring that students meet required proficiency standards.

- Concerns have been expressed by parents, teachers, and community agencies on the "fairness" of mandated, high-stakes testing.
- Schoolwide interventions on cooperative learning have yielded positive results, but only after at least 2 years of the intervention being in place.

ACTIVITIES

1. Reflect on your own experiences of small-group work when you had to work with peers, either in a school situation or during your college years, on a specific task. Consider the following questions as you reflect on your experiences: Why was the group established? How did the members each work out what they were going to contribute? What sorts of social skills were needed to manage the group discussions? What did you notice about the size of the group? How did you feel about this small-group experience? If you were to have another small-group experience, are there any things that you would do differently?

2. Spend some time observing an informal group at a social gathering. How can you gauge whether members are interested in the topic under discussion? Is one member dominating the rest of the group or do all members appear to have opportunities to participate? What do you notice about members' nonverbal body language? Do you notice differences in the way culturally different people communicate verbally and nonverbally?

3. Try to observe a group of students working formally together in small groups. What do you notice about their seating arrangements? What can you observe about how the division of labor has occurred with the group task? What do you notice about their discussion? Is one member dominating or are all members able to participate? Do you notice if there are any status issues in the group? If so, how has the group dealt with them? Are the members working productively together to produce a group product? See if you can construct a matrix listing all the behaviors you observed and your comments about each.

4. Interview two teachers about high-stakes testing. Ask them about the preparation they undertake for the testing (e.g., time involved, training students to respond to different test items). Does the testing affect what they teach? How do students respond to the tests? Do they regard them as a challenge or do they worry about the consequences? What benefits, if any, have they noticed from testing? If they could change the current testing regime, what would they do? How do the teachers' responses correspond to the issues discussed in this chapter?

SUGGESTIONS FOR FURTHER READING

Abrams, L., Pedulla, J., & Madaus, G. (2003). Views from the classroom: Teachers' opinions of statewide testing programs. *Theory Into Practice, 42*(1), 18–29.

Slavin, R. (1999). Comprehensive approaches to cooperative learning. *Theory Into Practice, 38,* 74–79.

Sloane, F., & Kelly, A. (2003). Issues in high-stakes testing programs. *Theory Into Practice, 42,* 12–17.

CHAPTER 2

Key Components in Establishing Successful Cooperative Groups

INTRODUCTION AND LEARNING OBJECTIVES

It is clear that placing students in groups and expecting them to work together will not necessarily promote cooperative learning. Groups need to be established so that children understand how they are to work together, contribute, accept responsibility for completing their part of the task, and assist each other's learning in an environment that is supportive of its members (Johnson & F. Johnson, 2003). Groups that have been established so these elements are present are referred to as structured cooperative groups; when these elements are not evident or are only partially evident, the groups are referred to as unstructured cooperative groups or small groups (Gillies, 2006). This distinction is important because it affects how students work and interact together (Gillies, 2003a).

Unstructured cooperative groups have many of the characteristics of the traditional, whole-class setting where there is no goal interdependence (i.e., requirement that students work together to achieve a group goal), so students work individually or in competition with each other to achieve their own ends. Hence there is often no motivation to act as a group or exercise joint efficacy to solve a problem or accomplish a task, share ideas, or promote each other's learning (Johnson & R. Johnson, 2003). This chapter deals with how to establish cooperative groups so students experience the benefits widely attributed to this approach to teaching and learning. The key components of successful cooperative groups are outlined along with specific strategies to enable teachers to build them into their class curriculum.

Case Study 2.1

An Example of Cooperative Learning in a First-Grade Classroom

I'll never forget the first time I saw cooperative learning in a classroom. I was a school counselor, monitoring the placement of three children with moderate intellectual disabilities in a Grade 1 classroom from an early intervention special education preschool. There was some concern about how these children would cope with the demands of a mainstream class given their high support needs with speech and language, personal management, and fine and gross motor skills difficulties. My concerns, though, were soon allayed as I sat and watched them participate in a cooperative learning lesson in their classroom. The children were sitting on the carpet around the teacher who had just read them a farmyard story and this had led to an animated discussion among the children about the animals in the pictures. When the discussion drew to an end, the class teacher told the children that she now had a task that they were going to complete in small groups. Basically, their directions were to work together to paint a farmyard scene that their small group would show and discuss with the larger class group at the end of the lesson.

The children were divided into groups of three and given a sheet of paper and a set of paints with the directions that someone was to draw the farmyard and the barn, someone else the duck and the pond, and someone else the farmer and his dog. The three tasks were explicitly identified, although the children had to decide who would complete each part. It was made very clear that the group task would not be completed until each child had completed his or her part. The children worked in mixed-ability groups, so the three children with high support needs were in different groups.

Once the groups were identified, the children very quickly decided who would do what task. As there was only one paintbrush, each child took turns working on completing his or her part of the picture while the others looked on and offered advice. The children talked enthusiastically about the task, laughed and giggled with each other, and offered help when they perceived it was needed, pointing to different parts of the picture and making suggestions about what to include. I was very impressed with how easily the children with high support needs participated with the other children and how readily these children accepted them.

Meanwhile, the teacher moved around the groups ensuring the children had the resources they needed and providing encouragement for their efforts. At the completion of the lesson, each group stood up and presented its work to the whole class, with each child, including the children with high support needs, discussing what he or she had done. This activity was followed by the teacher discussing with the children what they had learned from working together.

Follow-up discussions with the teacher revealed that she often used cooperative group activities as a way of involving the children with each other so they learned to listen to others, consider their ideas, share materials, and reach agreement on what they needed to do to complete the task. These were skills that she believed the children needed to learn if they were to participate fully in the classroom.

The scenario depicted above provides a clear example of how the teacher established cooperative group work in her classroom that was inclusive of all children, including those with disabilities. In the first instance, she organized the children to work in small groups with three members each. Discussions with the teacher later revealed that she believed that groups of two or three were ideal for very young children and, in this case, she had orchestrated the groups so that they consisted of children of different abilities and where possible were of mixed gender.

Before the groups commenced their task, the teacher had discussed the group rules, such as the importance of helping each other, sharing the materials, listening to what others had to say, and offering suggestions. Emphasis was placed on the need to work together to complete the task and using clear speech and good manners when seeking help or materials. To ensure that the children understood what was required, the teacher asked different children to model how they would pass the materials around, seek help from each other, suggest ideas, and so on. These examples were discussed with the children to ensure that they understood what behavior was being modeled and why it was important.

The teacher conveyed enthusiasm about the task, and she commented on how she was looking forward to what each of the groups would be able to show her and the class when they finished. In doing this, she was creating an expectation in the children about the group task they were to complete. The children had enjoyed the farmyard story they had heard, and this was their opportunity to work with their peers to complete an activity based on that story.

By providing each group with only one set of paints and one brush, the teacher created a situation that ensured that the children would share resources. In this way, they were linked interdependently together because they were unable to complete the task unless they shared the paints. They were also linked interdependently with the small tasks each member of the group had to complete (i.e., each had to paint a different part of the farmyard), and it was this interdependence that ensured that the children interacted as they contributed to the group picture.

In order to monitor the children's progress, the teacher moved around the groups, checking that they understood the task, discussing different aspects of the painting, and generally engaging with the children in a friendly and personal way. The children, in turn, responded positively to the interest the teacher showed and were eager to share their pictures and point out their achievements to her.

At the completion of the activity, each group was given an opportunity to show its picture to the class and discuss what members had drawn. This enabled the children to recount the story, important for their comprehension of it, and recall the contributions each had made in depicting their picture. In so doing, the children were engaging in group processing, monitoring what they did and how they did it. When children do this, it encourages them to think at the metacognitive as well as the cognitive level, which assists their understanding and promotes learning (Johnson, Johnson, & Holubec, 1990). Moreover, the group processing enabled the children to realize what they had accomplished and to receive feedback from their teacher and their peers on what they had achieved.

Given the success with which the teacher implemented cooperative learning in this classroom, questions naturally arise:

- What is cooperative learning?
- Why is it so successful with groups?
- What are the key components that seem to be important for its success?
- How long should students be expected to work in cooperative groups?

COOPERATIVE LEARNING

Cooperative learning is a pedagogical practice that involves students' working together in small groups to accomplish shared goals. In cooperative learning, each group member is required not only to complete his or her goal but to ensure that others do likewise if the group is to achieve its goal. The technical term for this dual responsibility is *positive interdependence,* and it is the most important component of cooperative learning (Johnson & F. Johnson, 2003). The other key components that will be discussed are: *promotive interaction, individual accountability, interpersonal and small-group skills,* and *group processing.*

Positive Interdependence √

Positive interdependence exists when group members are linked together in such a way that one cannot succeed unless others do, and they must coordinate their efforts to ensure that everyone completes his or her specific goal. In fact, it is argued that when students are placed in groups where positive interdependence does not exist, the students will not perceive that they are working cooperatively and will either work in competition with each other or individually to achieve their own goals.

Although numerous researchers have observed that individuals in groups will work either cooperatively or competitively with others, Morton Deutsch (1949) was the first to investigate the distinction between these goal-oriented approaches. He hypothesized that if individuals are working together to attain a group's goal, they will perceive themselves to be more psychologically interdependent than individuals who are working in competition with each other or by themselves, and this will have implications for how they interact.

In a now famous study conducted with first-year college students, Deutsch (1949) set out to determine how individuals perceive they are linked when they experience cooperation or competition. Using 10 groups of five students each, he randomly exposed them to either a cooperative or a competitive condition where they worked on a set of problem-solving tasks. In the cooperative condition, students were told they were to work together to solve the problems, and the group that came up with the best average for working together would be excused from one term paper and would automatically receive an A for that paper. The students in the competitive condition were told that the student who was ranked the highest for the contributions made to his or her group would be excused from one term paper and would automatically receive an A for that paper.

Each group was then observed and rated on the basis of their discussion, orientation, self-centeredness, involvement, communication, attentiveness, and acceptance or rejection of each other's ideas. In addition, the group participants completed a weekly questionnaire after each group meeting to elicit their perceptions of the feelings in the group, level of cooperation, individual and group productivity, interest in the activities, and reactions to others' contributions.

The students in the cooperative condition were rated by their observers as having a stronger sense of "group cohesiveness," were more attentive to what others had to say, communicated more effectively, were more motivated to achieve, and were more productive than their peers in the competitive groups. Moreover, these observations were confirmed by the students' responses to the weekly follow-up questionnaire. The results of this study challenged traditionally held beliefs that students who work in competition to receive awards work better than students who cooperate and promote each other's learning.

TYPES OF INTERDEPENDENCE

Johnson and Johnson (1990) extended Deutsch's (1949) work on interdependence and argued that there are two types of interdependence: outcomes interdependence and means interdependence. *Outcomes interdependence* exists when students are striving to achieve a goal or reward for their efforts, while *means interdependence* exists when students needs to share resources, fulfill different roles, or complete tasks in order to achieve the group's goal. Examples of the different types of interdependence are evident in Case Study 2.1 where the teacher required that each group painted a picture (outcome interdependence), but in order to do so, group members had to share the one set of paints and brush, and each child had to paint a specific part of the picture (means interdependence). If the teacher had not established the group's goal (i.e., to paint the picture) and structured the groups as she did, the children would not have understood that unless they cooperated and worked together, neither they nor their group would be able to achieve what they were expected to achieve. It is this notion of sinking or swimming together that provides the motivation to cooperate and facilitate each other's learning.

Johnson, Johnson, and Holubec (1990) propose that the group goal can always be supplemented with group rewards so that the group that manages to complete its task within a given period may earn additional points that can be traded at a later date for some special privilege (i.e., free time). Moreover, Johnson (2003) argues that while positive goal interdependence is sufficient to generate higher achievement outcomes than engendered by individual effort, the combination of goal and reward independence tends to increase students' achievements more than goal interdependence alone. When positive resource interdependence (i.e., group members share materials) is used in isolation from positive goal interdependence, positive resource interdependence produces the lower individual achievement and problem-solving success (Johnson, Johnson, & Stanne, 1989). In short, positive goal and reward interdependence tend to be additive, so teachers may need to consider different ways of structuring reward interdependence in groups to enhance students' potential achievements from positive goal interdependence alone.

Practical Activity

Ways of Structuring Positive Interdependence

Elementary School

★ Expert researchers. Each child has a responsibility to research a key part of the group task and report back to the group on the information obtained. A variation of this is Jigsaw, where each child takes responsibility for becoming an expert on a specific aspect of the task. Children then leave their group and join others from other groups who are also seeking information on that topic. When they have obtained the information they need, they then rejoin their own groups and proceed to teach others what they have found. This information is then incorporated into the group's task.

★ Paired learning. Children work in pairs to research specific information, clarify their understandings (i.e., children interview each other to ensure each understands the information they have been researching), or problem-solve together before reporting back to their group.

★ Resource interdependence. Children share the materials or personnel available to the group. This may include children's sharing not only art materials, computers, books, and other material resources but also each other's personal resources such as artistic talents, technological skills (i.e., abilities to search for information on the computer), organizational skills, and so on.

Middle School

★ Allocate students to groups so that each brings different expert skills. For example, some students may have specific technological and media skills while

(Continued)

(Continued)

others may have oracy and organizational skills that are needed if the task is to be completed successfully.

★ Students are required to undertake different tasks (e.g., find specific information) and bring that information back to their groups to share with the members. This may involve students' leaving their first group to acquire the specific information from a second group (i.e., this group is working on obtaining the same information) before bringing it back and sharing it with the first group.

★ Members work in pairs to complete an aspect of the group's larger task. Each pair (in a four-person group) shares their completed task with the other pair, and the group members work together to ensure that the parts contribute to the larger task.

High School

★ Establish the task so there are a number of subtasks that need to be completed first. This may involve students' working in pairs as part of a larger group of four students to research information on a particular topic. Each pair discusses their information with the other pair to determine how it will be integrated to accomplish the group task.

★ Allocate different resources to students that they need to use to be able to contribute to the group task. This may involve some members' conducting interviews on a specific issue while others use the Web and library resources to find specific information relevant to the topic. Students meet as a group to contribute their information and develop a group response to the task.

★ Establish the task so individuals who have developed expertise on specific topics are required to contribute to the group to help members complete their task. This may involve students who have particular technological skills (e.g., search skills), presentation skills (e.g., artists, actors), or editing skills (e.g., writing scripts) contributing to the production of the final group product.

Promotive Interaction

Promotive interaction involves students' encouraging and facilitating each other's efforts as they work together. Students do this by providing information and assistance, constructive feedback to help improve performance, and access to resources and materials needed to complete tasks. When children dialogue together, they learn to use language to explain their ideas and experiences, negotiate meaning around a task, and develop new ways of thinking and behaving that they may not have previously considered (Mercer, 1996). Other benefits include an awareness of what other children do not understand and the need to provide explanations or assistance that can be more readily understood. This willingness to engage with others not only benefits the recipient but also the helper. Giving help encourages reorganization and clarification that may help the person explaining to understand the material better and construct more elaborate cognitive understandings than he or she held previously (Webb & Farivar, 1999). Moreover, when children demonstrate goodwill toward others and a willingness to promote each other's learning, they are more likely to feel accepted and valued, less anxious and stressed, and more willing to reciprocate and help others in turn.

Teachers can facilitate children's interaction in groups by ensuring that they sit in close proximity to other group members so they can hear what is being said, see each other's faces, and participate in discussions with their peers. When children have opportunities to engage with their peers in this way, they learn to read each other's nonverbal body language, respond to each other's social cues, and engage in verbal repartee with their peers about the work they are completing. Examples of how teachers can promote interaction among students are provided below.

Practical Activity

Ways of Promoting Interaction

Elementary School

★ Seat children facing each other. Groups of three or four children are ideal because the children can hear and see each other and follow the discussion with ease. Students discuss how they will complete a particular task or present a vignette on a story they have read or heard.

★ Have children work in pairs with one child interviewing another about his or her favorite television program, game, or fun-time activity. Switch roles so that the interviewer is now the interviewee. At the end of the activity, the children report back to the class on what each found out about the other.

(Continued)

(Continued)

★ Teach children how to dialogue together so they learn how to seek information, share ideas, and deal with disagreements. Mercer, Wegerif, and Dawes (1999) believe for dialoguing to be effective, children need to be taught basic ground rules for generating *exploratory talk*. These rules are: (a) all information is shared, (b) the group seeks to reach agreement, (c) the group takes responsibility for decisions, (d) reasons are expected, (e) challenges to ideas are accepted, (f) alternative ideas are discussed, and (g) all group members are encouraged to speak by other members. There is value in spending time negotiating a set of ground rules to help children engage in discussions prior to commencing any group activities.

Middle School

★ Assign students to two-person groups and have them interview each other about their favorite sport, hobby, or activity. Each two-person group then joins with another pair to make a group of four. Students, in turn, introduce each other to the group, informing the members of their partner's favorite sport, hobby, or activity.

★ Give the students the first line of a limerick (make sure they understand it is a five-line rhyme) and have them work in their four-person groups to complete it. Groups then read their limericks to the class. This is an activity that can produce a lot of laughter as students often perform the limerick at the same time.

★ Give students a "story topic" and have them contribute a sentence each until they have made up a story about it. Give the students about 5 to 7 minutes to elaborate on their topic before discussing the outcome with the larger class. This activity can also be used as an icebreaker to help group members adjust to each other before settling down to work together.

High School

★ Promote discussion. Using numbers or colors, students are randomly assigned to small groups of four. Students with a specific number or color are then asked to introduce themselves and discuss an interest they enjoy (e.g., film/video/band). This type of activity helps to break the ice before they start to work together.

★ Students complete tasks within their groups and then share their findings with other group members. Group members ask questions about the task the student has completed. When all four students have presented their work, the group discusses how the information will be integrated into the final group product.

★ Students work in pairs on a particular task and then share their information with the other pair in the group. Each pair quizzes the other pair on the information presented (question starters can be used to stimulate ideas) and discusses how it can be included in the group product.

Individual Accountability ✓

Individual accountability involves group members' accepting personal responsibility for their contributions for attaining the group's goal. This includes not only being responsible for completing one's individual task but also ensuring that others complete theirs. It has been suggested that when positive interdependence is well structured in a group, members will feel more personal responsibility for contributing to the collective effort and be less likely to freeload on the efforts of others (Johnson, 2003). The shared responsibility that positive interdependence creates within a group where individuals realize they are accountable to their peers for their efforts helps to increase their motivation to perform well.

Another way in which individual accountability can be established involves the teacher's setting external requirements for completing specific tasks and then checking to see that these requirements have been met. Johnson, Johnson, and Holubec (1990) maintain that checking is important because it ensures that each student is contributing to the group's efforts, enables the teacher to provide feedback to individuals and groups on members' contributions, and helps group members avoid redundant efforts.

Practical Activity

Ways of Ensuring Individual Accountability

Elementary School

★ Peer assessment. Help each group develop specific criteria for assessing the contribution of others. For example, the teacher could help the children to develop criteria for assessing an unsatisfactory contribution, a satisfactory contribution, and a very worthwhile contribution when evaluating a task or process.

★ Teacher assessment. The class teacher assesses the contributions of each child and discusses the child's assessments with the group. Strategies such as getting children

(Continued)

(Continued)

> to use different colored pens or complete specific tasks are some ways in which each member's contribution to the group can be readily assessed.
>
> ★ Group assessment. Students are assigned different roles so they need to coordinate their efforts to complete the task. Such roles can include a motivator (keeps group members on task and focused), a researcher (locates relevant information for others to read), scribe (jots down the main ideas discussed by the group), and reporter (prepares and presents the group's work to the class). While all children would fulfill all roles at different times, the student named in a particular role would have primary responsibility for that role.
>
> *Middle School*
>
> ★ Peer assessment. The teacher helps students understand how to develop criteria that can be used to assess the contribution of each member to the group. Assessments can range from "made a contribution" through to "contributed some worthwhile ideas."
>
> ★ Teacher assessment. This involves the teacher's giving feedback to each group on her or his observations of members' contributions; feedback that is constructive and positive is always well received. For example, comments such as, "I liked the way you all wrote a short passage that contributed to the task you were working on" to, "I wonder if you can think of some additional ideas you may need to extend this point?"
>
> ★ Group assessment. Students agree to complete specific tasks or roles (e.g., researcher, reporter, organizer, or writer), with the group providing feedback to each member on how he or she performed the task or role. It may be necessary to provide students with some sentence stems to help them reflect on how they might structure their feedback to members. Sentence stems that are designed to elicit positive feedback may start with, "I liked the way you . . ." However, students also need to be able to critique each other's work; the following sentence stem may help them to do this in a nonconfrontational way: "I can see that you're trying to do . . . but I wonder if you could also think about doing . . . ?"
>
> *High School*
>
> ★ Peer assessment. Students develop criteria for assessing the contributions of others. Examples of how this has been done in the past could be provided to help students

understand the process. For example, contributions or effort could be rated as: on the way, some good ideas, well thought through, and so on.

★ Teacher assessment. These can be conducted informally as the teacher monitors each group's progress and provides feedback to members on their contributions.

★ Group assessments. These may involve students' undertaking specific roles/tasks (e.g., media manager, production manger, resource manager) and then having the other members of the group provide feedback on the contributions made. If ground rules for discussion are negotiated before students start, this type of assessment can be very productive and helpful.

Interpersonal and Small-Group Skills ✓

Placing children in groups and telling them that they are to cooperate does not ensure that they will use the interpersonal and small-group skills needed to work effectively together. These skills must be explicitly taught if children are to benefit from their small-group experiences. In a study that investigated the effects of structured and unstructured cooperative groups on children's behaviors and interactions, Gillies and Ashman (1998) found that when children had been trained to work together, as they had been in the *structured groups* where they were taught interpersonal and small-group skills, they were consistently more cooperative and helpful than their peers who had not been trained to cooperate. If children are not taught how to interact appropriately with each other, they are more likely to encounter conflict and difficulties with cooperating as they work together in small groups. The skills that facilitate students' interactions are as follows:

Interpersonal skills

    a. Actively listening to each other

    b. Stating ideas freely

    c. Accepting responsibility for one's behaviors

    d. Providing constructive criticism

Small-group skills

    a. Taking turns

    b. Sharing tasks

c. Making decisions democratically

d. Trying to understand the other person's perspective

e. Clarifying differences

Johnson, Johnson, and Holubec (1990) propose that if students are to cooperate to achieve their mutual goals, they must

a. Get to know each other and trust each other

b. Communicate accurately

c. Accept and support each other

d. Resolve conflicts constructively

In fact, Johnson (2003) maintains that individuals must be taught the interpersonal and small-group skills needed for successful cooperation, and they must be motivated to use them if they are to facilitate learning in others. Moreover, providing students with individual feedback on how they use these skills not only helps to create more positive relationships, but it also helps to increase students' achievement. When children are not taught these skills, they are more likely to experience difficulties with building trusting relationships, communicating effectively with each other, and resolving conflicts through constructive means.

Specific examples of the interpersonal and small-group skills and how teachers can teach them are outlined in Table 2.1.

Practical Activity

Ways of Ensuring That Children Learn These Interpersonal and Small-Group Skills

Elementary School

★ Teacher role-plays a particular skill (e.g., someone who pushes into a waiting line) and asks the children to identify what should have been the appropriate behavior. This gives the teacher the chance to discuss what that behavior should look like and what it should sound like. A child is then chosen to model the appropriate behavior. The teacher uses this opportunity to ask the children how they might feel if someone pushed in and how they might feel if someone behaved appropriately. The importance of helping children to understand that their actions (behaviors), thoughts, and feelings are very important for their sense of personal well-being, and when one aspect of how they behave, think, or feel is affected, it affects their whole selves.

★ Children role-play appropriate behaviors, and the teacher and children discuss what the behavior looked like, what it sounded like, and how the children felt. This will give the children the chance to become aware of the positive feelings that can flow from being courteous to others.

★ Have the children construct their own list of appropriate interpersonal and small-group behaviors. This allows the children to accept ownership of the behaviors they are going to use when they get into their small groups to work on their activity. The teacher may need to augment this list if the children omit some important behaviors.

Middle School and High School

★ Teacher leads a class discussion on the types of student behaviors that are important if students are to work successfully in groups. Adolescents prefer to negotiate rules or expectations for behavior rather than have them imposed. Guidelines for group behaviors could be developed and posted on the class Web site or notice board or pasted in each student's notebook. Examples of group behaviors may include: listens to others, no put downs, democratic decision making, discusses differences and tries to settle them, shares resources.

★ Students may need to be taught how to manage conflict or express dissension. Giving "I-messages," that is, focusing on the issue and not the person, is one way of helping students learn how to express concern/disagreement. This is particularly important with adolescents who can sometimes be hypersensitive to comments from their peers. An example of an I-message is: "I feel concerned when you make those comments."

Group Processing ✓

Group processing is critically important for student learning as it allows members to discuss how well they are achieving their goals and maintaining effective working relationships. In a study that investigated the impact of group processing on the achievement of 48 high-ability high school seniors and beginning college students who worked in one of four conditions (cooperative learning with no processing, cooperative learning with teacher-led processing,

Table 2.1   Examples of Interpersonal and Small-Group Skills

Skill	What Does It Look Like?	What Does It Sound Like?
1. Listening	Eye contact	Yes; I see; Ah! Mm! (Verbal encouragers)
2. Stating ideas clearly	Scan group, face group	I think . . . ; My thoughts are . . .
3. Accepting responsibility	Scan group, face group	I-statements
4. Giving constructive criticism	Eye contact	I liked that idea, but have you thought that you could do it this way too?
5. Taking turns	Eye contact, facing group	I've had my go . . . ; It's your turn to have a go.
6. Sharing tasks	Pass the materials, allocate jobs.	Have we all got something?
7. Understanding others	Appropriate facial gestures	Do you mean . . . ? Are you saying . . . ?
8. Clarifying differences	Eye contact, face group	I'm not sure I understand . . . ?

cooperative learning with teacher- and student-led processing, and individual learning) Johnson, Johnson, Stanne, and Garibaldi (1990) found that students had greater problem-solving success and higher achievement gains when they participated in either teacher-led or student-led group processing discussions than students who worked cooperatively with no processing or individually, although the cooperative learning with no processing condition outperformed the individual learning group.

Group processing involved the students' ensuring that everyone in the group engaged in one of three social skills: (a) summarizing group members' ideas and information, (b) encouraging members to participate in group discussions, and (c) checking to ensure that decisions made by the group were supported by members. Possible explanations for the results obtained included: The focus on *metacognitive thinking* increased members' abilities to achieve, group processing assisted members to gain insights into how to behave more effectively, and feedback on social skills increased the frequency of their use. Additional benefits of group processing include helping members to maintain good working relationships, develop cooperative learning skills, receive constructive feedback on their contribution and participation, and provide opportunities to celebrate the success of the group (Johnson & R. Johnson, 2003).

Practical Activity

Ideas for Group Processing

Elementary School

★ Group members spend 10 minutes at the completion of their group activity identifying: (a) what they have accomplished (learned) and what they still need to accomplish. This may involve their listing the information they still need to obtain to help the group accomplish its goal and (b) how they managed their working relationships (i.e., the process of learning). Key questions to stimulate this reflection may need to be provided to the children on cue cards (i.e., *What did we learn today? What do we still have to do? How did we work as a group? Did everyone contribute?*).

★ The teacher directs the group processing by posing some questions that are designed to get the children to think metacognitively about their groups' learning experience: What was the problem? What was your plan? How did you solve it? What will you do now?

★ Students produce a picture or play or present a brief summary to the class of what they accomplished. Using concrete materials such as pictures, constructions, or short recounts helps young students to remember more readily what they did, sequence their achievements, and correctly acknowledge the contributions of others.

Middle School and High School

★ Students spend 5 minutes in their groups reflecting on what they have accomplished and what they may still need to do. Simultaneously, members need to check each other's thoughts on how they managed their relationships in the group. Questions such as the following may stimulate discussion: How did we manage our relationships with each other? Was there anything in the way we worked together that you think needs to change? What would you like to happen differently next time?

The following box presents a specific example of how students and teachers can evaluate group processes:

Example of a KWL Processing Activity

K (Know)	W (Want)	L (Learned)

What I know.

What I want to know.

What I've learned.

Table 2.2   Example of Students' Thoughts About How the Group Worked

Each of the statements below will ask you how the group worked. Next to each statement is a number. Circle your answer.

Circle number 1 if this almost never happened.

Circle number 2 if this seldom happened.

Circle number 3 if this sometimes happened.

Circle number 4 if this often happened.

Circle number 5 if this almost always happened.

1. All group members felt free to talk.	1	2	3	4	5
2. People listened to one another.	1	2	3	4	5
3. Group members were asked to explain their ideas.	1	2	3	4	5
4. Some members tried to boss others.	1	2	3	4	5
5. Group members tried to help others.	1	2	3	4	5
6. Everyone had a say in the decisions that were made.	1	2	3	4	5
7. The members worked well as a group.	1	2	3	4	5
8. Each member had a job to do.	1	2	3	4	5
9. I felt OK about being in this group.	1	2	3	4	4

How Long Should Students Work in Cooperative Groups?

Given the importance of establishing cooperative groups that have the key components outlined above, teachers often seek clarification on the length of time groups can be expected to work together and how groups can be helped to move on so there is positive closure at the completion of an activity. These are valid questions; as Tuckman (1965) observed, group members do bond or form attachments that they may be reluctant to break at the completion of a set activity or period of time working together. This is because as group identity evolves, members pass through a series of stages that progressively help them to gain a sense of who they are and what they can do. The five stages that Tuckman identified included: *forming, storming, norming, performing,* and *adjourning.*

The forming stage is characterized by members' experiencing some uncertainty as they begin to work out what they need to do to accomplish the task. This is followed by the storming stage, where group members often experience some tension as they work through their ideas on accomplishing the task. The following stage, performing, is probably the most productive stage as members settle down and work on accomplishing the task at hand. In the final stage, adjourning, members realize that they have accomplished the task and it is time to move on. This stage of adjourning has also been described as a mourning stage because group members may feel somewhat saddened by the break up of the group.

A sense of sadness or loss is often experienced by creative artists who may have been brought together to produce a theatrical production in which members of the group have worked closely and in synchrony with each other over an extended period of time, developing close professional and personal relationships. In this situation, directors need to be aware of the importance of helping the team to move on positively. Likewise, in schools students can develop strong working and personal relationships, particularly if they have worked together for long periods of time. Teachers need to be aware of this and ensure that students transition smoothly from the group experience. This can be done by ensuring that students have opportunities to work formally and informally together on different tasks across the school day so the contact they have with each other is maintained. In many cooperative learning situations, groups tend not to last longer than 4 to 6 weeks, which seems to be an ideal length of time to work together on classroom-based tasks. Extracurricular groups may experience longer periods of time as a group, however, and members may experience more noticeable difficulties as they transition to other groups or activities.

> ## Five Key Components for Structuring Cooperative Learning Groups
>
> Positive interdependence: Group members are linked together, so for one to succeed, they must all succeed.
>
> Promotive interaction: Group members facilitate each other's learning through discussion.
>
> Individual accountability: Group members are held accountable for their contributions to the group task.
>
> Interpersonal and small-group skills: Group members use appropriate social skills when working together.
>
> Group processing: Group members discuss what they have achieved and how they are managing their working relationships.

BRINGING IT ALL TOGETHER: UNDERSTANDING THE RESEARCH

A plethora of research on cooperative learning over the past three decades has unequivocally demonstrated the success of this approach to learning (Cohen, 1994; Slavin, 1996). Cooperative learning has been used successfully to promote learning achievements across diverse curriculum areas from kindergarten to college. In a review of the research on cooperative and collaborative learning with 4- to 8-year-olds, Vermette, Harper, and DiMillo (2004) concluded that children gain cognitively and socially from peer-mediated learning experiences, and Hertz-Lazarowitz (2004) reported that storybook writing was enhanced when Grade 1 children worked in small cooperative groups as opposed to working in whole-class settings. Terwel (2003) reported on a series of studies that he and his colleagues conducted at the high school level that investigated the effects of cooperative learning on cognition and motivation for students participating in mathematical interventions. The overall conclusion from these cooperative learning interventions was that they produced positive outcomes in both learning and motivation for the students involved, although students in classes and small groups where there was a higher average ability level performed better than students in classes and small groups where the average ability level was lower. This finding led Terwel to conclude that ability composition counts, whether in a school, a class, or a small group, and low-ability students, in particular, need to be taught to use the social and cognitive skills needed to promote interactions in mixed-ability groups.

McWhaw, Schnackenberg, Sclater, and Abrami (2003) found that students at the college level had much to gain from this approach to learning provided they had been trained to work constructively together, understood the purpose of the activity, believed the group product was attainable and their own contributions were important, and the physical and psychological demands placed on the group were not excessive.

In a study that compared the experiences of college students during cooperative learning and large-group instruction, Peterson and Miller (2004) reported that cooperative learning can lead to greater cognitive involvement; higher levels of motivation, including higher engagement; greater perceived importance of the tasks; and more optimal levels of cognitive challenge in relation to skill. These findings led the authors to conclude that carefully designed and monitored cooperative learning tasks can help students engage more actively in their learning experiences. However, the tasks should provide a challenge to students and should require the use of skills they feel capable of using to maximize their involvement in the tasks.

Low-Ability Children

Children with low ability also benefit from cooperative learning experiences. In a review of eight studies that investigated children's academic achievement and social behavior from Grades 5 to 11 across seven subject areas, Shachar (2003) found that although children from all three ability levels (high, medium, low) benefited from cooperative learning, low-ability children consistently emerged as those who derived maximum benefit from their cooperative learning experiences, and that these benefits included academic and social gains. In the academic area, these gains were apparent across the curriculum in English, science, mathematical reasoning and information processing, chemistry, and social studies in elementary and high school students.

Affective Development

In the affective areas, cooperative learning experiences have been found to enhance the development of positive social attitudes toward other group members (Battistich & Watson, 2003; Jordan & Le Metais, 1997), including students with emotional and behavioral disorders (Ryan, Reid, & Epstein, 2004); motivation to learn (Sharan & Shaulov, 1990); and more positive attitudes toward school (Shachar, 2003), and contribute to an enhanced sense of psychological health and well-being (Johnson & Johnson, 2000). In fact, it has been argued that cooperative learning experiences are crucial to preventing and alleviating many of the social problems related to children, adolescents, and young adults (Johnson, Johnson, & Stanne, 2000).

WHAT IS COOPERATIVE LEARNING?

Cooperative learning involves children's working together to accomplish shared goals, and it is this sense of interdependence that motivates group members to help and support each other's endeavors (Johnson & R. Johnson, 2003). When children work cooperatively, they learn to give and receive help, listen to other children's ideas and perspectives, reconcile differences, and resolve problems democratically. However, placing children in small groups and telling them to work together does not guarantee that they will work cooperatively. Groups need to be structured to ensure that members will work interdependently if students are to reap the benefits widely attributed to this approach to learning (Gillies, 2003c). Once children understand they are interdependently linked and they must coordinate their efforts to achieve the group's goal, they will begin to use interpersonal and small-group skills that will facilitate their efforts.

Although older children and adults may demonstrate these skills with ease (simply because of their maturity and exposure to life events), children often need to be specifically trained to use these skills, and they need to have the opportunity to use them if they are to obtain maximum benefit from their cooperative learning experiences. In a study of 192 sixth-grade children who participated in trained and untrained cooperative groups, Gillies and Ashman (1996) found that the children in the trained groups (i.e., children were trained to collaborate to facilitate each other's learning) were consistently more cooperative and helpful to each other, used more inclusive language (i.e., language designed to encourage participation by others), and gave more elaborated help to each other than children in the untrained groups (i.e., children were told to help each other but were not trained in how to do so). Moreover, the trained groups exercised more autonomy with their learning, recorded greater satisfaction with their participation in their groups, and obtained higher learning outcomes than their untrained peers.

It appears that highlighting the skills that promote *collaboration* and providing opportunities to use them help children not only to gain a better metacognitive understanding of how and when these skills are used, but also a sense of self-confidence with their learning. Interestingly, Gillies and Ashman

(1996) found when the children were asked to comment on their perceptions of their small-group learning experiences, the children in the trained groups had a clearer understanding of the group as one in which they were able to participate, share ideas, and make joint decisions.

It seems that children's sense of *personal agency* or control as learners is enhanced by cooperative learning experiences in which they are provided with opportunities to be active participants in their own learning, contribute and share ideas, facilitate the learning of others, and evaluate their actions and achievements in an environment that is supportive of their endeavors (Bandura, 2001). Gillies (2003a) found that when these conditions exist, junior high school students had stronger perceptions of their cooperative, small-group work as being enjoyable and providing them with the opportunity to do quality work together—perceptions that are highly motivating and conducive to learning.

THE ROLE OF THE TEACHER IN ESTABLISHING COOPERATIVE LEARNING

The role the teacher plays in establishing cooperative learning in the classroom is critically important for its success (see Chapter 7 for a detailed discussion of the teachers' responsibilities). This involves being aware of how to structure cooperative learning groups, including their size and composition; the type of task set; expectations for student behavior; individual and group responsibilities; and the teacher's role in monitoring both the process and outcomes of the group experience (Johnson & Johnson, 1999).

1. *Ensure that groups are structured so the key components (outlined above) are evident: positive interdependence, promotive interaction, individual accountability, interpersonal and small-group skills, and group processing.* When teachers structure their groups so these components are present, children work more effectively together, they provide more help to each other, and their achievements are higher than in groups where these components are unstructured (Gillies & Ashman, 1996). When students work in unstructured groups where positive interdependence has not been established, there is little motivation to promote each other's learning, exercise responsibility for one's own and other's learning, and exhibit the social skills that promote good relationships among members because students are primarily focused on achieving their own goals rather than the group's (Johnson, 2003). In a study of junior high school students who worked in structured and unstructured cooperative groups in three subject areas, English, mathematics, and science, Gillies (2003a) found

that students in the unstructured groups were less cooperative and provided less verbal help and assistance to each other than their peers in the structured cooperative groups. Similarly, Gillies (2004a) found that high school students who worked in unstructured groups in mathematics were less willing to work with others on assigned tasks and they provided less help and assistance to their peers. Moreover, the students in the unstructured groups reported less of a sense of group cohesion and social responsibility for each other than their peers in the structured groups. In short, both of these studies illustrate the importance of ensuring that groups are structured if students are to reap the social and academic benefits of cooperative learning.

2. Determine the size and the ability and gender composition of the group. Research conducted by Lou et al. (1996) on the size and composition of small groups indicated that small groups (i.e., 3–4 members) are preferable to larger groups, possibly because if groups are too large, they tend to be less personal and students will not participate. Moreover, small groups ensure everyone is included. Similarly, consideration needs to be given to the ability composition of groups. Lou et al. found that low-ability children learned significantly more in mixed-ability groups, while medium-ability students learned significantly more in homogeneous groups. High-ability students, however, learned equally well in mixed-ability or homogeneous groups. It appears that low-ability students benefit from the tutoring they receive from their high-ability peers, who tend to be quite active with the help they provide in mixed-ability groups, whereas their medium-ability peers may act as neither tutor nor tutee, making mixed-ability groups less beneficial for these students. Medium-ability students perform significantly better in homogeneous groups where they are more verbally active and possibly benefit from the detailed and elaborative help they give and receive from each other.

The ability composition of groups has been widely investigated, but the information available on the gender composition of groups is more limited. In an early study that did investigate gender composition and its effects on interaction and learning, Webb (1984) found in gender-balanced groups that males and females were equally interactive and showed similar levels of achievement. In majority-male groups, however, females tended to be ignored while males showed higher achievement than females. In majority-female groups, females directed most of their interaction to males to the detriment of their own interactions and showed lower achievement than males. The results of this study led Webb to suggest that children interacted better and learned more in gender-balanced groups or in all-female groups.

In contrast, Gillies and Ashman (1995) found the effects of different ability and gender compositions on members' behaviors and interactions were minimal when students worked in structured cooperative groups. It appeared that as the group members had more experience working in their groups, they became more responsive to the needs of each other, irrespective of the ability and gender composition of the group. This meant that by the conclusion of the study there were no significant differences between the different ability and gender group combinations in their behaviors and interactions. This further strengthens the importance of ensuring that when students work together, they work in groups that are well structured.

In a *meta-analysis* of peer-assisted learning interventions (i.e., where children work in small groups of 2–6 members), Rohrbeck, Ginsburg-Block, Fantuzzo, and Miller (2003) reported that interventions that had same-gender dyads and groups had significantly higher achievement effects than interventions with mixed-gender dyads and groups. The authors, however, caution that care should be taken when interpreting the findings because of the limited number of studies on same-gender groups included in the meta-analysis. In sum, the research on gender composition in groups is equivocal and further studies need to be conducted to clarify this issue.

3. *Set a task that will encourage the children to interact together.* For example, in some tasks, such as many computational tasks, children only need to exchange information and explanations or request assistance as they work together. Cohen (1994) suggested that these types of tasks involve low levels of cooperation because they require only that the children share information or decide how to divide their efforts so that each member contributes to the final group product. In effect, the type of discourse they engage in is limited by the nature of the task. In contrast, high-level cooperative tasks require students to interact about the process and to discuss planning, decision making, and the allocation of jobs as well as substantive content. These types of tasks are often open and discovery-based; they have no set procedures to follow or solutions to find so children are forced to interact together if they are to solve the problem. In these situations, group interaction is vital to productivity, and it could be expected that the children would engage in more productive discourse as they worked on the problem at hand. In a study of the behavior and interactions of children in structured and unstructured groups in Grades 1 and 3, Gillies and Ashman (1998) found that children in the structured groups in both grades used higher-level cognitive strategies in their interactions than their peers in the unstructured groups. These findings suggest that well-structured cooperative tasks where children have to interact together promote higher reasoning interactions.

4. *Ensure that tasks that are set are inclusive of all students.* This means that the appropriate modifications are made to tasks to ensure that children with

learning difficulties or disabilities are able to participate as well as students with challenging behaviors. This latter category may include students who have emotional and social difficulties who may initially have problems working in a group of four students. In these situations, consideration may need to be given to having these students work in pairs for short periods of time (5–10 minutes) on specific tasks until they are able to cope with the dynamics of the larger group.

5. *Inform the class of the group experience and discuss with them clear expectations of acceptable behaviors, including task-focused behaviors and interpersonal behaviors.* This can be achieved through class discussion where the students can generate their own list of rights and responsibilities as class participants as well as the types of interpersonal and small-group behaviors they believe will facilitate the smooth running of the groups (Webb & Farivar, 1994). Johnson and Johnson (1999) believe that it is very important that teachers explain the social skills that need to be used if groups are to run smoothly. While elementary teachers can discuss their expectations with their students, high school teachers need to be prepared to negotiate the ground rules for acceptable group behaviors with their students. In this way, students are more likely to be prepared to accept a code of behaviors that they believe they have developed as opposed to one that's been imposed on them. The list of social behaviors outlined below is intended only as a guide:

- We listen when others talk.
- We state our ideas freely and clearly (no put downs).
- We offer constructive comments on others' ideas.
- We accept ownership of our own behaviors.
- We share work-tasks fairly.
- We resolve problems democratically.
- We try to understand the other person's perspective (point of view).

It is advisable to write these as positive behaviors so the focus is on what members can do to contribute to the smooth running of the group, rather than as negative ones that students may perceive as an attempt by the teacher to exert control over group members. It is also advisable to review these group behaviors frequently with students so they understand clearly the expectations for appropriate behavior that are held by their teacher and their peers.

In forming groups, teachers also need to be mindful of the dynamics of different group combinations. For example, some students will have difficulties working with others, and it is often advisable to ensure that they are included in groups where they are more likely to work successfully than in groups where they are likely to be in conflict.

6. Students need to understand that they have responsibilities both to themselves and to their group members when they work together. Each student will be responsible for completing that part of the task assigned to him or her and for sharing the information with others in the group. Group responsibilities include ensuring that everyone has a specific task and that all members in the group need to complete their tasks before the group's goal is achieved. This requirement ensures that there is no social loafing and that everyone is held accountable for their contributions. In addition to being responsible for completing the above tasks, students sometimes like to take on specific roles: for example, organizer, motivator, recorder, researcher, reporter. With older students, the following types of roles may be more appropriate: production manager (i.e., helps to organize the group's report), human resources manager (i.e., helps to harness the members of the group and encourage their efforts), technology manager, resources manager (i.e., collates information for the group to use). These roles are not imperative and can be negotiated. Because the roles are allocated, students can be held accountable for their individual contributions to the group and, by doing so, they learn that social loafing will not be tolerated.

7. Students need to be taught to monitor the group's progress, including their own contributions, as well as how well the group is maintaining effective working relationships. This involves identifying what members' actions are helpful or unhelpful so they can make decisions about what behaviors to continue or change (Johnson & Johnson, 1990). The following types of questions can be used to help individuals self-monitor and groups self-evaluate:

Individual self-monitoring

- How am I doing?
- What have I accomplished?
- Is this making sense?
- How does this link with what I've learned before?

Group self-evaluation

- What did we do that was helpful?
- What can we improve?
- What do we still need to do?
- How did we manage our relationships with each other?
- How can we do things differently next time?

These types of questions encourage children to think metacognitively about their own learning as well as how members are contributing to attaining the group's goal. There is evidence that children can be taught explicit strategies for monitoring their thinking during learning and that this has a positive effect on their academic progress. Mason (2004) found that when children who had difficulties reading were taught to integrate and self-regulate comprehension strategies throughout the reading process, they performed better than students who participated in reciprocal questioning techniques with only their teacher.

Manset-Williamson and Nelson (2005), in a study of the effects of explicit strategy instruction on comprehension for upper elementary and middle school students with reading delays, found that when children had received explicit strategy training, they made significantly greater comprehension gains than students who had not received such training but had participated in guided reading instruction only.

Likewise, Desoete, Roeyers, and De Clercq (2003), in a study of Grade 3 children who participated in a metacognitive intervention designed to enhance mathematical problem solving, found the metacognitively trained group achieved significant gains in the acquisition of metacognitive trained skills and mathematics problem-solving knowledge over children who had participated in other training interventions. In effect, the research clearly demonstrates that when children are taught metacognitive skills and strategies, they are able to use these strategies to enhance their comprehension and problem-solving abilities (Boekaerts & Corno, 2005).

Similarly, children engaging in group processing learn to review their contributions, receive feedback from other group members, develop more precise understandings of what they know and may need to learn, and develop learning plans that will help them to accomplish their goals (whether the group's or their own). In effect, group processing sharpens students' awareness of what is happening and enables them to see that they can be active in any decisions they make. Moreover, there is evidence that the process of monitoring the academic performance of others can improve the monitor's own task behavior and academic skills (Topping & Ehly, 2001). When children help others to learn, they often have to reorganize and clarify the information they are explaining and in so doing often develop new perspectives and construct more elaborative cognitive understandings than they held previously (Wittrock, 1990).

Teachers need to monitor students' group work actively and provide constructive feedback on the group's progress, including feedback on each individual's efforts. Johnson and Johnson (1999) propose that this should include systematically observing and collecting data on each group as it works and, when needed, intervening to assist students in completing tasks accurately and in working together effectively. The following types of questions can be used to stimulate feedback to groups and individual students:

Groups

- How well organized was the group to deal with the task?
- How relevant was the information to the task?
- What was the standard of the work (satisfactory, good, very good)?

- Did group members spend time researching the topic?
- Did members have opportunities to share their ideas?
- Did group members listen to the ideas of others?
- Did members participate in group decisions?
- Did members work independently as a group?

Individuals

- What did you like about what you did in the group?
- What would you like to change or improve?
- What did you learn from your experience in the group?
- What is your plan now?

These questions are not prescriptive, but are designed to encourage children to reflect on what they have been doing and what they have learned from their experiences. Reflections are important because they help students relate what they have learned to their previous understandings and determine how their learning and problem-solving strategies might be reapplied (Hmelo-Silver, 2004). King (1994) found that when children were taught to provide explanations and make connections between new information and what they had learned previously, they engaged in higher-level discussions and more complex knowledge construction than peers who had been taught to provide explanations only. Similarly, Fuchs et al. (1997) found that when elementary students were taught to build relations between their current knowledge and new information during peer-mediated learning, they provided more conceptual explanations to each other than peers who had not been taught to make these links.

The process of asking and answering questions and making links to previous knowledge highlights the importance to students of thinking about what they have achieved and what they have learned from their experiences. When children engage in activities that encourage them to think about their thinking, or to think metacognitively, they learn to become reflective thinkers, which, in turn, teaches them to think more deeply and flexibly about the issues under discussion and to use their knowledge to plan.

There are a number of ways in which the class teacher can encourage students to reflect on their group's effort; one involves encouraging students to keep a reflective journal of their experiences. A reflective journal allows students to consider what they've experienced, how well they collaborated with the group, and how effectively they directed their learning (Hmelo-Silver, 2004). Stimulus prompts or questions, such as the ones outlined above, can help focus students' efforts, and this, coupled with opportunities to discuss their responses, can assist children to galvanize their thoughts and consolidate their thinking on the group learning experience. Moreover, it can provide the class teacher with the opportunity of reviewing the children's comments and responding to them.

McInerney and McInerney (2002) propose that students can be trained to become more conscious, purposeful learners through writing statements in class about their learning. The teacher reflects on their journal entries and writes a response that the children read before making their next entry. The benefits of these reflective activities are to encourage students to become more active in their learning by questioning what they do not understand, including the purposes of classroom activities and the effectiveness of their own work habits. In effect, these types of activities teach students how to accept more responsibility for their own learning.

CHAPTER SUMMARY

The research suggests that cooperative learning works best when

- Groups are well structured.
- Groups are small in size (probably no more than 3–4 students).
- Low-ability children work in mixed-ability groups, and medium-ability students work in same-ability groups (high-ability students do equally well in any grouping arrangement).
- Groups are gender-balanced or same-gender groups, particularly for girls.
- Tasks are established to promote discussion (i.e., open and discovery-based tasks).
- Teachers play a key role in monitoring students' group work and providing constructive feedback.

ACTIVITIES

1. Interview two classroom teachers who have used cooperative learning; ask about their perceptions of what they needed to do to establish cooperative learning in their classrooms. In particular, ask questions about the way the groups are structured, the composition of the groups, the types of activities undertaken by the children, and the types of learning that occur. Consider how the teachers' responses compare with the information you've gleaned from reading this chapter.

2. Arrange to visit a classroom where cooperative learning is used. Note the following: types of activities the children undertake during cooperative learning; how the children are made accountable for their efforts; the size and composition of the groups; and how the teacher monitors the children's progress. Pay particular attention to any groups that are gender-imbalanced. See if there are differences in the way the students interact. If the groups are mixed-ability groups, are all the children interacting with each other?

3. Construct a matrix of the types of behaviors you saw as you observed the cooperative groups and note the frequency with which each occurs. For example, how frequently did you observe group members' providing verbal and nonverbal assistance to each other? Did you observe any conflicts or disagreements among the members? What did you notice about their time on-task and off-task?

4. How does the teacher verbally cue the students on their group work? What type of feedback do they receive? For example, was the feedback very directive so students understood what they needed to do, or was it more facilitative? Try to jot down examples of the different types of feedback teachers provided to the students.

5. Reflect on your experiences in class. Have you had the opportunity of working in a small group with others? If that was a positive experience for you, what worked well? If not, perhaps you can suggest what you would do if you had the opportunity of working together again. Consider issues of how the group was established, the task members undertook, guidance provided for the activity, and the contributions of other members.

SUGGESTIONS FOR FURTHER READING

Gillies, R., & Ashman, A. (Eds.). (2003). *Cooperative learning: The social and intellectual outcomes of learning in groups.* London: RoutledgeFalmer.

Jacobs, G., Power, M., & Inn, L. W. (2002). *The teacher's sourcebook for cooperative learning.* Thousand Oaks, CA: Sage.

Johnson, D., & Johnson, R. (2003). *Assessing students in groups: Promoting group responsibility and Individual Accountability.* Thousand Oaks, CA: Sage.

Johnson, D., & Johnson, R. (1999). Making cooperative learning work. *Theory Into Practice, 38,* 67–73.

CHAPTER 3

*Teachers' Discourse to Promote
Student Thinking and Learning*

INTRODUCTION AND LEARNING OBJECTIVES

Teachers play a key role in promoting interactions among students and engaging them in the learning process, and cooperative learning is widely recognized as a pedagogical practice that can be employed in classrooms to stimulate students' interest in learning through their involvement with their peers. When children work cooperatively, they learn to give and receive information and develop new ideas and perspectives on how others think and communicate in socially appropriate ways. It is through interacting with others in reciprocal dialogues that children learn to use language differently to explain new ideas and realities and, in so doing, to construct new ways of thinking and feeling (Mercer, 1996). Cooperative learning provides opportunities for children to actively interact with others, negotiate new understandings, and appropriate new and creative ways of thinking about topics under discussion (King, 1999). In effect, cooperative learning provides opportunities for children to coconstruct new knowledge in an environment that encourages them to test out their ideas free from the constraints of a wider class group.

When You Have Finished This Chapter You Will Know:

- How teachers' interactions with their students are shaped by the learning environment
- How teachers can use specific verbal strategies to scaffold and challenge students' thinking
- The different types of mediated learning strategies teachers use to promote understanding and learning in students
- How students model the dialogues that teachers use
- The constructivist theories that underpin students' learning in small groups

Case Study 3.1

Teacher's Dialogue With a Small Group of Students

The teacher (T) and students (S) are examining a picture of a brass rubbing of some nobility who lived during medieval times.

T: See this area here? Let's have a go. I love the dresses, they're so ornate. Why do you reckon they would have had long dresses and all the gear on their head? (*T. challenges children to think of some reasons why people who lived in medieval times wore the clothes they did*)

S: Because of their religion.

T: It might have been because of their religion. (*T. validates and acknowledges student's response*) In some places they do cover their faces and everything, but I think there was another reason why they dressed up. (*T. probes for additional ideas*)

S: Some people cover their hair so nobody can see their hair—that's what they did.

T: It's their customs and religion, that's right. Have you got any other ideas why they got dressed up like this with their head covered and veils and . . . and the material looks really, really heavy, ornate . . . (*T. keeps probing for reasons*)

S: To impress

T: Yes, to impress their husbands maybe. Do you have any other ideas? (*T. continues to probe for reasons*)

S: Yes. Because it's very cold.

T: Yes, that's great. It can get very, very cold in England. (*T. acknowledges and validates student's response*)

S: My grandma told me my dad was born in England so I have a little bit of English blood.

T: If you have a look at the photo of them, you'll see them all dressed warmly. So when you look at the lady, she's dressed really warm. So in the cold she'd be lovely and warm. Now if she lived in a hot climate, what do you think would happen? (*T. challenges children to try to make links between the information they have been reading about and what they know from previous work*)

S: She'd be hot. She's get all sweaty and sticky.

T: I wonder if you can think of what might be different if she decided to live here? What do you think might be different? How would it be different? (*T. challenges children to think metacognitively about how the types of clothes may have been different*)

Case Study 3.1 provides an extract of a short interaction between a teacher and a small group of children who are examining a picture of a brass rubbing of a group of medieval nobles and the clothes they wore. This activity is part of a medieval theme the children are investigating in their social studies program.

In this extract, the teacher (T) challenges the students (S) to think of some reasons why the individuals depicted in the brass rubbing would be wearing the clothes they are (Turn 1). When one of the students suggests a reason, she acknowledges and validates that attempt while continuing to probe for additional ideas or reasons (Turns 3, 5, and 7). When another reason is given, she acknowledges and validates that effort also (Turn 9), but continues by challenging the children to try to make links between what they know about their own climate and the clothing these medieval people in Europe wore. Finally, she builds on the children's responses to try to get them to think metacognitively about how the situation may be different and why it would be different in the Australian context.

Questions that encourage children to make links between previous understandings and current learning help them to learn to monitor and regulate their understanding of the material and their ability to extend their learning by going beyond that material to construct new knowledge (King, 2002). Throughout this dialogue, the teacher continues to challenge the children's thinking while encouraging and supporting their endeavors: "Yes, that's great" (Turn 9) was made with enthusiasm and emotion so the student clearly understood that she appreciated the response provided.

TEACHERS' DISCOURSE DURING WHOLE-CLASS, SMALL-GROUP, AND COOPERATIVE LEARNING

In many ways, the teacher's discourse depicted in Case Study 3.1 is typical of that used by teachers in classrooms where cooperative learning has been implemented. This discourse is quite different from that used by teachers during whole-class teaching or small-group learning.

Whole-Class Versus Cooperative Learning

Hertz-Lazarowitz and Shachar (1990) investigated the difference in 27 elementary teachers' discourse as they alternatively implemented *whole-class instruction* and cooperative learning in their classrooms. The authors noted that during cooperative learning the teachers used language that was more friendly, encouraging, and supportive of their students' learning than during whole-class teaching when their language was more authoritarian and impersonal and where they spent more time directing, questioning, and disciplining their students. The difference in the discourse was so marked that Hertz-Lazarowitz and Shachar argued that when teachers established cooperative learning where they had to deal with a number of small groups rather than one large one, they became engaged in a complex process of linguistic change that affected how they interacted with their students. This observation was particularly interesting given that all the teachers had participated in extensive professional development on how to establish groups for cooperative learning in their classrooms.

Small-Group Versus Cooperative Learning

In a follow-up study that built on the Hertz-Lazarowitz and Shachar (1990) study, Gillies (2006) investigated whether there were differences between the discourses of teachers who implemented cooperative learning as opposed to *small-group learning* in their classrooms. This distinction in how students are grouped is important because small-group learning has many of the characteristics of whole-class learning where children are not linked interdependently around a goal but often work individually to achieve their own goals. This is in contrast to cooperative learning, where children are interdependently linked so they must work together to achieve the group's goal, participate in group discussions, share resources, and learn to resolve disagreements democratically.

The Gillies study involved 26 teachers and 303 students in Grades 8–10 from four high schools in Brisbane, Australia. All participating teachers agreed to embed cooperative learning pedagogy into a unit of work once a term for three school terms. Audiotapes of the teachers' and students' discourses were collected during these lessons, transcribed, and analyzed. The results showed that when teachers used cooperative learning, 18.2% of their talk involved *mediated-learning behaviors* or behaviors designed to promote thinking and foster learning in students; 20.5% involved asking open and short questions, although the open questions were more designed to elicit an expected response; and 6.3% of their talk was directed at disciplining the students. In contrast, when teachers implemented group-work only, 12.5% of their talk involved mediated learning behaviors, 13.7% questioning, and 12.9% disciplining.

These results showed that when teachers implemented cooperative learning, they engaged in nearly 50% more mediated learning and questioning behaviors and recorded fewer than half the disciplinary comments of those teachers who used group work only. These findings provide strong support for the Hertz-Lazarowitz and Shachar (1990) study that found when teachers implement cooperative learning, it changes the way they interact with their students.

Moreover, like Hertz-Lazarowitz and Shachar, Gillies (2006) found that the teachers' manner was more personal and friendly as they interacted with the students during their cooperative learning activities. Comments such as: "You're really thinking hard about that. That's great," "I like the way you're looking at both points of view before you're making your decisions," and "Jason, that's a really imaginative word that you've used to describe that scenario" are typical of the types of personal and friendly discourses the teachers used.

Communication Skills and Cooperative Learning

Given that the research clearly indicates that teachers' discourse is affected by the organizational structure of the classroom so that when cooperative learning is implemented, teachers use more mediated learning interactions or language designed to promote thinking and foster learning, Gillies (2004a) investigated whether teachers could be trained to use specific communication skills to enhance children's thinking and learning during cooperative group work.

This study (Gillies, 2004b) involved 30 elementary teachers and 826 students drawn from 11 schools across Brisbane. All the teachers participated in a 2-day workshop designed to introduce them to the key components of cooperative learning (i.e., positive interdependence of task/goal, individual accountability, promotive interaction, the interpersonal and small-group skills, and group processing) and how to embed these components in their classroom curriculum. In addition, half the teachers were trained in those communication skills that are designed to challenge children's thinking and scaffold their learning. Examples of these communication skills are seen in the box on page 66.

Although all the teachers were trained to embed the key components of cooperative learning into their classroom curriculum, the results of this study (Gillies, 2004a) showed that the teachers who had been taught specific communication skills to promote thinking and to scaffold children's learning engaged in more mediated learning behaviors (12.0% for the communications skills group vs. 7.6% for the cooperative group) and asked more questions (39.7% for the communications group vs. 21.2% for the cooperative group) than those teachers who did not receive the communication skills training. Moreover, while the teachers who had been trained in specific communication skills still asked questions that tended to elicit short-answer responses, Turner et al. (2002) argue that these types of questions can be effective if used in combination with instructional *scaffolding* or, as occurred in this study, mediated learning (i.e., those verbal behaviors designed to challenge children's thinking and scaffold their learning).

Communication Skills Teachers Were Trained to Use

Types of Communication Skills	Examples of Skills
Probing and clarifying issues	• *Can you tell us a bit more about what you found out when you investigated that issue further?* • *Have you thought about using this information to help you work through that dilemma?*
Acknowledging and validating	• *That's a really great effort. You've worked hard to put that information together.* • *I like that word. It creates a sense of mystery about the plot.*
Confronting discrepancies and clarifying options	• *You seem to be saying . . . but I notice you've actually got something different here. I wonder how you reconcile the anomaly.* • *I'm not sure I understand what you mean by that. Perhaps you can explain it more clearly to the group?*
Tentatively offering suggestions	• *I wonder if you've thought about doing it like this?* • *Perhaps you could try it to see what happens?* • *Have you thought about . . . ?*

It appeared that by training teachers explicitly to use the communication skills outlined above, they learned to think about how to interrogate students' thinking and learning, and this, in turn, helped them to monitor their own mediated learning behaviors—what they should say and how they should say it. Interestingly, the teachers who participated in the communications skills training were four times less likely to have to discipline students as they worked in their groups than the teachers who did not participate in this training. It may be that when teachers use discourse that clearly demonstrates interest in what students are doing, students, in turn, are more likely to remain engaged with the task at hand.

Types of Mediated Learning

In order to provide a clearer picture of the different types of mediated learning behaviors the teachers used, Gillies and Boyle (2006) analyzed transcripts of the teachers' discourse as they interacted with the children. The mediated learning behaviors they identified were designed to challenge children's understandings, encourage their thinking, and help them to connect their ideas to previous learning. Moreover, the teachers were observed to work at making these connections by encouraging the children to cooperate and to discuss ideas together and by setting tasks that required the children to draw on their prior knowledge and understandings. Examples of the mediated learning behaviors the teachers used are outlined below.

Types and Examples of Mediated Learning Behaviors Used by the Teachers

Mediated Learning	Examples
1. Questions basic information to challenge children's thinking	*Tell me a little bit more about the characters in the story.*
2. Challenges children to provide reasons	*So tell us a bit more about how you solved that problem.*
3. Metacognitive: thinking about thinking	*How do you find out what else you might still need to consider?*
4. Confronts discrepancies to highlight inconsistencies in thinking	*I hear you saying this . . . but now you've said . . . I'm not sure I understand your position.*
5. Prompts student by pointing to potential help	*I think I'd check that out again, because sometimes there are other possibilities (i.e., answers) you'll need to consider too.*
6. Prompts student to focus on issue	*You'll need to look at those issues and identify the one to focus on.*
7. Tentatively questions to provide another perspective for consideration	*Have you thought about . . . as a way of dealing with that topic?*
8. Asks open question	*What do you think you'll do now? How do you think that may help?*
9. Scaffolds connections between information, ideas.	*Remember what we discussed yesterday about the indigenous people who lived . . .? Think about what we're discussing now . . . Can you see any similarities and differences?*
10. Validates and acknowledges students' efforts	*You've thought very carefully about how you responded to that topic. There are some really imaginative ideas there. That's great.*

Pedagogical Practices That Promote Thinking

In follow-up interviews with the teachers who had participated in the communication skills training, all commented that they believed it was important that children are taught to think both cognitively and metacognitively if they are to become proficient at problem solving and learning. Moreover, they believed that they did this by actively challenging the children to justify their opinions and by encouraging children to reflect on what they knew and what they still needed to know. By challenging the children to justify their reasons and make them explicit, the teachers were promoting high-level processing of information and thinking (King, 1999). Furthermore, when children have to do this publicly (albeit in the small group), they learn to sharpen their own understandings and to express their ideas in ways that others can understand and will accept as well reasoned and valid. In so doing, they contribute to the development of their own and others' understanding and learning (Rojas-Drummond & Mercer, 2003).

Scaffolding was another important pedagogical practice that the teachers reported using to promote children's thinking and learning. Teachers reported doing this by prompting children to consider different issues and perspectives or by modeling problem-solving strategies. The following comments were made by teachers who recognized the importance of modeling problem solving to their students:

> "You've got to be on the ball all the time and making every effort to model how it's done. I find modeling is very helpful as it gives the kids an idea of what they need to do."

> "I find if I model it for them—talk them through the steps, then they have a go and then I phase out . . . they seem to get the gist of what they need to do."

The teachers further reported that scaffolding also included making connections between information and ideas while all the time validating and acknowledging children's efforts. The following are examples of how teachers reported scaffolding connections to help encourage the children to think more comprehensively about the issues:

> "Remember what we discussed yesterday. We were talking about making sure that we had an understanding of . . . (key issues). Well, today you need to have a look at how they compare to what you discuss today (key issues on a related topic)."

"You could consider what he's had to say (group member) and consider his ideas along with what others have suggested. Put them together and you might come up with a fabulous idea." (*Teacher helping children understand how they could coconstruct new understandings from considering different ideas or information*)

Helping students to link previous understandings to current information is critically important if they are to be able to analyze and integrate different ideas and go beyond prescribed material to coconstruct new knowledge (King, 1999). The process involved is complex as it requires students to engage in critical thinking, problem solving, and decision making (King, 2002). These are processes that teachers can actively facilitate through their *dialogic exchanges* with students during cooperative learning. Case Study 3.2 provides an example of a class teacher challenging a group's thinking during a cooperative small group task.

Case Study 3.2

An Exchange Between a Teacher and One of the Small Groups in Her Fifth-Grade Class

The teacher (T) is challenging the children to think about how they might deal with the problem below.

Background: Students(s) are required to come up with a solution to a problem where a car has gone over the edge of the cliff and they are first to arrive on the scene. They are required to develop a plan of action and represent their plan (e.g., a sequence of pictures), which they will then discuss with the larger class group.

T: Now you've got to decide how she's going to get them out of this mess, because she's the only one who is conscious.

S: They could be dead, I think.

T: Yes, but we don't know that so we assume they're not. So if it were you and you saw two people in the front who looked as though they were asleep, what do you think you might do? (*T. prompts students to think of the actions they might take*)

S: I would, if it were a busy road, I would go up and call out.

T: True, but is there something you might do before that? (*T. challenging students to think of how they might sequence their responses*)

S: Try and wake them up. See if they're conscious.

T: Yes, see if they were conscious or if they were dead. If they weren't dead, what could you do next that could help them? . . . Think about that TV show the other day where we saw how the emergency people rescue people who get into difficult situations. (*T. scaffolds connections between information*)

S: Go up to the road and stop some cars. Get them to help you. Call the police, the ambulance.

T: They might be hurt or uncomfortable in some way. What would you do? Can you see what you would do if they were hurt? And that it was someone who was near and dear to you? (*T. probes the students to see if they can think of an immediate response*)

S: Check out whether they're alive. Their pulse.

S: Check their breathing, blood pressure.

T: Yes, that's part of it. I don't know about blood pressure. What else is obvious? (*T. scaffolds links between the different pieces of information provided in the scenario*)

S: I know if you're alive your tongue would still be pink but if you're dead your tongue would be relaxed.

T: But if you were lying unconscious and I wasn't sure whether you were dead or not, what could I do? What else do you think you would do? (*T. challenges students to think of response*)

S: Shake you gently.

T: Little things like that to see if you were dead or alive, and then if they were alive, what could you do that might help them? Think about what you know here. (*T. scaffolds links between information*)

S: Make sure they can breathe . . . that their mouth isn't blocked up with blood.

T: Make sure they're not vomiting in their mouth or something. Is there anything else you'd do? (*T. probes students to think of other responses*)

S: If they were dead their tongue would be black because all the blood goes to it.

T: But if they were not dead and you could get them to come around what would you do next? (*Pause*) Well, what do you normally give people if they've been hurt or upset? (*T. scaffolds links between previous information and its relevance to the current situation*)

S: Comfort.

T: Yes, that's important. How do you do that? What might you say? (*T. probes students to identify a response*)

S: Say you'll be OK. Keep telling them you'll help.

T: What else do you think these people would need? (*T. challenges students to consider other responses*)

S: Water.

T: Water, right! What else could you check out? Most cars carry these. (*T. prompts students*)

S: First aid kit.

T: Most modern cars these days carry one. So perhaps that's how you should start out. And once you know they're OK she could go off and get help, but if they were dead that's a different scenario, isn't it? Can you imagine how you'd react if they were dead? What would you do? What would you think? So you've got to decide if they're dead or alive. (*T. challenges students to think metacognitively*)

In Case Study 3.2, the teacher demonstrates a number of mediated learning behaviors that promote thinking in students. These include prompting (Turns 3, 9, 26), probing (Turns 9, 18), and challenging (Turns 5, 14, 24) the students to think of possible responses to the road accident scenario. The teacher also scaffolds links between information (Turns 7, 12, 16, 20), and she encourages them to think metacognitively (Turn 28) when dealing with the problem at hand. When these mediated learning behaviors that promote thinking are taught explicitly, students learn to take these behaviors on board and model them in their small-group discussions with each other (Gillies & Boyle, 2005).

To illustrate what the students were doing in their groups, an extract from a continuous discussion that occurred in one of the small groups in the above teacher's classroom is presented in Case Study 3.3. This extract lasted only a few minutes, and it occurred after the dialogue reported above.

Case Study 3.3

A Discussion Among Students in a Small Group

The students (S) are discussing how they would solve the problem of a car that has gone over a cliff and they are the first to arrive on the scene.

S: OK, what do you think she (person in the car) did? (*S. challenges others to think of a response*).

S: She punched out the back window, climbed out and up to the rocks . . . she had to get away and get help.

S: If she went on to the road, what about the people in the car?

S: That's right. (*S. acknowledges and validates other's idea*) They could die.

S: What do you think you would do, Jason? (*S. challenges group members to suggest a response*)

S: I'd get help . . . go to the shop and phone the police and ambulance.

S: Yeah, but they could be badly injured and they'd die in the meantime. . . .

S: They could be badly injured and need help?

S: Yeah, but isn't it better to get help first . . . get the ambulance and the police to come and help them. . . . Like we saw before (*referring to TV program about a car accident*). (*S. links information*)

S: You'd have to go and check them out and see if they're dead or alive . . . you'd have to go down and do that (*referring to climbing down the hill*).

S: But that could waste time, I think you'd be better trying to get help . . . go to the nearest shop and phone the police and ambulance.

S: Yeah, but they could die in the meantime, bleed to death . . . there could be a fire, the car could explode.

S: OK, let's make a decision here. What do you want to do first? (*S. challenges others to make a decision*)

S: You'd need to go down the hill and check them out. If there were two of us, one could go and get help and the other could go down the gully.

S: Yeah, he's right. (*S. acknowledges and validates other's idea*)

The students' dialogue demonstrates that they modeled many of the types of mediated learning behaviors that their teacher had used as she interacted with the groups. For example, they challenged each other's opinions (Turns 1, 5, 13), acknowledged each other's points (Turn 4, 15), and attempted to link new information to previous understandings (Turn 9). Moreover, they did this in an environment that was task oriented and open to others' ideas and suggestions.

It was interesting to hear the students modeling many of the mediated learning behaviors that their teacher used to scaffold learning and challenge understanding, particularly given that they, unlike their teacher, had not been trained to use communication skills to challenge thinking and promote learning. It can only be assumed that they relied on the cooperative group context and their teacher's discourse to understand the relevance of these skills to their learning needs. Gillies and Boyle (2005) found that students were successful at scaffolding and challenging each other's learning during small-group work if their teachers first modeled these behaviors in their interactions with their students. It seems that when students work in cooperative small groups where they feel supported and free to try out new ways of thinking and talking, they need only a minimum of encouragement to model some of the mediated learning behaviors they have heard their teachers use.

In order to illustrate how teachers interact with older students to challenge their thinking, scaffold their learning, and encourage them to make links between different bodies of knowledge and cognitive understandings, the following scenario of a Grade 11 teacher interacting with a small group of students in her class is presented (Case Study 3.4). The students have been working on a science unit that has included some detailed cases on genetic abnormalities in humans. Concurrently, the students have been exposed to some of the ethical and moral dilemmas doctors and scientists confront as they deal with life-and-death decisions relating to different genetic abnormalities in humans. The students have also been studying codes of ethical practice to help them understand the principles that underpins these codes.

Case Study 3.4

An Exchange Between an Eleventh-Grade Teacher and a Small Group of Students

They are discussing what they would do if they were confronted with the decision of aborting a 24-week-old fetus that had been diagnosed with Down syndrome.

Background: The students have information on this genetic abnormality, including information on how this type of genetic abnormality occurs, the types of tests that are used to screen and diagnose this condition in an unborn child, and the long-term quality of life prospects for a child with Down syndrome.

S: How reliable is amniocentesis? Is it really reliable?

S: It's pretty reliable. It's more reliable than the different screening tests we read about. You know the ones they do when they check the mother's blood.

T: You probably need to just check that out again and make sure you're clear on that issue because it sounds as if it's going to be pretty important for your discussion (*T. prompts students on a key issue to consider*).

S: I would need to be pretty sure that the test was reliable before I'd consider aborting it.

S: I agree, although . . . but if the test was reliable I'd be inclined to abort. It wouldn't be fair to bring up a child that didn't have a fair chance at life, a child that was mentally retarded.

T: I wonder if you're considering that from your perspective. I wonder if these children might think differently? (*T. challenges students to consider another perspective to the issue*)

S: OK. We seem to have a couple of different perspectives that we need to consider if we're going to make a decision. Like. Jessie [student] thinks that she'd need to be clear that the test was reliable but you (*pointing to another student*) think that even if it was reliable, you'd still abort 'cause it wouldn't be fair to not have a good quality life.

S: Yes, but there's also the ethical issue of aborting a fetus that is fully human. Have you seen pictures of fetuses at this stage of their development? They look like small babies.

S: That's true. This is really quite complicated. I'm not sure I'd want to make that decision.

S: The family thinks she should abort. They're worried about whether they can support such a child.

S: Yep! Surely things can't be that bad. You know you'd get a lot of support from agencies. There's Down syndrome help groups. I've seen them on the Web and there's special schools for these children.

T: These are important points, and you need to consider them carefully. (*T. acknowledges and validates students' points*) Have you thought about the doctor's position and how he stands ethically? (*T. scaffolds links between different pieces of information provided in the scenario*)

S: Yes, that's important. He's bound by a code of professional practice and he may not want to be involved in an abortion.

T: I wonder if there are other pieces of information you may need to bring together to help inform your discussion? (*T. prompts students to consider linking information*)

S: Well there's also the mother's health. If she doesn't want the baby, she shouldn't be expected to have it, especially if it's mentally handicapped.

T: That's an issue. (*T. acknowledges student's issue*) I wonder if there are other issues that you might need to consider about the mother's health? (*T. prompts the students to consider other health issues*)

S: Well, there's also the issue of if she aborts, she may not be able to have another child. Sometimes, women can be left sterile after abortions.

T: Yes, that's true. (*T. acknowledges student's point*) How are you doing with the information you have? Is there anything else you need to consider? (*T. encourages the group to think metacognitively—to think about their thinking*)

Although the students in the scenario in Case Study 3.5 are more sophisticated in the way they talk and how they consider the issues, the teacher still uses a number of mediated learning behaviors to extend their thinking on the topic. These include prompting (Turns 3, 14, & 16), challenging (Turn 6), and scaffolding (Turn 12), as well as encouraging the students to think metacognitively (Turn 18) to ensure that they have considered whether there is any additional information they may need to include. While the teacher's role in mediating the students' discussion is more subtle than the role of the teacher with the younger children (Case Study 3.2), she nevertheless is quite active in prompting, challenging, and scaffolding students' thinking to help broaden their perspectives on the dilemma at hand. This is important because without the teacher actively monitoring the discussion, the students could end up with a less-than-informed or a limited perspective on the factors that affect the dilemma.

Because this teacher has good rapport with her students, they respond well to her interest in their discussion and her efforts to extend their thinking. For example, the response that was given after the teacher had challenged the children at Turn 6—*I wonder if you're considering that from your perspective. I wonder if these children might think differently?*—immediately triggered the following response in the student at Turn 7, indicating that she has grasped the importance of considering additional perspectives: *OK. We seem to have a couple of different perspectives that we need to consider if we're going to make a decision. Like. Jessie (student) thinks that she'd need to be clear that the test was reliable but you (pointing to another student) think that even if it was reliable, you'd still abort 'cause it wouldn't be fair to not have a good quality life.*

A similar response occurs after the teacher has asked the group to consider the doctor's position and how he stands ethically (Turn 12) when the student acknowledges the importance of the suggestion by stating: *Yes, that's important. He's bound by a code of professional practice and he may not want to be involved in an abortion.* In short, the teacher's probing, challenging, and scaffolding influenced the students' responses and thinking.

The following extract (Case Study 3.5) is presented to illustrate what the students discussed after the teacher moved on to another group. The dialogue represents only a few minutes of this group's discussion, which occurred directly after the dialogue reported above.

Case Study 3.5

A Group Discussion Among Eleventh-Grade Students

They are discussing whether they would or would not consider aborting a fetus with Down syndrome.

S: OK, let's see what we've got so far. We know Down syndrome means that the child will be mentally retarded and this will affect the quality of its life. Some of us think she should have an abortion but some say no. The family wants her to abort but the doctor has an ethical dilemma to confront. Is that how you see it?

S: Yes. (*all students agree*)

S: We seem to be thinking about everyone else in this discussion but I wonder how the girl feels. Perhaps we need to think about her for a minute? (*S. tentatively proposes that the group considers another perspective*)

S: Sure, you're quire right. We haven't thought about her much at all. (*S. acknowledges and validates this suggestion*)

S: How do you see her situation? (*S. asks open question to elicit a clearer perspective on the issue*)

S: I really think this is very difficult because she's probably experiencing a lot of pressure from all sides. She's also got to consider what she wants too. Not just what everybody else wants.

S: Sure. You're right. (*S. validates another's point*)

S: How do we get round this, folks? (*S. challenges the group to think of solutions to the dilemma*)

S: I'm not sure we're going to be able to do that. I mean, it looks as though it's irresolvable.

S: Yes, but this is an issue that many people deal with every day. I'm not sure we can say we can't deal with it?

S: Is it better to try to think of some suggestions that have already come up and then we can look at them and try and work out what to do? (*S. challenges group to link information to work out a solution*)

It is interesting to observe how the students modeled many of the mediated learning behaviors that their teacher had used in their interactions with each other. While this would not have occurred solely from this brief interaction with their teacher, it was typical of the types of *dialogic exchanges* this teacher had with other groups in the room where she used a number of mediated learning behaviors to help students focus more clearly on the issue, consider different perspectives, and link relevant information to the issue under discussion to help obtain a better understanding of the dilemma. This teacher, like the teacher depicted previously, working with the Grade 5 students, had also been trained in the communication skills designed to challenge students' thinking and scaffold their learning; however, the students had not been trained to use these skills, so it can only be assumed that these students also saw the relevance of these skills to their own group context and emulated their teacher's dialogic exchanges in their interactions with each other. Certainly, Gillies and Boyle (2005) observed that this is what younger students did with a minimum of encouragement. It appears that when students work collectively in groups, and they are motivated to do so, they will engage in more facilitative interactions with their peers as they work on solving the problem at hand (Johnson, 2003).

Other Ways of Challenging Students' Thinking and Facilitating Interactions

Bloom's Taxonomy (1956) has traditionally been used by many teachers to develop questions that stimulate children's thinking in progressively more challenging ways. Questions posed range from those that tap basic recall through to those that require more evaluative responses. In class situations, teachers often try to ask questions that not only test recall and comprehension but also aim to stimulate higher-level thinking, such as those that challenge students to analyze, synthesize, and evaluate information. The following are examples of a series of questions a teacher may ask to help students think more deeply about information, in this case, weather systems:

1. Knowledge: List . . . (three types of weather systems)

2. Comprehension: What. . . . (damage could occur if our school was in the path of a tornado)?

3. Application: Using the information you've collected about a tornado, make a brochure to alert people to the precautions they should take if a tornado approaches.

4. Analysis: Compare two types of weather systems . . .

5. Synthesis: Design a house that would remain standing if a hurricane hit.

6. Evaluation: A powerful hurricane is threatening your home and you have to be evacuated. You can take only six of your belongings. What would you save and why?

The above questions tend to be hierarchical because they are ordered from simple to complex and from concrete to abstract. While this approach to stimulating students' thinking has been used extensively in schools, this is not the only way students can be helped to think and understand. Wiggins (1998) proposes that there is no one way of demonstrating *understanding* because understanding is multidimensional, encompassing very different interpretations of meaning. According to Wiggins, there are five overlapping yet separate aspects of understanding that need to be uncovered through schooling. These aspects derive from the different meanings attached to the word *understanding* and include being able to do the following:

1. Explain (This includes the ability to provide sophisticated explanations and interpretation of events)

2. Apply (This includes knowing how to apply knowledge effectively in different situations)

3. Take perspective (This includes being able to see things from multiple vantage points)

4. Empathize (This includes the ability to get inside another person's feelings and frame of reference)

5. Reflect (This includes knowing ourselves and understanding our prejudices)

These aspects of understanding are not hierarchical as in a *taxonomy* and are often developed simultaneously as students learn to uncover rich understandings of the material being presented or concepts being explored. Interestingly, teachers often use Bloom's taxonomy and Wiggin's approach to uncovering meaning to stimulate students' thinking and maximize their understandings—critically important for facilitating interactions.

CREATING THE LEARNING ENVIRONMENT

Research reports on the importance of creating learning environments where students feel safe, are able to participate, and can contribute to group discussions without fear of ridicule or mockery from their peers. When students believe they can contribute and are valued by others, they are more likely to feel motivated to continue to participate and stay engaged with the task. Moreover, the sense of "group" that students develop as a result of their cooperative learning experiences helps to foster a strong sense of social cohesion whereby members care about one another and will help each other learn (Slavin, 1996).

In summarizing the research on the benefits of cooperative learning to psychological health, Johnson and F. Johnson (2003) noted that cooperativeness, or the willingness to work with others, is positively related to a number of indices of psychological health, such as emotional maturity, well-adjusted social relations, strong personal identity, ability to cope with adversity, social competencies, and basic trust in and optimism about people. Johnson and Johnson reported that this occurred because, when students make an effort to cooperate, they realize that they are accepted by their peers, know that they have contributed to their own and others' success, and have learned to perceive themselves and others in more realistic and complementary ways (i.e., each individual has unique abilities).

In a study of junior high school students' experiences of cooperative learning, Gillies (2004b) found that students in cooperative groups demonstrated more care and concern for each other and were more willing to promote each other's learning and accept responsibility for each other's achievements than students who worked in small groups only (i.e., groups that have not been taught cooperative learning). These attitudes help to build a sense of group identity, promote prosocial norms among members, and create an environment conducive to learning. It is this sense of collective agency where members believe they can work together to produce desired effects that is highly motivational, as it contributes to group members' sense of autonomy or control over their own learning (Bandura, 2001; Goddard, Hoy, & Woolfolk Hoy, 2004).

Practical Activity

Ways of Creating a Cooperative Learning Environment

Elementary School

★ Use good verbal encouragement or language that lets students know that they are being heard. For example, "Mm!, Ah!, Sure, I see, Yes."

★ Use nonverbal body language that communicates a willingness to listen to students. For example, appropriate eye contact and body posture that is open and nonthreatening.

★ Use open questions with a pause to allow students time to process the question and respond. For example, "What do you think might have happened if . . . ?"; "Where do you think the characters were intending to go . . . ?"; "How were the . . . ?." Pausing after the question is very important as it

(Continued)

(Continued)

allows students time to reflect on what was asked and cognitively reorganize their thoughts to generate a possible response.

★ Use empathic listening and speaking skills to communicate an understanding of a student's thoughts or feelings about an issue. For example, "It sounds as if you've had a rough time . . ."; "How did you feel when that happened to you?"; "I can see that you're looking exhausted from it all."

★ The use of humor is a good stress and tension reliever, and it allows students to see their teacher in another light. Paradoxical techniques are particularly funny as children often like the humor conveyed by saying the opposite of what is meant. For example, "We don't need to worry about having lunch. We can all live on fresh air." This comment may be made (in a very friendly way) to encourage children to be a little quicker in getting themselves out for lunch.

★ Discuss clearly with the students their rights and responsibilities as members of the group or small team. The format in the box below is provided as a guide to stimulate discussion. Teachers can do this exercise as part of a brainstorming activity where they help the students to identify the rights and reciprocal responsibilities that each has as a member of the group. Students are often very forthright in identifying their rights as class members and can often very readily list them; however, getting them to identify reciprocal responsibilities is often difficult. It is important that students recognize that while they have rights as individuals in the classroom, they also have responsibilities to themselves and to each other as members of a learning community.

Rights and Responsibilities of Members of a Group

Rights to Learn	Responsibilities in Learning
1. I have a right to learn.	1. I have a responsibility to help others learn.
2. I have a right to contribute.	2. I have a responsibility to help others contribute.
3. I have a right to receive respect.	3. I have a responsibility to respect others.
4. I have a right to be safe.	4. I have a responsibility to help others feel safe.
5. I have the right to be able to do the best I can.	5. I have a responsibility to help others produce the best they can.

★ Ensure that the classroom is well lit and the general physical layout is open, friendly, and stress free. Posters on the walls can often act as stress relievers and promote discussion on topical issues such as key sports figures, current movies, key cartoon characters, and so on. When rooms are decorated in this way, students often feel more relaxed and able to enjoy their surroundings.

Middle School and High School

★ Create an environment that enables students to move around different work stations so they can access information, seek help, and produce individual and group products with ease. For example, access to the Internet may be critical for searching for information and downloading relevant materials. If students are working in groups, they need room to move freely around other groups as they seek help from others. They also need access to tables or floor space where they can lay out their work and prepare their group's report.

★ Negotiate expectations for group and classroom behaviors before students begin working in their groups. If this is done in a consultative and friendly manner, students are more likely to respond positively to any negotiated rules or parameters for behavior. Having students identify the types of behaviors they would expect from others is one way of helping students to generate their own list of behaviors they expect to see others demonstrate. Generating their own list of behaviors is more likely to promote ownership of them and a sense of responsibility to practice them.

★ Taking a personal interest in students by asking about their weekend or their favorite game is one way of helping to build connections and letting students know that their teachers are interested in them as individuals. Language used during these exchanges is often very relaxed and friendly and enables students to see another side of their teacher. Be prepared to share some of your own thoughts, as teachers, with your students so they can understand what your position or your opinion may be on topics of mutual interest (e.g., sports, movies, books).

★ Organize some icebreaking activities so students can get to know each other before they begin to work more formally together. This is particularly important for adolescents, who are often very sensitive about how they are likely to be perceived by their peers. Such icebreaking activities may include: finding out three things about a person in your group and then introducing that person to the wider class; completing a limerick from the first stimulus line; and identifying and discussing your funniest experience.

(Continued)

)

rganize to hold debates between groups on topical and humorous subjects. Ensure that speakers understand that what is being discussed is to be presented in a lighthearted manner. Have the remaining groups identify key aspects of the presentation that they liked and discuss these at the end of the debate. The teacher would need to help students highlight aspects of the debate that fulfilled the goal of the debate—to have fun. This type of exercise enables a teacher to demonstrate many of the mediated learning behaviors discussed above, such as acknowledging and validating students' efforts, challenging their perspectives, scaffolding their learning, and helping them to connect ideas and think metacognitively.

BRINGING IT ALL TOGETHER: UNDERSTANDING THE RESEARCH

There is no doubt that students learn by interacting with more competent others in their environment. Parents play a key role in helping very young children to learn and to communicate their needs. As children grow and develop, others such as teachers and peers play a key role in their learning and development. Through social engagement with others, children learn new ways of talking and of constructing meaning from their experiences. This process of constructing meaning on how children learn can be explained from two perspectives—personal and social constructivism.

Personal constructivism, originally proposed by Piaget (1950), involves the individual's reflecting on and organizing experiences to create order and adapt to the environment (Lisi & Golbeck, 1999). Personal constructivism emphasizes the intrapersonal dimensions of learning, and, in particular, the belief that knowledge is not transmitted directly from one individual to another, but rather is mediated through interacting with others. Exchanges that bring differing viewpoints into a child's awareness are likely to give rise to a state of cognitive conflict, because children have to keep their own points of view in mind while taking account of other incompatible perspectives. In this way, a state of disequilibrium is created that forces the child to *decenter* or consider the perspective of others in order to reduce the cognitive tension that has arisen.

When children disagree with others, two important realizations occur. First, they are forced to reexamine their own points of view and reassess their validity, and, second, they learn that they must justify their own points of view and communicate these clearly if these are to be accepted as valid. In so doing, children reevaluate and restructure their own perspectives on the basis of new information and are strongly motivated to reconcile contradictions. The interaction with others is a trigger to social and cognitive change, although the change itself is achieved by the individual.

The sociocognitive conflict that arises when different cognitive approaches are undertaken for the same situation was illustrated in a series of studies by Doise and Mugny (1984) and Mugny and Doise (1978). Children who were not yet able to conserve spatially were required to reproduce a model village of several houses but with each house having a different orientation. As the children were not yet capable of the spatial transformations required to preserve the front/back and left/right relations, they produced an egocentric copy of the village. In order to demonstrate the superiority of collaborative performances over individual ones, the children were paired on this task, and one child was required to make front/back and left/right transformations (despite having been selected because of an inability to do so) in placing the houses while the other child was required only to make the 90° rotations (something that most children of this age can do). Thus, any misplacement of a village house by a child who was required to make the more difficult transformations (front/back and left/right) would have created a problem for the other child, because the correct answer would have been obvious. The misplacement of the house would have challenged the children to reevaluate their own performances, including the perspective of the other child.

Analyses of the children's responses indicated that two types of interactions occurred. One led to compliance when the child simply applied the solution the other gave. This is called a relational solution to the problem; the child places an emphasis on maintaining the personal relationship to the detriment of his or her cognitive growth (Doise, 1990). The other interaction led to sociocognitive conflict where children had to defend their own solutions while being required to consider other erroneous solutions at the same time. This situation caused consternation among those children who did not have the cognitive capabilities necessary to solve the problem but who were perturbed by the unacceptable solution proposed by the other children. While looking for a solution, these children tended to verbalize their strategy and the issues they faced and, in so doing, made progress toward resolving the problem.

These studies showed that the simultaneous confrontation of different perspectives leads to the integration of new cognitive structures (Doise, 1990). By structuring situations in which challenge occurs, children are confronted with cognitive schemas or ways of thinking that are contradictory to their own. In order to reestablish internal equilibrium, the child is forced to confront these contradictory ways of thinking and integrate them into more elaborate cognitive formulations (Mugny & Carugati, 1989).

Children who know the correct answer can still learn from those who, seeing the problem from different angles, offer incorrect solutions. The gains made during the paired performances (by the children who were challenged to reevaluate their answers) were structurally superior to those of the group members taken individually, and generalized to individual performances on posttests indicating that the children were able to think through their own solutions as well as those of their partner before deciding on a final response. The results were interpreted in terms of *cognitive conflict*. When children are confronted with a conflicting solution, even if incorrect, it may provide them with some dimensions of a progressive elaboration of a cognitive mechanism new to them (Doise & Mugny, 1984; Mugny & Doise, 1978). In effect, the perturbing feedback provided by interaction with others initiates a process of *intellectual reconstruction* in the child as he or she seeks to accommodate and assimilate new ideas and understandings. Although sociocognitive conflict is important, the main work of constructing new knowledge is done at the intra-individual level by the child through solitary reflection (Damon, 1984; McInerney & McInerney, 2002).

In contrast, *social constructivism* proposes that children are introduced to new patterns of thought when they engage in dialogues with others. Social constructivism, originally proposed by Vygotsky (1978), emphasizes the interpersonal dimensions of learning and, in particular, the role more competent adults or children play in helping the child gain mastery over the cultural tools and signs that are important to his or her cultural group. However, although the environment or the context provides the habits and forms these cultural behaviors take, it is the individual who is actively involved in mastering these cultural behaviors and acquiring them as his or her personal property.

Vygotsky (1978) maintained that interaction with others is critical for the development of higher cognitive functions in children. During these interactions, more capable and older others mediate the child's environment by focusing attention on relevant environmental information and providing the tools for solving problems (e.g., speech, memory strategies). In other words, children are introduced to new ways of thinking and patterns of thought when they engage in dialogues with more competent others. Eventually, after repeated exposure to these exchanges, the child's thinking and communication processes become internalized, and it is through this internalization of processes that skills are incorporated into the child's mental system. Hence, when two children enter into a peer relationship, it is not only the information that is internalized from interactions but also the fundamental cognitive processes that are implicit in the communication (Vygotsky, 1978).

Internalization occurs as a child learns to adjust his or her definition of a situation to accommodate a "situation definition" that those involved in the interaction share (Wertsch, 1984). Thus, as adults use speech and gestures that are tied to the definition of a situation that exists for children, children adjust their understanding of that situation to develop a common understanding of social reality. This process occurs through mediation when adults or more capable peers mediate the environment for children by supplying the culturally available tools of thought that children eventually internalize. Once internalization has occurred, the child retains the ability to reproduce these jointly produced cognitive performances, and the achievement becomes part of the child's actual capabilities rather than merely a potential skill that can be realized only through interaction (Damon & Phelps, 1989).

By studying the interaction patterns between mothers and their young children, Wertsch (1984) identified four levels through which children progress from other-regulation to self-regulation, beginning with the young child responding in a way that is not related to the task, followed by realizing there is some connection to the adult's speech and the task, accepting more responsibility for regulating his or her own activity and being able to respond to the demands of others, through to finally being able to perform the task without any strategic assistance from the adult. Wertsch argued that children are motivated to progress from one level to the next because of the need to establish and maintain coherence between their actions and the adult's speech.

Coherence is created by children's adjusting their understanding of situations so their understandings are consistent with their behaviors. The child follows the adult's directions and constructs an understanding of the relationship between speech, definition of the situation, and behavior. Thus, children may perform the task even though they may not understand what they are being asked to do. Wertsch (1979) found that adults use directions that children do not understand and then guide the children's responses. Cazden (1983) later observed that as the child's learning developed, the strategy or routine that was provided by the teacher was progressively altered and replaced by one that enhanced the learner's mastery of the complex behavior. Children learn to understand the task situation because they have performed it under the guidance of the adult (Rogoff, 1990). In a tutoring relationship, more-capable peers provide the speech, situation definition, and behavior that mediate or scaffold the child's understanding of the task. However, while more-capable others mediate or scaffold understanding of a task, it is the child who acts on this information to negotiate meaning and appropriate learning for him- or herself (Palincsar, 1998).

In summary, there are two different perspectives on how children learn in interaction with others. The first perspective, personal constructivism, proposes that collaborative learning experiences can help participants to discover new knowledge and solutions by challenging their partial and incomplete perspectives on a problem. When children generate different cognitive approaches for the same problem, a state of sociocognitive conflict exists that forces children to decenter to consider the perspectives of others in order to restore equilibrium. By structuring situations in which cognitive conflict is likely to arise, Doise and Mugny (1984) and Mugny and Doise (1978) found children demonstrated different cognitive competencies that they could not perform individually. These changes could not be attributed to imitation, because the children were able to generalize them to other related tasks. Children at an intermediate level of mastery showed progress after interacting with a child of less skill. Thus, peer interactions work mostly to trigger a change, although they do not provide the substance of change. It appears that it is the opportunity to coordinate and coconstruct a solution from incomplete perspectives that is an important aspect of peer interactions and that contributes to cognitive growth.

Teachers promote cognitive growth in children when they use language that challenges their understandings, confronts discrepancies in their thinking, and requires them to them to justify their reasons (Gillies & Boyle, 2005, 2006; King, 1999). When teachers do this, the cognitive tension it creates in children forces them to revise and reconsider their own understandings, to reconcile contradictions, and, in so doing, to develop new understandings and learning.

The second perspective on how children learn, social constructivism, proposes that more-capable peers and adults mediate children's learning by providing language and strategies for problem solving. These skills are then incorporated into the children's mental systems where they become part of their own cognitive repertoire. More-capable peers also benefit from the interaction with others because they are challenged to restructure and reformulate their own knowledge in order to explain it to their less-able peers, which, in turn, facilitates cognitive growth.

Teachers foster cognitive growth in children when they create situations that give children the opportunity to interact with others where they learn to exchange ideas, model patterns of thinking and reasoning, and solve problems. King (1999) argues that as a result of these interactions, individuals learn new ways of thinking and talking and of constructing new understandings and negotiating meanings. Gillies (2004a) found that teachers model many of these patterns of thinking and reasoning when they prompt children to focus on issues, engage in questioning designed to suggest tentative alternatives, scaffold connections between information, and promote metacognitive thinking.

CHAPTER SUMMARY

The research on teachers' discourse suggests

- Teachers' discourse during cooperative learning is more personal and friendly and less authoritarian and impersonal than it is during whole-class instruction or unstructured small-group instruction.
- Teachers use more mediated learning behaviors during cooperative learning than during small-group instruction.
- Teachers' mediated learning behaviors are designed to challenge children's understanding and thinking and help them to connect ideas to previous learning.
- Mediated learning behaviors include: prompting, challenging, confronting, questioning, and scaffolding children's thinking and learning.
- Children model the mediated learning behaviors they hear their teachers use in their interactions with each other during cooperative learning.
- Personal and social constructivism helps to explain children's learning during cooperative learning.
- Personal constructivism occurs when children encounter ideas that are different from their own, and they are forced to examine these alternative ideas in order to reduce the cognitive tension they experience and reconcile these ideas with their own.
- Social constructivism occurs when children interact with others and are introduced to new ideas and new patterns of thought until eventually, after repeated exchanges, these ideas and patterns of thought are internalized.

ACTIVITIES

1. Role-Play:

   - Divide into triads.
   - One person talks, one person listens, and the last person observes.
   - Discuss an event/topic of interest for a few minutes.
   - The observer notes the behaviors and interactions that facilitate the discussion.
   - The triad debriefs and members share their perceptions of the discussion.
   - Rotate so each person has a chance to be the observer.
   - Identify the skills and behaviors that facilitated and inhibited the interaction. List those skills and behaviors and be prepared to discuss them with the larger class.

2. Arrange to visit an elementary classroom where the teacher uses cooperative learning. See if you can make a note of the following types of discourse as they are used: asking open questions, prompting children to think of possible solutions, challenging children to think about issues, and scaffolding information to help children's understanding. Write down one example of each type of interaction. How did these different types of discourse facilitate or inhibit the interaction between teacher and students?

3. Observe a small group of elementary students as they work cooperatively together. Make a note of the following ways they might help each other: provide detailed help to others in the group, respond to a child's request for assistance, challenge each other, and acknowledge other's ideas or efforts. Write down an example of each type of interaction.

4. Arrange to interview a high school teacher who uses cooperative learning. In particular, ask for examples of how he or she might try to facilitate students' learning. How does the teacher commence the cooperative activity? What types of directions or instruction are given to the students? What does the teacher say to students to facilitate their understanding of issues? Are these comments directive or more circumspect? How do the students react to the comments? See if you can identify how these comments match what the research says about the types of discourses teachers use when they implement cooperative learning in their classrooms. What are the similarities and the differences?

5. Arrange to interview a small group of high school students who have had experience with cooperative learning. Ask the students about their interactions with their teachers. For example, do the teachers direct the students or do they make suggestions about how to deal with a problem? Give an example of what teachers might say. What do teachers do if they see something that is glaringly incorrect? Do they draw it to students' attention and suggest they correct it or do they just suggest that students may need to look at that again? How do the students interact with each other in their group? See if the students can give examples of what they might do when something needs correcting, some additional work needs to be done, someone is not pulling his or her weight, or they need to sort out a disagreement. See how the students' responses match the ways students may interact with each other if they have seen appropriate modeling from their teachers.

SUGGESTIONS FOR FURTHER READING

Gillies, R. (2005). The effects of communication training on teachers' and students' verbal behaviors during cooperative learning. *International Journal of Educational Research, 41,* 257–279.

Gillies, R., & Boyle, M. (2006). Ten Australian elementary teachers' discourse and reported pedagogical practices during cooperative learning. *Elementary Journal, 106*(5), 429–451.

King, A. (2002). Structuring peer interaction to promote high-level cognitive processing. *Theory Into Practice, 41,* 33–40.

CHAPTER 4

*Strategies to Promote
Student Discourse*

INTRODUCTION AND LEARNING OBJECTIVES

The importance of social interaction as a way of promoting thinking and discussion during cooperative learning is well recognized and has been the focus of a number of studies over the past 20 years as researchers have sought to identify the types of help that are beneficial to student learning. One of the first researchers to investigate help-giving behaviors and their effects on student learning was Noreen Webb, who, in a series of studies (Webb, 1985, 1991, 1992), examined children's verbal interactions as they worked together in small groups and found that explanations or detailed help received in response to requests for help was related to achievement gains for both the giver and the receiver. In contrast, help that was unelaborated or minimal did not contribute to students' achievement outcomes. Webb proposed that when students give elaborated help to each other, they are forced to reorganize and restructure their own understandings and, in so doing, often construct more elaborate cognitive understandings than they had previously. However, giving non-elaborated help does not involve as much cognitive restructuring and, hence, is not strongly related to achievement gains for the explainer or the recipient.

Recently, Webb and colleagues (Webb & Mastergeorge, 2003; Webb, Troper, & Fall, 1995) have focused on the conditions that must exist for help to be fully understood and useful for those requesting it. These conditions are that the help given must be relevant to the student's need for help, and it must be timely, correct, and sufficiently detailed to enable the student to correct his or her misunderstanding. In addition, Webb and colleagues have argued that the help received is beneficial only if the student requesting it understands the explanation given and has the opportunity to apply it to solve the problem at hand. When students have the opportunity to apply the explanations they have received, it may help them not only to generate their own internal understandings and principles for solving the problem, but it may also make them more conscious of the need to monitor their own problem-solving skills. Furthermore, when students attempt to solve problems, it may raise the group's awareness of their lack of understanding or the need to provide them with additional help. Students are often more aware than their teachers of what others do not understand, are able to focus attention on the relevant aspect of the problem, and can provide explanations that can be readily understood.

In short, it is apparent that children can help each other to learn; however, it is important that they provide high-quality help and that this help is provided at an appropriate time so the student who needs it is able to use it. Meloth and Deering (1999) maintain that high-quality talk emerges with only low frequency when left to emerge naturally or as the by-product of cooperative learning. Teaching children to dialogue together so they can provide high-quality help when it is requested is very important if the help is to be effective in facilitating students' learning. For help seekers, this involves teaching students to be active in the learning process, to ask questions, and to persist in asking them until the help required is received. For help givers, this involves giving help that is detailed and ensuring that the help given is understood (Webb & Mastergeorge, 2003).

When You Have Finished This Chapter You Will Know:

- The different dialoguing scripts that can enhance students' interactions in small groups
- How students can be taught specific interaction strategies to enhance their dialoguing and reasoning during small group learning
- How different dialoguing scripts can be used to elicit different types of thinking and learning
- The theories of personal and social constructivism and situated and generative learning that can be used to help understand how children learn in social contexts

STRATEGIES FOR HELPING
STUDENTS TO DIALOGUE TOGETHER

Reciprocal Teaching

Reciprocal teaching, developed by Ann Brown and Annemarie Palincsar (1988), was designed to help students learn to generate questions to assist their comprehension of written text. During reciprocal teaching, students work in small cooperative groups with each member having the opportunity of leading the group and employing a number of specific strategies to assist comprehension. These strategies are as follows:

- Predicting (What do you think this story is about?)
- Questioning (What are these characters doing?)
- Clarifying (What do you mean by that? I'm not sure I understand what you're trying to say.)
- Summarizing (Let me see if this is what you have been saying . . . ?)

The purpose of these strategies is to help the children think about the text and direct the discussion to assist comprehension. For example, the purpose of predicting is to get the children to try and see if they can hypothesize what the text is about. Then, as the children listen to the predictions of others, they learn that others' perspectives may differ from their own. This forces them to *decenter* to consider these perspectives, and, in so doing, they are forced to accommodate the conflicting information and recognize that others have ideas that may be valid. The leader (each student has a turn at this role) then reads the text, which allows the students' predictions to be confirmed or challenged. If challenged, the student is forced either to justify his or her original prediction or reconcile it to the passage as it is read. As each section of text is discussed, the leader generates a question to which the group members respond with possible explanations or further questions as they seek to clarify their understandings of the text.

As the group works through each section of the text, the leader summarizes the main issues and provides opportunities for others to talk about the summary. Word meanings and confusing text are clarified before the students predict what might happen in the next paragraph. This process is repeated as each new section of the text is read. While reciprocal teaching was originally developed to assist students who had difficulties reading, it has been used widely to assist students to develop skills needed to comprehend text.

Case Study 4.1

An Example of the Four Reciprocal Teaching Strategies

Whale Calf Stranded in Rough Conditions

Rescuers struggled for over 10 hours yesterday to return a newborn humpback whale calf to the sea from an island off the coast of Maine. The calf had become separated from its mother and beached itself on the eastern side of the island. Local wildlife services were alerted and a frantic rescue operation swung into action. Rough seas and blustery conditions made the effort more difficult as each time the calf was pushed back to sea, it was beached by the rough conditions. Finally, with a break in the rough weather, rescuers managed to push it back out to sea where it was reunited with its mother. At last report, mother and calf had rejoined a whale pod heading north along the coast.

Teacher (T): Look at the title of this passage. What do you think this passage is about? (*T. asks the children to try to predict what the passage is about*)

Student (S): It's about a whale rescue.

T: Yes. How do you know that?

S: Well, it talks about the whale being stranded. That's stuck on the beach.

T: Does anyone else want to add anything to that? (*T. seeks additional information that may help to strengthen the prediction*)

S.   (*reads the passage*).

T: What do you know about the weather conditions?

S: Rough.

T: Yes, is there anything else that you can add to that?

S: Currents—strong and rough. Kept blowing the baby whale back in.

T: Are there any questions you'd like to ask about the passage?

S: Why did it take so long to rescue the baby whale?

T: That's a good question. Does anyone want to answer that question? (*T. encourages the children to clarify the concern*)

S: You got to get the people together . . . the sea was rough . . . it was hard

S: The baby whale kept getting blown back in.

T: Now, my summary of this passage is about how a newborn whale calf was reunited with its mother after being washed ashore. (*T. models how to summarize the main theme of the story*)

Case Study 4.1 provides an extract of a class teacher modeling the four reciprocal teaching strategies with her students. Brown and Palincsar (1988) chose these strategies because they represent the types of activities successful readers regularly employ to assist their understanding of text. That is, successful readers predict and hypothesize what might happen, they pose questions and seek clarification on issues they do not understand, and they try to connect information in the text with what they may already know to construct meaning from it.

Initially, the teacher models the process with the children and they practice the strategies with the teacher providing feedback, modeling, and coaching until the children have mastered the strategies and can perform them independently. During this process, children are exposed to multiple ways of processing information as they dialogue among themselves and model ways of talking and reasoning about the passage under discussion. These multidirectional exchanges help students to think about the strategies they are using and learn to comment on them and the content they are learning. Eventually, through repeated exposure to the use of these strategies in their groups, children learn to internalize them and they become part of the repertoire of skills they use to help process text.

Brown and Palincsar (1988) reported teaching reciprocal teaching strategies to junior high school students in remedial classes whose reading comprehension was 2 to 5 years below their grade level. After initial training in the reciprocal teaching strategies and 20 days' practice, the students' comprehension levels improved markedly. Interestingly, the students generalized the strategies to other classes and tasks distinctly different from the original training task, thereby indicating that they had successfully mastered them and felt confident to use them in other contexts to enhance their understanding of text.

These findings led Brown and Palincsar (1988) to propose that the success of this approach could be attributed to the training the children received in how to think, the expert support or scaffolding they received as they learned how to use each skill, and the collaborative context in which the children practiced these skills. In effect, reciprocal teaching helps children learn how to dialogue together to construct meaning and understanding from text. From a Vygotskian perspective, children learn from interacting together using language as a tool to mediate their understandings and scaffold their learning. The concept of the zone of proximal development (i.e., the difference between a child's independent problem-solving level and the level of potential development as determined through problem solving in conjunction with a more capable peer or adult), where more-able students assist less-able students, has a prominent role in the learning that occurs as children use a range of verbal prompts, questions, and probes to clarify misunderstandings and promote learning.

Reciprocal teaching has also been used successfully in a range of educational settings. Hart and Speece (1998) used reciprocal teaching with college students who were at risk of academic failure and compared them to a group of students who participated in cooperative learning groups where students were not trained to use reciprocal teaching strategies. The reciprocal teaching groups performed significantly better than their peers in the cooperative groups on reading comprehension and strategy acquisition measures. Moreover, the poorer readers in the reciprocal teaching groups performed significantly better than poorer readers in the cooperative groups, in effect demonstrating that this structured approach to dialoguing together can be used effectively with students in the postsecondary school years.

Alfassi (1998) investigated the effects of reciprocal teaching in comparison to traditional methods used in remedial reading in large intact high school remedial reading classes. The results showed that the students who participated in the reciprocal teaching classes obtained higher postintervention comprehension scores than their peers who participated in traditional reading instruction. Similarly, Lederer (2000) found that reciprocal teaching improved the reading comprehension performance of elementary students with learning disabilities in comparison to a control group of students with learning disabilities who were not trained to use reciprocal teaching strategies.

More recently, Palincsar and Herrenkohl (2002) reported on a project they conducted to promote student engagement and collaboration during inquiry-based science instruction where they used reciprocal teaching strategies to help students develop explanations about scientific phenomena. This was followed by a set of audience roles that were designed to promote student interaction during the whole-class reporting stage. During this report-back stage, some students in the audience were responsible for checking the reports for clarity between predictions and theories; others were responsible for reporting on the summary of the findings; and others focused on the relationship among the group's prediction, theory, and findings. Palincsar and Herrenkohl found that the use of these strategies and roles helped to do the following:

- Support classroom discussion
- Advance student theorizing
- Influence student thinking on scientific issues
- Promote conceptual understanding

Moreover, the audience roles that the students undertook contributed to sharing meanings and developing common understandings with the wider classroom group.

In sum, reciprocal teaching involves the explicit teaching of the steps of predicting what a passage of text is about, posing questions to help clarify issues in the text, and summarizing the main points of the group discussion. The process is iterative as members seek to develop a common understanding of the text under discussion. Initially, this process is modeled by the teacher who teaches the *reciprocal teaching* strategies to the students. As the students develop competence with them, they gradually assume leadership of the group and use the strategies as a way of developing a shared understanding of a passage of text (Palincsar, 1999). Reciprocal teaching has been used with a range of students from elementary school to college level to successfully promote discussion and thinking in students.

Practical Activity

Ways of Teaching Reciprocal Teaching Strategies to Students to Enhance Students' Discourse and Develop a Greater Understanding of a Passage of Text

It is important to note that these strategies will need to be introduced over a number of sessions, modeled by the teacher, and practiced by the students if students are to develop proficiency with them. Moreover, while the focus in the examples below is on gaining a better understanding of a text passage, these strategies are very portable and can be used to help students gain a better understanding of a group project, of independent research, or to provide feedback to others on the work they have completed.

Elementary School

★ Predicting
  The class teacher discusses with students how we use the clues around us to try to predict what is going to happen next. For example, when we try to predict the weather, we use clues like looking at the cloud cover, feeling the wind speed, and measuring the temperature to try to predict what the weather may be like for the remainder of the day or week. Similarly, when we try to predict what a book is about, we look at the picture on the cover or some of the pictures inside to see if we can predict what the book is about. We also look at the title of the book to see if that provides any clues. This short discussion should then be followed by the presentation of a passage that the students are

(Continued)

(Continued)

going to read. The teacher reminds the students to use the clues they have discussed to see if they can predict what the passage is about.

★ Questioning

The teacher reminds the class that when they need to find information, they ask questions. For example, if they were unsure about when the next bus might arrive, they could ask the clerk at the bus depot a question such as: "Do you know what time the next bus is due?" In class, the teacher will often ask students questions to check on their understanding of the work. Questions not only help students find out more about a topic, but they also enable them to make sure they have understood what they have read. Questions are used to help focus on important information in a passage rather than focusing on trivial details or unimportant information.

Time may need to be allocated during each reading session to help students learn to become adept at posing and answering questions about the text they have read. Having students work together to read a passage and then ask each other questions is one way to consolidate their understanding of how to ask and answer questions to enhance their comprehension.

★ Clarifying

Students are reminded that if they are unsure about any aspect of the passage they have read together, they need to ask questions and persist in asking questions until they have clarified their understandings. It is important that students understand that it is OK to ask questions and that their reading partner will try to help clarify their concerns. When students seek clarification on an issue, they often ask the following types of questions: "*I'm not sure I understand that. Can you explain that to me?*" "*I don't know what they mean. Can you help me with this?*" Students need to understand that it is important to seek clarification on issues they do not understand and that their partner understands the importance of trying to assist.

★ Summarizing

The ability to summarize key information is a very important skill; without it, students will not fully understand what they have read. Summarizing involves picking out the main points or key information and presenting that in one or two sentences. Students will need to be taught how to pick out the main points in a short passage and recount them either orally or in written form.

The strategies of predicting, questioning, clarifying, and summarizing that are used in reciprocal teaching are cyclic and need to be used repetitively as students work their way through the text. Ongoing reminders at the beginning of each reading lesson and feedback at the end on how they used these strategies will help students to develop automaticity with using them.

Middle School and High School

The reciprocal teaching strategies are the same but they are introduced at a more sophisticated level because of the cognitive maturity of the students. While it is recommended that the four strategies be introduced, described, and modeled by the teacher to the whole class, students will need to have time to consolidate their understandings of how to use them by practicing them in their small groups. It is also suggested that the strategies be introduced in the following order because summarizing in which students write a brief overview of an issue is often viewed as more task appropriate for adolescents than predicting that involves some oral rehearsal and guesswork, which students may be reluctant to do until they feel more confident in what they know and understand about the passage:

★ Summarizing
   This strategy is introduced first. It focuses on helping students realize that they need to attend only to the key issues and that they must delete minor and unimportant details. Ensure that they understand that they need to state the main idea if the author has stated it or surmise what it is if it has not been provided.
★ Questioning
   Students are taught that they need to try to think of the types of questions teachers may ask students about the passage. Such questions may include: cause and effect relationships, compare and contrast relationships, questions about key ideas and themes, and questions that require students to draw inferences about the passage they have read. Activities such as asking student to write three or four questions will cover one or two of the different types of questions that they could ask about the passage and will help them to develop a clearer understanding of the importance of asking questions.
★ Clarifying
   This strategy can be taught by having students identify words or concepts that are difficult to understand and having them highlight them in the text. Students then ask other group members for assistance in clarifying their understandings. Questions such as the following let other group members know that the help seeker does not understand the problem and is seeking assistance from other group members: "*I don't think I understand . . . Can you help me with this one?*" "*This is a bit confusing. Does anyone know what*

(Continued)

(Continued)

it means?" Students need to understand that it is important to seek help from others and to persist in seeking such help until they receive it. Other group members also need to understand that they have a responsibility to help clarify any concerns that are raised.

★ Prediction
Students are taught to try to determine what might happen next, based on what they already know about the passage. This strategy requires students to consider what they have learned about the story so far and to use that information to try to predict what may happen in the future.

Practical Activity

Ideas for Establishing Audience Roles During the Report-Back Stage of Each Small Group's Presentation

Elementary School

★ Teacher instructs the class to listen carefully as each group reports back to the class on its project.

★ The students in the class are asked to recall three positive aspects of each group's report that has been presented and to provide reasons why they identified these aspects. Feedback organizers such as the following may be used to help students present their ideas: *"I liked the information that group presented. . . . because . . .";* *"I think that that was a really good idea because . . ."* Three students each recall one positive aspect of the presentation and their reasons for choosing that aspect.

★ The class teacher asks the class to comment on the reasons that different class members have provided. Comments such as the following may be used to lead this discussion: *"What do you think about that point?"* *"Do you think the reason presented is acceptable? Why?"*

★ The class teacher then identifies a member from each small group and asks them to reflect on their group's process. For example, what did they think worked well and what might they need to improve? These children are then asked to present these reflections to the wider class group. The children's reflections, like the recall, need to be well reasoned.

Middle School and High School

★ Assign students audience roles that they need to fulfill during the report-back stage of each group's presentation. These roles may include: checking the reports for clarity with regard to the relationships between hypotheses and theories; ascertaining the clarity of the summary of findings; and determining if the group had discussed the relationships between their hypotheses, theory, and findings. The different roles can be undertaken by individuals or small groups of two or three students who work together to produce a small-group report on the feedback they are going to provide to the group presenting their work to the class.

★ Criteria need to be developed so that students who have audience roles are providing constructive feedback on the group's presentation. The following is a suggested format for providing feedback:

Criteria	Needs to Be Clearer	Clear	Very Clear	Questions Raised
Overview of study				
Relevance of hypotheses				
Research questions				
Elaboration of theory that underpins the research				
Presentation of findings (e.g., tables, graphs, illustrations)				
Discussion of findings				
Implications for future research/investigations				

★ Debriefing needs to occur so that the group that received the feedback has the opportunity to comment on it. This may involve acknowledging its value, or it may involve clarifying misunderstandings.

Collaborative Strategic Reading

Collaborative strategic reading (CSR) consists of a set of strategies designed to enhance students' understanding of text. In many ways, CSR is not dissimilar to reciprocal teaching where children are taught four basic strategies to assist their comprehension: making predictions prior to reading (preview strategy), monitoring reading and learning to enhance vocabulary development (click and clunk strategy), identifying main ideas (get-the-gist strategy), and summarizing key ideas (wrap-up strategy) (Vaughn, Klingner, & Bryant, 2001).

The following outlines each of these strategies and how they are taught:

- *Preview strategy.* This strategy is designed to help students learn to activate background knowledge so they can make informed predictions about the text. To do this effectively, students are taught to scan the text and search for clues, such as pictures, headings, key words and phrases, to try to predict what the text is about. In fact, Vaughn et al. (2001) maintain that once this strategy is mastered, students can use it across other subject areas prior to instruction to try to predict what the lesson is going to be about.

- *Click and clunk strategy.* This involves teaching students how to monitor their own reading and to "click" when they recognize material they know and to "clunk" material, words, or concepts they need to find out more about. Students work together in small groups to read a specific passage and discuss their clicks and clunks to help each other enhance their understanding of the passage.

- *Get-the-gist strategy.* This strategy is designed to help students identify the main idea expressed in the passage by teaching them to focus on identifying the main idea, summarizing it in their own words, and stating it in 10 or fewer words. When students do this, they learn to focus on the most important idea and exclude unnecessary details. Get-the-gist strategy is practiced every two paragraphs as a way of helping students to monitor their understanding of what they are reading.

- *Wrap-up strategy.* This occurs at the end of the text when students are taught to think of the types of questions a teacher would ask about what they have read. The purpose of this strategy is to teach students to focus on the main ideas that emerged from the text and to assist with comprehension.

The following questions are adapted from Vaughn et al. (2001) and are designed to assist students to wrap up their ideas more readily: *How are . . . and . . . the same and how are they different? What is your understanding of what happened . . . ? What do you think might happen if . . . ? How would you compare . . . with . . . ? What did you notice when . . . ?*

The above four strategies (preview, click and clunk, get-the-gist, and wrap-up) are introduced one at a time and modeled by the teacher before students practice them in their small groups. When students have mastered the preview strategy, the click and clunk strategy is introduced, modeled, and again practiced in small groups. This process continues until the students have learned all four strategies.

Bryant and colleagues (2000) reported using collaborative strategic reading as part of a multicomponent reading intervention strategy with students with reading disabilities, low-achieving students, and average-achieving students in the middle years and found that all students' reading outcomes (i.e., word identification, fluency, and comprehension) increased significantly as a result of the intervention, although a subgroup of very poor readers made little progress. Moreover, teachers reported that the percentage of their students who passed high-stakes tests increased from the previous year as a result of their participation in the intervention (Vaughn et al., 2001).

Klinger, Vaughn, Arguelles, Hughes, and Leftwich (2004) examined teachers' yearlong implementation of CSR in five elementary classrooms and found that students in the CSR classrooms improved significantly in reading comprehension when compared with students in the control classrooms. Furthermore, when students were compared by achievement level (i.e., high/average, low, or learning disabled), all students, irrespective of achievement level, outperformed their peers in the control condition. Moreover, those students in classrooms where teachers implemented CSR with high integrity (i.e., the teachers explicitly taught the students the strategies and ensured the students modeled them with each other) outperformed those children in classrooms where teachers implemented CSR with low integrity (i.e., the teachers taught the strategies to the students but were not consistent in ensuring the students modeled them with each other).

In short, Bryant et al. (2000) and Klinger et al. (2004) demonstrate that CSR has the potential to benefit all students, irrespective of achievement level. Moreover, these benefits are likely to be additive when teachers ensure that students are explicitly taught the four CSR strategies and are given the opportunity of practicing them in their small groups.

Practical Activity

Ways of Introducing CSR to Students to Enhance Their Understanding of Text

Elementary School

★ Place students in groups of two and give each pair a short passage to read. Instruct students to look at the passage to see if they can guess what it is

(Continued)

(Continued)

about. Remind students to scan the passage for clues such as: *What does the picture tell you about the story? Look at the title to see if there are some key words that provide some clues?* The teacher will need to remind the students to work with their partner to see how many clues they can find. Discuss these clues with the wider class.

★ Get students to read the passage and identify what parts click; that is, what information do they understand or do they remember from their past experiences? Remind students that when this happens, the information is clicking and they are beginning to make links to what they already know or understand. However, when they read words or ideas that do not click, they will need to clunk them. Clunking involves identifying those words or ideas that they do not understand. Students can underline them or use a highlighter to draw attention to them. The clunks need to be discussed with their partners to see if they can work out what they mean; if not, they need to discuss them with the wider class. The class teacher will need to monitor students to check on how they are using this strategy and determine if there are any aspects that need to be clarified.

★ After the students have read one or two paragraphs, they sum up in their own words what the gist of the passage is. Each partner then comments on whether he or she agrees with this short summary. If not, each partner outlines what he or she thinks the gist of the passage is until they are able to reach agreement. This strategy is repeated throughout the reading until they have finished the passage. It may be appropriate for the class teacher to ask different groups to share what they identified as the gist of different sections of the passages they read so others can hear how it is done.

★ At the end of the passage, the students are encouraged to generate a list of questions they could be asked about the passage they have read. This is called the wrap-up strategy, and it is designed to help students focus on the key ideas that emerged and in so doing develop a clearer understanding of the text. Once all of the groups have generated their questions, they could then share them with the wider class group.

Middle School and High School

★ Discuss with the class the importance of using preview clues to try to determine what the passage is about. These clues include not only reading the title but also the abstract or introductory paragraph if the passage is lengthy. If it is a book, previewing will include scanning the table of contents and reading any reviews of the text on the front or back cover. The teacher may need to discuss how different disciplines (i.e., math, science, English, social studies) have different ways of helping readers understand what a passage or text is about. For example, in science, readers will often preview the article by reading the abstract and glancing at the tables or figures. In contrast, when previewing a social studies text, readers will often glance at the pictures and the headings and subheadings to predict what it is about.

★ Demonstrate how students can reflect on what they have read and link any ideas or concepts to previous knowledge and understandings. For example, statements such as: "*I know what that means*" or, "*I've read about that before*" are ways in which students can let their partner know that the information has clicked. When they are unsure of any words, ideas, or concepts, however, they need to identify them as clunks that require help from their partner. Statements such as: "*I'm not sure what that means. Do you know what it is?*" or, "*I think you'll need to give me a hand with this one. It doesn't make sense to me*" are ways of letting their partner know that they will need help to work it out. It is important that all group members understand that they are expected to work with each other on solving clunks. The class teacher will need to monitor the groups' activities and provide assistance when needed.

★ Students are taught how to identify the gist of the passage by summarizing it in 10 or fewer words. Examples of how this is done need to be provided so students can see how this strategy can be used as an effective way to develop an ongoing summary of the material they are reading. Examples of different groups' summaries can be shared with the class.

★ Once the students have completed reading the text, they need to see if they can identify some questions that someone who had not read the text would ask. This will involve students in recounting the summaries they had previously made, thereby testing their comprehension of the text. Moreover, when students have to consider the other person's perspective, they are forced to cognitively restructure their thinking, which often helps them to get a better understanding of it. Students should be encouraged to share their questions with the wider class so everyone has the opportunity to comment on them.

Scripted Cooperation

Scripted cooperation, developed by Donald Dansereau and elaborated further by Angela O'Donnell (see O'Donnell, Dansereau, & Rocklin, 1987),

involves children's working in pairs on an academic task. In scripted cooperation, each partner is asked to play a specified role, such as listener or recaller,
and to play these roles in a specific order. O'Donnell (1999) argues that the
scripted role plays are very important because they help to prompt the use of
cognitive processes that may not necessarily occur otherwise. Furthermore,
they can limit negative social interactions as the children focus on the cognitive
requirements of the scripted roles they are asked to perform.

In *scripted cooperation,* the children work together to acquire information
about the task. This may involve reading a particular passage and discussing it
or seeking background information from a text. The children work collaboratively to obtain the information and to promote each other's understandings of
it. Once this is achieved, they put their notes aside and one partner assumes the
role of the recaller while the other acts as the listener. The recaller then summarizes the information that both students have collected, while the listener's
role is to try to detect any misinformation and seek clarification on any aspects
of the recall that are unclear. Both students then work together to elaborate on
the material under discussion until they arrive at a common understanding of
what they have been reading and discussing. The children then change roles so
the recaller is now the listener and vice versa. The process of reading, recalling,
listening, and elaborating is repeated many times as the children work their
way through the task. The opportunity for the children to engage in the role
of the listener, where they have to actively monitor the recall for accuracy
and understanding, and the role of the recaller, where they have to reorganize
and restructure their thoughts in order to explain them to their partner, ensures
that the children engage in a range of metacognitive activities. These activities
are known to enhance student comprehension of text and facilitate learning
(O'Donnell, 1999).

Scripted cooperation has been used with students in elementary, high
school, and college/university settings in a range of lessons involving text comprehension through to the retention of procedural and technical information
required in university courses. While the original research into scripted cooperation was conducted with university students to test the viability of different
scripted and nonscripted dyads in dealing with learning procedural information (see O'Donnell et al., 1990), research in recent years has focused on how
this approach works in elementary, middle, and high school settings to enhance
students' acquisition of information in specific subject or content areas, including text comprehension.

Meisinger, Schwanenflugel, Bradley, and Stahl (2004) investigated interactions in Grade 2 students during partner reading sessions and found that being
provided with basic partner-reading script instruction was associated with better

social cooperation during reading sessions. During partner reading, students alternated roles of reader and supporter throughout the reading, with each role requiring a specific cognitive activity such as taking turns, reading along, staying on task, and providing help to their partners. In this context, the children were asked to play certain roles in a particular order, which imposed a script on how they interacted about the passage. The authors found that the script helped to promote high-quality interactions among partners and enhanced thinking and meaning-making.

Rahm (2004) reported on a case study of how meaning-making occurred among seven 14-year-old students and a museum guide through their participation in a science exhibit. Individual students' meaning-making and forms of participation in the dialogue during their visit were examined. This included an analysis of the students' articulations, their manipulations of the exhibit, and the concordance between their talk and exhibit manipulations. The discourses that emerged from interactions among group members, between different members and the exhibit, and between the group and the museum guide and the exhibit were also examined. This examination included the role of talk, gestures, and gaze as well as the way in which talk and manipulation of the exhibit contributed to meaning-making for the students. His examination of the data led Rahm to conclude that meaning-making occurred as the students engaged in conversations with others, manipulated the exhibit, and had opportunities to observe others manipulating it. The challenges the students confronted as they tried to understand how to manipulate the exhibit forced them to deconstruct and reconstruct their understandings and link them to prior knowledge and learning in order to be able to observe the lighted display that the exhibit could be used to create. Although the students in this study did not engage in formal scripted dialogues, they nevertheless did engage in dialogic exchanges that were critical to helping enhance their thinking and meaning-making of the phenomena under investigation.

In a study of college students that examined the role of different types of scripts to help students dialogue together as they worked on a computer-based activity, Weinberger, Ertl, Fischer, and Mandl (2005) found that social scripts rather than epistemic scripts, which specified how students work on a given task, were substantially more beneficial with respect to the individual acquisition of knowledge. In fact, epistemic scripts can at times impede knowledge acquisition. The authors proposed that social scripts may serve to reinforce collaborative learning mechanisms where students learn to contribute and discuss divergent perspectives and to refine and restructure their own ideas in order to evaluate and eventually integrate the various perspectives. In contrast, epistemic scripts appear to function more as checklists, so students do not need to integrate divergent perspectives but only focus on the strategy they have been given for solving the problem at hand.

In sum, scripted cooperation involves children's working together to acquire information on a task. Each partner alternatively plays a specified role such as listener or recaller where they each have opportunities to read, recall, listen, and elaborate on the task at hand. The listener has the job of monitoring the other's recall for accuracy and understanding, while the recaller is often forced to reorganize and restructure his or her thoughts in order to explain them to a partner. Each of these roles involves a range of metacognitive activities known to enhance student understanding and contribute to learning. Scripted cooperation is a structured way of dialoguing together to enhance understanding of a task.

Guided Reciprocal Peer Questioning

Guided reciprocal peer questioning was originally developed by Alison King (1990) to assist college students' learning of expository materials presented in classroom lectures. In order to enhance peer interaction and learning, King provided students with a *generic* list of questions designed to guide them in generating their own task-specific questions on the lecture materials. Initially, the students worked individually on compiling their list of questions and then used them to ask and answer each other's questions on the lecture materials as they worked together in small cooperative groups.

The following is the list of generic questions King (1990, p. 669) provided:

- How would you use . . . to . . . ?
- What is a new example of . . . ?
- Explain why . . . ?
- What do you think would happen if . . . ?
- What is the difference between . . . and . . . ?
- How are . . . and . . . similar?
- What is a possible solution to the problem of . . . ?
- What conclusions can you draw about . . . . ?
- How does . . . affect . . . ?
- In your opinion, which is best, . . . or . . . ? Why?
- What are the strengths and weaknesses of . . . ?
- Do you agree or disagree with the statement . . . ? Support your answer.
- How is . . . related to . . . that we studied earlier?

King (1990) found that students using this guided reciprocal questioning procedure asked more critical thinking questions, gave more detailed explanations, and demonstrated higher *achievement* with the material under discussion than students who just discussed the lecture material with each other or who used an unguided reciprocal peer questioning approach (i.e., students were trained to ask and answer question but were not provided with the list of generic question stems to guide their generation of questions). King argued that the generic question stems helped students generate their own list of critical thinking questions designed to elicit elaborated explanations. To be able to answer these questions, students had to think extensively about the material, organize it, and integrate it into their own existing understandings, and it was this process of reorganization and restructuring and connecting to existing knowledge that promoted comprehension and learning.

In a follow-up study with pairs of fourth- and fifth-grade students who were taught to ask and answer each other's self-generated questions, King (1994) found that students who had been taught to ask and answer self-generated questions and link their responses to prior knowledge or experience outside the immediate context of the class lesson engaged in more complex knowledge construction than their peers who had been taught to engage in lesson-based questioning only or those who were only trained to provide elaborated responses to questions from their partners. King concluded that although self-generated questions help promote complex knowledge construction, questions designed to access prior knowledge and experience are more effective in enhancing learning than lesson-based questioning only.

The following question stems were given to the children in the experience-based and lesson-based groups to help them generate their own list of questions about the teacher-presented class lesson:

Comprehension Questions

- Describe . . . in your own words.
- What does . . . mean?
- Why is . . . important?

Connection Questions

- Explain why . . .
- Explain how . . .
- How are . . . and . . . similar?
- What is the difference between . . . and . . . ?

The following connection questions are different and designed to draw upon experience-based knowledge or lesson-based knowledge:

Experience-Based Connection Questions:

- How could . . . be used to . . . ?
- What would happen if . . . ?
- How does . . . tie in with . . . that we learned before?

Lesson-Based Connection Questions:

- How does . . . affect . . . ?
- What are the strengths and weaknesses of . . . ?
- What causes . . . ?

(King, 1994, p. 345)

ASK to THINK-TEL WHY Strategy

In a more recent extension of her work, King (1997) has developed the ASK to THINK-TEL WHY strategy, which is an inquiry-based model of peer tutoring. This model builds on her previous work on guided reciprocal peer questioning and is designed to promote higher-level complex learning, or in effect, the construction of new knowledge. The ASK to THINK-TEL WHY strategy involves a tutor and tutee of similar ability and competency engaging in structured reciprocal roles where each partner has the opportunity of using open-ended question starters to prompt his or her partner to think about the topic under discussion. The tutor acts as a *cognitive coach* who, through a series of sequenced questions, scaffolds the tutee's thinking and learning to progressively higher levels.

The five types of questions that King (1997) identified as part of this sequence of questions designed to promote higher-level thinking include the following:

- Review questions ("Describe . . . in your own words.")
- Probing questions ("Tell me more about . . .")
- Hint questions ("Have you thought about . . .")
- Intelligent-thinking questions ("What is the difference between . . . and . . . ?")
- Self-monitoring questions ("Have I covered all the points I need to?")

The advantage of this type of sequence is that it encourages children not only to focus on summarizing and elaborating information but it also helps them to ask cognitively challenging questions or questions that encourage children to draw on previous understandings and knowledge and connect it to the issue under discussion. In generating these types of connection questions, King (1999) maintains that questioners need to think about how ideas in the task relate to each other, and responders must be able to generate a response that connects the ideas together or provides rationales or explanations to justify the response. Because responders have been taught to provide elaborated responses such as explanations, justifications, and rationales to the questions they are asked, they realize the importance of explaining, justifying, and rationalizing how they have connected ideas and information to support their responses. In so doing, students often develop new ways of explaining and arguing their points as new knowledge is often generated and the quality of the discourse is enhanced. As partners engage in the question-asking-answering process that is typical of the interactions in the ASK to THINK-TEL WHY strategy, they learn that each question posed is often highly dependent on previous responses that have been given and that these, in turn, help to shape following questions. In this sense, the partners are highly dependent on each other in these reciprocal dialogues for scaffolding and guiding each other's learning. King maintains that this reciprocity of questioning and answering creates a *transactive process* where the partners are equal participants in providing mutual assistance and mutual learning. This transactive process is clearly evident in the dialogue recorded in Case Study 4.2.

Case Study 4.2

Example of Fifth-Grade Students Dialoguing Together Using the ASK to THINK-TEL WHY Questioning Strategies

Damien: OK. Tell me what you know about the tsunami that hit Indonesia. (review question)

Shelley: A tsunami is a large wave that was caused by an earthquake in the sea and it created these waves that were very high that hit the coast and destroyed the houses. Lots of people were killed and houses and shops destroyed. A tsunami hit Indonesia on the day after Christmas and caused a huge disaster. It was like the Krakatau eruption only not as bad but pretty bad. (statement showing comprehension)

Damien: Is there anything else that you need to say about the tsunami and its effects? (*probing question*)

Shelley: 'Cause many people lost their homes and couldn't work, the Red Cross had a big fund-raising appeal to help the people who lost their houses and farms. (*statement showing integration of concepts of cause and effect*)

Damien: Can you tell me more about the tsunami? You said it was a big wave. How big? (*probing question*)

Shelley: It was a very big wave—about 60 feet high and it had a lot of mud and trees and stuff it collected. It looked like liquid mud and it moved very fast. It was moving faster than a train or cars. People got caught up in its power. Everything got swept along in it. (*statement showing integration of concepts of speed and power using the example of train and cars to give a sense of how quickly it moved and the force of its power*)

Damien: You mentioned the Krakatau eruption. What is the difference between the two? (*thinking question*)

Shelley: Krakatau was a volcano that exploded in the 1900s and blew ash and rocks into the air. Lots of people got killed and it caused a tsunami too. (*statement showing comprehension of difference*)

Damien: How were they similar and how were they different? (*thinking question*)

Shelley: I know that they both caused a tsunami and they both caused lots of loss of life. That's how they're the same. They happened in different centuries. That's how they're different. (*statement showing integration of concepts by linking different aspects*)

Damien: Have you thought about how they were different in how they started? (*hint question*)

Shelley: Krakatau was a volcano that exploded and the tsunami—the one on the day after Christmas—was caused by an underwater earthquake. That's how they're different. (*statement showing integration of concepts of difference*)

Damien: Is there anything else that you can think of about how they're the same and different? (*probing question*)

Shelley: They're both natural forces that no one can do anything about. (*statement showing integration of concepts of both being natural events*)

Damien: How did you decide that? (*thinking about thinking*)

Shelley: I realized that you can't stop a tsunami—it's too powerful and you can't stop a volcano exploding. No one can plug it up. (*statement showing integration of concept of power of natural forces*)

Damien: That's good thinking.

In Case Study 4.2, Damien acts as the tutor, posing questions designed to encourage Shelley, the responder, to think about the passage under discussion and provide elaborated or detailed responses. Damien's role is only to ask questions. He does not explain or give answers to any of the questions, while Shelley's role is to explain and not to ask questions. King (1999) maintains that by encouraging the tutor to ask thinking questions only, the responder is more likely to respond with explanations and other elaborations or the kinds of responses that are known to promote learning for the responder.

In the dialogue between Damien and Shelley, Shelley is initially asked to state what she knows about the tsunami, and she responds with a detailed review of the information she has been reading (see Turn 2). Damien follows with a probing question to see if there is anything else she wants to add to her description of the tsunami. His question provides a hint that he'd like her to discuss the effects of the tsunami in more detail (see Turn 3). Shelley responds with more elaboration on the effects of the tsunami on people's livelihoods than she had in her original recount (see Turn 4). Damien continues to scaffold Shelley's responses as he probes her on the size of the tsunami. This probe helps Shelley respond in more elaborate detail as she verbalizes her integration of different concepts on speed and power that help to illustrate how quickly it moved and the force of its power (see Turn 6).

Damien follows this up with a thinking question that seeks to have Shelley identify the difference between the tsunami and the Krakatau eruption. Shelley responds and Damien builds on this response by asking her how these two events were similar and how they were different (see Turn 9)—in effect, asking her a thinking question that involves a compare and contrast assessment. This prompts Shelley to respond with a statement that illustrates she is able to integrate concepts by linking different aspects of the tsunami and the eruption—an elaborative response. Damien decides that he needs to provide Shelley with a hint question to get her to focus on the difference between these natural events (see Turn 11). The response provided by Shelley is a clear statement showing the integration of concepts of difference (see Turn 12) that she had not shown in her first response in Turn 10. Damien continues to probe to see if there is anything else she wants to add (see Turn 13). Shelley makes a statement showing integration of concepts of both being natural events that are uncontrollable (see Turn 14). Damien asks Shelley a metacognitive question on how she arrived at that decision. Shelley's response demonstrates that she has integrated the concepts of power and natural forces and evaluated the evidence and concluded that these events are too powerful to stop.

Self-Regulated Strategy Development

Self-regulated strategy development (SRSD) is an approach to helping students improve their writing performance by teaching them specific strategies on how to dialogue together to improve their writing, as well as strategies to help them monitor and self-regulate their performances. SRSD was developed by Steve Graham, Karen Harris, and Linda Mason (2005) and involves students' working in pairs through a five-stage process during which students are taught two genre-specific strategies to enhance writing, the general planning strategy in which these two strategies are embedded, and the self-regulatory strategies needed to monitor the writing process. The five stages in the process are the following.

1. *Develop background knowledge.* The *mnemonic* POW—Pick my ideas (i.e., choose a topic to write about), Organize my notes (i.e., organize ideas into a writing plan), and Write and say more (i.e., change the plan while writing)— is taught to give the students a three-point plan for how to write. This strategy is followed by the teacher's discussing the characteristics of a good story with students, noting that stories are interesting and fun to read and are made up of several parts that must make sense when they are read. Finally, students are taught the mnemonic WWW (who, when, where), What = 2, How = 2 (Graham & Harris, 2005) to help them remember the seven key parts of a story:

- Who are the main characters?
- When does the story take place?
- Where does the story take place?
- What do the main characters want to do?
- What happens when the main characters try to do it?
- How does the story end?
- How do the main characters feel?

Students practice using the above strategies until they are memorized.

2. *Discuss it.* Students practice finding the key parts of a story in their own stories and identifying how many parts their stories contain. The idea is to encourage students to realize that their stories need to contain all key parts needed to make sense (i.e., introduction, different key ideas, conclusion). During this stage, students are also introduced to the concept of goal setting where they learn that their goal when writing stories is to include all parts, that each part needs to read well, and that the story must make sense.

3. *Model it.* Students are introduced to the idea of using self-talk to assist them as they plan and write a story. This involves the teacher's modeling the following types of self-talk statements as he or she works through the planning and writing process with the students:

- What do I have here? (problem definition)
- What comes next? (planning)
- Does that make sense? (self-evaluation)
- I really like that part (self-reinforcement)
- I'm almost finished (coping)

Students use these *self-talk strategies* as they work with their teacher on composing a story. Once the story is completed, the teacher and the students discuss whether their story includes all the key parts needed for it to make sense, as well as the relevance of the self-statements that were used to help direct the story's development.

4. *Support it.* Students work in pairs to plan a story incorporating all the key parts. Once this is achieved, each student writes his or her own story. Students then read their stories to each other, examining the parts they have included and discussing the personal self-talk statements that they used.

5. *Independent performance.* Students work on planning and writing stories using the planning and self-monitoring strategies outlined above to help scaffold their performance. During this stage, students reflect on their use of the strategies, particularly the goal they set for themselves to write a story that included all the key parts. The teacher and peers continue to provide support to students as needed.

While the five stages of the SRSD are designed to help struggling elementary students enhance their writing performance, the strategies (with age-appropriate adjustments) can also be used effectively with middle and high school students who experience similar difficulties with writing. Moreover, when students work with peers to support the use of these strategies, there is evidence that the strategies are more likely to be maintained and generalized (Graham & Harris, 2005).

BRINGING IT ALL TOGETHER: UNDERSTANDING THE RESEARCH

In Chapter 3, I discussed how children learn new ways of talking and thinking about issues when they interact with others. This chapter provided an overview of the constructivist perspective on how children learn from their experiences and noted that although both personal and social constructivism differ in the emphasis placed on the intrapersonal and interpersonal dimensions of learning, both acknowledge that learning is mediated through interacting with others. When children interact together they are exposed to different cognitive perspectives and ways of using language that challenge them to consider these other ideas and forms of expression so that, eventually, after repeated exposure to these exchanges, these thinking and communication processes become internalized as part of their *mental schemata* or ways of organizing their world.

Wertsch (1979) maintained that internalization occurs as children learn to adjust their understandings to accommodate a shared understanding of a situation. From this perspective, the context or setting within which understanding and learning develop is critical because it recognizes that an individual's reasoning, thinking, and problem solving are not only attributable to the individual but also to the social context, such as the group, within which the individual operates (Gage & Berliner, 1998). Vygotsky (1978) argued that the social context for learning is so strong that higher mental functions appear first at the *inter-psychological* or social level and only later at the *intra-psychological* or individual one. However, to move from other-regulation as occurs at the social level to self-regulation at the individual level, scaffolding by a more competent peer or adult is often needed. This occurs when more competent peers or adults operate within the *child's zone of proximal development* to maximize his or her potential for learning.

The five strategies for enhancing student discourse discussed earlier—reciprocal teaching, collaborative strategic reading, scripted cooperation, guided reciprocal peer questioning, and self-regulated strategy development—are different approaches to scaffolding children's thinking and learning during small-group work. While each strategy adopts a unique set of techniques to promote dialogue and thinking within groups, all are designed to scaffold children's learning by providing a set of roles or questioning techniques that guide students' exploration of the task at hand. For example, some of the strategies encourage questions that promote review, comprehension, and clarification of information that helps to guide respondents to developing a better understanding of the issues under discussion, while others encourage questions that are thought provoking and require respondents to think deeply about the issues and integrate them with prior knowledge to construct new understandings and knowledge (King, 2002).

The ASK to THINK-TEL WHY peer tutoring model (King, 1997) is explicitly designed to promote higher-level complex thinking by having tutors ask a sequence of questions designed to help tutees link information and knowledge and provide justifications and rationales to support their responses. King (1999) maintains that higher-order thinking takes place only when learners go beyond the factual information presented to generate relationships among those facts and to make inferences and generalizations that are not readily foreseen. In so doing, tutees are often challenged to find new ways of constructing meaning from the task and explaining their responses in ways that others will accept as valid. Moreover, when children are required to defend or elaborate on their solutions to a problem, it forces them to reconsider and reorganize their arguments in the light of others' perspectives or available information. This process often leads to the emergence of a more mature resolution of the problem than had previously been considered (Brown & Palincsar, 1988).

The types of questions the ASK to THINK-TEL WHY peer tutoring model (King, 1997) proposes encourage children to assess their own understanding as well as their thinking processes as they generate their responses. Wittrock (1990) argues that the mind is not a passive consumer of information, but actively constructs its own interpretation of information and draws inferences from that. Furthermore, he believes that children must be taught those metacognitive strategies that will assist them to organize, monitor, and control their *generative thought* processes. Certainly, the ASK to THINK-TEL WHY model of peer tutoring (King, 1997) is designed to teach children to ask questions that require partners to explain or provide reasons for their responses. Moreover, as partners alternatively adopt the role of tutor and tutee, they learn to pose questions that encourage partners to think about their thinking while simultaneously learning to monitor their own responses. In effect, children learn to become more *metacognitively aware* of their own learning and how they must coordinate their contributions to the task they are jointly trying to resolve.

The use of reciprocal tutor and tutee roles promotes interdependence and mutuality as each partner is highly dependent on the other for scaffolding and guiding the other's learning. Learning in this context is situation specific; that is, it is dependent on the social context and the role each partner adopts. It is also dependent on the partners' being prepared to dialogue together using the "script" provided to challenge and scaffold each other's thinking. By making their thinking explicit, children learn to articulate their thoughts, argue their positions, and generate new ways of thinking about issues, and this, in turn, leads to the construction of new knowledge and learning.

CHAPTER SUMMARY

The research on students' discourse suggests

- Children benefit from giving and receiving explanations or detailed help.
- Help is useful if it is relevant to the student's need, timely, and of sufficient detail for the student to be able to use it.
- Children need to be taught to provide high-quality help when it is requested.
- The six strategies that help children dialogue together are: reciprocal teaching, collaborative strategic reading, scripted cooperation, guided reciprocal peer questioning, the ASK to THINK-TEL WHY strategy, and the self-regulated strategy development.
- Different questioning strategies can be used to elicit different types of dialogues during interactions, with some strategies focusing on comprehension and application while others focus on encouraging metacognitive thinking.
- Metacognitive questions prompt students to engage in higher-order thinking by providing explanations, justifications, and rationales that often lead to the construction of new understandings and knowledge.
- All six dialoguing strategies (reciprocal teaching, collaborative strategic reading, scripted cooperation, guided reciprocal peer questioning, the ASK to THINK-TEL WHY strategy, and the self-regulated strategy development) are designed for students to use as they work in small groups on specific tasks.

ACTIVITIES

1. Teach children to ask and answer questions that encourage critical thinking. Give the children a short passage to read as they work in dyads. Each child has a turn to be the questioner and the explainer. The children are given cards to prompt their dialogue. For example, the questioner has a card with five question stems on it that can be used to pose a question, while the explainer has some key phrases to remind him or her that explanations need to be detailed and provide one or more reasons for the response.

Question stems to prompt discussion:

What do you think . . . ?

How do you know that . . . ?

What is a possible solution . . . ?

Do you agree or disagree with . . .? Think of some reasons to support your answer.

Explanations need to:

Be detailed

Be on time

Provide reason(s)

At the completion of the activity, the teacher debriefs the children on how helpful the question stems and the explanation prompts were. Children need to be encouraged to provide reasons when they respond.

2. Teach children to ask thinking-about-thinking questions. The children pretend they have been to the world premier of a new movie. One child pretends to be a journalist and asks a series of questions about the movie for his or her paper. The types of questions that can be asked to probe a responder to think about the movie are:

- What did you think of the movie? Describe what you saw . . .
- Tell me more about the main character(s) and what you noticed.
- What is the difference between this type of movie and . . . ?
- How does it compare with others (movies) that you've seen?
- What advice would you give to others who intend to see the movie? Perhaps you could tell me why you would say that.

3. Students are assigned the task of interviewing a successful gold medalist from the recent Olympics. However, while other journalists have been plying him or her with questions about how it feels to be a successful medalist, your task is to take a unique angle to see if you can identify some other issues that you can conduct your interview on. You will need to brainstorm some ideas, agree on the type of topic for your interview, and then generate a list of questions that will explore and probe the topic with your subject. Role-play the interview with a classmate not in your group so others can provide you with feedback on whether your interview achieved its purpose.

SUGGESTIONS FOR FURTHER READING

King, A. (2002). Structuring peer-interaction to promote high-level cognitive processing. *Theory Into Practice, 41,* 33–40.

O'Donnell, A., & King, A. (Eds.). (1999). *Cognitive perspectives on peer learning.* Mahwah, NJ: Lawrence Erlbaum.

Palincsar, A., & Herrenkohl, L. (2002). Designing collaborative contexts. *Theory Into Practice, 41,* 26–35.

CHAPTER 5

Group Composition

INTRODUCTION AND LEARNING OBJECTIVES

Grouping students has become standard practice in many K–12 classrooms as teachers have realized that there are academic and social benefits that accrue to students from working with others, sharing ideas, discussing differences, and learning to deal with conflict in ways that are cognitively manageable and socially acceptable (Gillies, 2003a; Gillies & Ashman, 1998). Through social interaction with peers, students learn to challenge or accept the ideas of others and have their own ideas challenged or accepted in turn. It is by engaging in reciprocal dialogues that students are exposed to new ways of thinking and talking and constructing new understandings and learning (Mercer, Wegerif, & Dawes, 1999). Although teachers freely acknowledge the benefits of students dialoguing together on academic tasks, they often express concerns about the most appropriate ways to group students to ensure the discussions are productive and that learning will occur. These concerns have emerged, in part, from the pressure often exercised by adolescents who want more autonomy to work with their friends and teachers who may even feel that students will be rebellious if they are forced to work in groups that are not of their own choosing (Mitchell, Reilley, Bramwell, Solnosky, & Lilly, 2004). Pressure may also be exerted by parents of more able or gifted younger children who want them to be challenged by working with students of similar ability or aptitude (Cohen, 1994). Often these grouping practices run counter to teachers' own intuitive understandings of what works best for different students in different learning situations. The purpose of this chapter is to discuss the evidence emerging from the research on classroom grouping practices found to enhance socialization and self-concept; to promote thinking, problem solving, and learning; and to reconcile them with practices that can be readily implemented in classrooms.

When You Have Finished This Chapter You Will Know:

- The advantages and disadvantages of same- and mixed-ability groupings
- The conditions under which mixed- and same-gender groupings may be appropriate
- When and how friendship groups may be constructed and used
- How to deal with issues of status in small groups
- Ways of harnessing the potential of different interest groups
- Ways of using the computer to enhance small-group discussion and learning

HARNESSING THE POWER OF THE GROUP: PRODUCTIVE SMALL GROUPS

Case Study 5.1

Students' Perceptions of Mixed-Ability Groupings in Their Classroom

T: You've spent most of this term during social studies working together in your group. I was wondering if you could tell me a little about how things worked out for you, personally? (*children were directed to respond from their own perspective and not from what they thought the group might like to hear*)

S1:   It was good. We all got on OK and we mostly helped each other. Do you agree with that? (S1. directs question to the group)

S2:   Yep! We mostly got on OK. We had some times when we didn't do so well but we mostly did OK.

T: Can you tell me a bit about what you think made it work for you? (*T. probes to try and encourage the students to elaborate on this point*)

S1:   I think when we had to work out the group rules that made it.

Ss: Yes.

S3:   We knew what we had to do if we didn't agree.

S1:   Also! Also! We are friends and we tried to do our best.

T: Were you friends before you worked in the group?

Ss: No . . . (all together) . . . not really . . .

S3:   We didn't play together—he played handball and I like soccer.

S4:   Yep! We didn't play with them (pointing to the two girls).

S2:   No, 'cause we do other things. We (pointing to S1) played jump rope . . . we have our own friends.

T: What have you learnt from the tasks you had to do? (*T. has set tasks that the children were required to research, construct a group report, and present it to the class. Each task took about two weeks to complete*)

S2:   We all had to do our jobs. We worked out what we had to do and we helped each other with it.

S3:   Him (pointing to S4) and me worked together on the computer.

S2:   Sometimes, he worked with me. (referring to S3)

T: Did you notice anything about the contributions you all made?

S1:   Yes, we all had different things we did . . . he's (referring to S3) good at finding things on the computer . . . he's a good drawer (referring to S4 who is talented at presenting pictures and creating designs). . . .

T: I wonder. Did you have any times when group members didn't contribute or pull their weight?

S3:   Not really because we all knew what we'd agreed to do and we stuck to our agreement.

S2:   Sometimes, sometimes, we had to remind a person to do something . . . but not very often. Mostly they just did it.

Note: T = Teacher; S = Student

Case Study 5.1 provides a short extract of a discussion between a teacher (T) and group of Grade 6 students (S) who have been working together in class over the past term. The teacher is trying to gauge the children's perceptions of how the group experience worked for each of them and what she may need to do to enhance the experiences they had. It should be noted that this teacher had excellent rapport with her students, and the students were very forthcoming in their responses. The four-person group above consisted of two boys (S3, S4) and two girls (S1, S2) who worked together in a mixed-ability (high-, middle-, and low-ability) group.

It is also clear from the students' responses that they felt they worked "OK" together (Turn 2, 3) and that they had become friends as a result of their small-group experience (Turn 8). In response to the teacher's query about what they learned from their group experiences, the children acknowledged that they knew they had to contribute (Turn 15) and that they had to help each other. This requirement appeared to make the children more aware of the different contributions each member could make to the group (Turn 19), with group members receiving public acknowledgment for being competent at using the computer or being a proficient drawer (Turn 19).

The extract above provides insights into the students' perceptions of how they cooperated. Although the extract captures only a small part of the dialogue that occurred, it is clear that the students had developed a concept of the group as a collective unit with their frequent use of *we* and *our*. It has been argued that when this concept of "group identity" has been established, it provides the momentum for members to work together, contribute to the collective effort, and promote each other's endeavors (Gillies & Ashman, 1996; Johnson & Johnson, 2000; Slavin, 1996). The notion that children work well together in mixed-ability groups is also evident in this group, with recognition being given to two of the members for their unique contributions that undoubtedly contributed to the status of the low-ability student (S4).

Ability Groupings

The observations described above are consistent with research on the benefits students derive from working in mixed-ability groups. In a meta-analysis of different grouping practices in classrooms, Lou et al. (1996) found that low-ability students learned significantly more in mixed-ability groups than in same-ability groups, medium-ability students learned significantly more in same-ability groups, and high-ability students learned equally well in either group combination (see Chapter 2 for a detailed discussion of ability groupings).

In a follow-up study, Webb, Nemer, Chizhik, and Sugrue (1998) also found that the ability composition of the group had an impact on student performance, with low-ability students benefiting from working in groups with students of medium- or above-average ability where they seemed to learn from the discussions that took place and were able to apply what they learned in follow-up testing. Contrary to previous findings that medium-ability students may participate less and learn less in mixed-ability groups, Webb et al. found that medium-ability students actively participating in the group discussions learned more, and it was this participation and, in particular, the explanations that students provided that contributed to their enhanced achievement scores. Interestingly, high-ability students generally performed better when they worked in same-ability groups than mixed-ability ones, although their performances did not suffer when they worked with low-ability students, and they were not disadvantaged by working with low-ability students. On balance, Webb et al. concluded that mixed-ability groups produce greater achievement than restricting high-ability students to same-ability groups, and that medium- and low-ability peers have much to gain from working with their high-ability peers.

Catering for Students With Diverse Needs

Mixed-ability groups provide opportunities for teachers to include a range of students with diverse needs (e.g., second-language learners, at-risk students, students with learning difficulties) who clearly benefit from the opportunity of working with others (Miller & Harrington, 1990). Sharan (1990) and Slavin and Cooper (1999) reported that cross-ethnic relationships were enhanced and academic learning was promoted when students worked in cooperative groups, and that children identified more friends outside their own racial and ethnic group than peers who had not worked in cooperative groups. Slavin and Cooper argued that when students are assigned to cross-ethnic groups, they are sent a strong positive message regarding the importance of cross-ethnic interaction, and this, in conjunction with the equal-status roles assigned by working in such groups, permits students to learn about one another. Similarly, Putnam, Markovchick, Johnson, and Johnson (1996) reported that students with learning disabilities were more likely to be accepted by their peers when they had the opportunity of working with them in cooperative groups, and Cohen, Lotan, and Catanzarite (1990) and Cohen and Lotan (1995) found that the use of status treatments where teachers implemented strategies to enhance the status of low-status students (i.e., usually the less academically able) during cooperative learning was associated with higher rates of participation of these students, which, in turn, contributed to significant gains in their achievement.

Given the above findings, what are the implications for teachers who are looking to grouping students in their classes? The following summarizes the research evidence on grouping students:

- Mixed-ability groups promote achievement gains for low- and medium-ability students.
- High-ability students are not disadvantaged by working with lower-ability peers.
- Second-language learners acquire language skills more readily when they work with peers in mixed-ability groups.
- Cross-ethnic relations and learning are promoted in mixed-ability groups.
- Students with learning disabilities are likely to be accepted by their peers.
- Status and learning for low-status children can be enhanced in mixed-ability groups.

Ideas for Establishing Mixed-Ability Groups

Elementary School

★ Teacher assigns young children to groups of three or four members, ensuring that children with different abilities or talents are included (i.e., artist, writer, humorist). The teacher would need to spend time with the children explaining what she means and actively identifying children who may have these abilities or talents. For example, comments such as the following may be appropriate: "Dana has a good sense of humor and I think he'd have some good ideas he could contribute to his group." Children discuss these attributes and use them to complete the task at hand (e.g., constructing a diorama to depict an interesting scene from a story the class has read; painting a picture with each child completing a section; participating in presenting a skit with each child responsible for part of the organizing—actor(s), director/coordinator, stage manager, costume manager).

★ Children are given colors (red, blue, yellow, green) and told to form a group, ensuring that each color is included in their group. Unbeknownst to the children, each color represents an ability level or a talent (e.g., red = high, blue = medium+, yellow = medium−, green = low). Children then complete the task they have been assigned.

★ Using the same colors (red, blue, yellow, green), the teacher structures the activity so that each student is required to perform a particular task (e.g., searching for specific information). Once they have located the information they were looking for, different colors pair up (e.g., red + green) to organize how they will present the information they have collected to the other pair in the group. This is one way of structuring peer support within the group to ensure that the less-able students receive scaffolding with the task.

★ Teacher assigns children to pairs so each pair consists of one above-average and one below-average student. Pairs join with another pair to make a group of four, thereby ensuring that there are two above-average and two below-average students in each group.

Middle School and High School

★ Teacher discusses the task with the students and informs them that they will be unable to complete it unless they include students who have different talents. For example, if the group is required to present a PowerPoint display to the class, students may need someone who is a technician (resolves difficulties with the computer, program materials), a researcher (conducts searches from different databases to locate information), manager (collects resources), and a presenter (responsible for organizing the group's presentation to the class). The recognition that different students have different talents provides status to those students and also makes others aware of the talents they can harness. It is recommended that the teacher, initially, constructs the groups to ensure that students with different talents are included. As the students become more aware of the different attributes of others, they can begin to exercise more control over the selection of members.

★ Students are given a line or lines of a limerick and are asked to find others with lines from the same limerick. This activity promotes a great deal of fun as they try to piece together the limerick and then present it to the larger class. This activity not only serves as an icebreaker, but it identifies the group's members. Students are often quite willing to accept this type of randomization in selecting members, whereas they may be reluctant to accept members the teacher identifies. The astute teacher, though, will see that each group consists of students with different talents or abilities by ensuring that lines from each limerick are given to students who reflect this diversity.

★ Each student is given one task to work on from a complement of three tasks that are required to be completed by the group. Students have to find the remaining members of the group to ensure that they can identify a theme/focus for their combined tasks. This is a reverse-order approach: Rather than identifying the subtasks, students have the subtasks and are required to identify the group's task. For example, the group task may be to investigate the packaging of cookies currently used by a company and make recommendations on future packaging, although they are not explicitly told that this is the group's task. Students may be assigned one of the following subtasks and asked to find other members of their group and then identify the overall task of their group from the individual tasks that they have been given: (a) the needs of the consumer when packaging cookies; (b) the expectations of the community for environmentally friendly packaging of cookies; and (c) ways to minimize the costs to the company of packaging its cookies.

Gender Groupings

As mentioned in Chapter 2, the research on the best gender groupings for students is still unclear, probably because the focus is often on the value of mixed-ability groups rather than trying to determine whether students work best in gender-balanced or -imbalanced groups. In the extract above (Case Study 5.1), the students (2 boys and 2 girls) were quite willing to work together as is evident from S2's comment, "Sometimes, he (S3) worked with me" (helped her on the computer). Moreover, as a consequence of their group experience, the students in Case Study 5.1 had become friends, which they were not previously. These comments are similar to those reported by Lyle (1999) of elementary students' perceptions of their experiences in mixed-gender and -ability groups (designed to improve their literacy levels), with most children commenting on the value of sharing ideas and learning from others. Furthermore, many students indicated that they had made new friends as a result of their experiences.

Interestingly, in a study of help-seeking behaviors of children in naturalistic class settings in elementary school, Nelson-Le Gall and DeCooke (1987) found that they are often more likely to seek help from same-sex peers than cross-sex peers even though girls are often perceived as more academically competent by both boys and girls and more likeable as helpers than boys. These findings led the authors to propose that gender appears to influence students' choice of peer helpers in elementary classrooms.

The perspectives of preadolescents who worked in mixed- and same-gender dyads appears to be similar with Strough, Swenson, and Cheng's (2001) finding that students who worked in same-gender dyads on a creative writing task reported a greater sense of affiliation, influence, and enjoyment than students in mixed-gender ones, possibly because friendship bonds were greater in same-gender dyads. Moreover, Strough et al. found that the more students perceived that they were able to influence each other, the better their task performance, with fewer punctuation and capitalization errors. These findings led the authors to propose that the preference for working in same-gender dyads may be because the students were preadolescents and this age group often prefers to avoid mixed-gender relationships (Sroufe, Bennett, Engluns, Urban, & Schulman, 1993).

Yet, while both Nelson-Le Gall and DeCooke (1987) and Sroufe et al. (1993) observed an apparent preference for same-gender interactions among both elementary and preadolescent students, Webb (1991) argued that it was the composition of the group, rather than gender per se, that affected the interactions participants had with each other. In groups where there were more boys than girls, Webb found that the boys tended to interact with each other and ignore the girl. In contrast, in groups where there were more girls than boys, the girls spent more time trying to involve the boy in the discussions, to the detriment of interacting with each other. In both of these groups, boys outperformed girls even though boys and girls did not differ in ability. When groups were gender-balanced, however, boys and girls were equally interactive in the help they provided, and the differences in achievement that occurred in the gender-imbalanced groups did not occur in these groups.

Teachers' Perspectives on Grouping Students

Given the issues raised by the research on gender groupings and the requirement that students are often expected to work cooperatively in groups, interest lies in investigating teachers' perceptions of what works best when they group students. Teachers' perspectives are important because they have firsthand experience of different situations and can often provide invaluable insights that inform research.

In interviews of 21 teachers in elementary schools who reported using cooperative learning, Antil, Jenkins, Wayne, and Vadasy (1998) found that most preferred to use a range of strategies to form groups. These included forming *heterogeneous groups* (the most popular form of grouping), allowing students to select their group members, random assignment, and groups of convenience (i.e., students sitting next to each other). Interestingly, none of the teachers referred to ability groups when they discussed heterogeneous groupings. While most of the teachers indicated that they deliberately formed heterogeneous groups some of the time, at other times they used strategies that might or might not result in such groups. It appeared that once they had decided to form groups for different activities, they chose strategies rather than groupings that would allow them to do so with maximum efficiency.

Gillies and Boyle (2006), in interviews with 10 elementary teachers who had used cooperative learning in their classrooms, also found that most teachers reported that they used heterogeneous groups (i.e., usually mixed-gender and -ability groups) because of the benefits that children derived from interacting with others with different ideas and talents. Furthermore, many of the teachers believed that by working in heterogeneous groups students learn that others have strengths and weaknesses that can be used to make valuable contributions to the group.

In short, while the research on gender groupings still requires further investigation, the following key issues have been identified to date:

- Students often prefer working in gender-balanced groups.
- Adolescents do not like to work in mixed-gender dyads.
- Gender composition of groups influences students' interactions.
- Students are more interactive and obtain higher learning outcomes in gender-balanced groups.
- Teachers use a range of strategies in grouping students, and gender considerations is only one.
- Teachers often structure groups to include students with diverse talents and needs.

Friendship Groupings

One question frequently asked by teachers dealing with group composition is, "Should friends be allowed to work together?" This probably occurs because students often place a great deal of pressure on teachers to form groups with their friends as they work on tasks that they may have a common interest in completing. Certainly, there is evidence that friendship with one's peers is important as a context for social, emotional, and cognitive development. Newcomb and Bagwell (1995), in an extensive review of children's friendship relationships, reported that friendships are characterized by: a pattern of positive interactions, with friends often achieving greater productivity in task-oriented activities; friends encouraging problem-solving efforts through cooperation and better understanding of the other's needs and abilities; and friends being more likely to try to resolve conflicts because their management is critically important to the development and maintenance of any friendship. Similarly, Hartup and Stevens (1997), in a review of the research on friendships and adaptations across the lifespan, reported that friends are both cognitive and affective resources who foster self-esteem and a sense of well-being. They also help to socialize each other, especially with achieving age-related tasks such as learning to display and regulate their emotions, and they provide supportive and intimate relationships that are important for an individual's personal growth and development.

Given the benefits obtained from having close friendships, how does this information translate into classroom contexts where teachers need to make decisions about friendship groups? Certainly, there is evidence that students who know and like each other benefit most from working together as they tend to accept more responsibility for their learning and are more motivated to achieve their goals than students who are not friends (Abrami, Chambers, Poulsen, DeSimone, & Howden, 1995; Kagan & Kagan, 1994). Moreover, in some cooperative approaches (i.e., Group Investigation), students are able to select group members on the basis of friendship and compatibility; this appears to work well, with students in these groups attaining greater achievement gains than peers who work in whole-class settings. Yet while there is some merit in allowing students to choose their group members because it gives them more control over their learning environment, in reality there are some drawbacks.

In a study of high school students' preferences for teacher-selected or student-selected groupings in science, Mitchell et al. (2004) found that students' preferences for choosing their own group members actually declined over the period of the study. When this was investigated further through student interviews, the authors found that although students reported that they liked the autonomy of being able to choose who they would work with, many realized that friends may not always be ideal group members because of the conflict that can arise from being a good friend and being a good team member. Students reported that friends often tended to talk and socialize rather than work, and if the group task became demanding this created some tension, with many indicating that they were reluctant to challenge a friend who was not contributing to the group, although this seemed to be more of an issue for females than males. Male students tended to characterize themselves as being assertive and more willing to speak up and reprimand those who were not willing to do their share.

Interestingly, Strough et al. (2001) also reported that while greater friendship was beneficial for performance earlier in the task, it was detrimental to performance later in the task in terms of errors that the students made on their collaborative writing task. It appeared that students may have been more concerned with the social aspects of the task rather than the performance itself. Students acknowledged that they lacked skill in judging effective team members, that is, those who would work and those who would not, with many admitting that it was better for teachers to select group members because they had more experience in choosing groups.

Another concern that students expressed was the consequences of not selecting a friend for inclusion in a group. When students are allowed to choose group members, they often choose them on the basis of perceived social success, athletic prowess, or academic competency, so many low-status students may not be included or are selected only as a last resort (Cohen, 1994). This also appeared to occur in the Mitchell et al. (2004) study. In effect, when students choose their own group members, they often promote or reinforce status hierarchies that currently exist, and this led some low-ability students to question the value of group work.

In short, while there is quite extensive research on the importance friendships play in supporting an individual's social, emotional, and cognitive development and growth and there is some evidence that friends who work together are more likely to exercise greater autonomy and motivation with their work, there is also some evidence that friendship groups may not be as beneficial to some students as others. In this regard, teachers are encouraged to use their discretion when deciding to establish friendship groups in their classrooms, to ensure that friends who work together do so productively and that no student is left to feel rejected or abandoned when he or she is not included. The following summarizes the research to date:

- Friendships are important for social, emotional, and cognitive development and well-being.
- Students can be more motivated when they work with friends.

- Choosing group members can allow students to exercise more autonomy over their learning; this is important for adolescents.
- Friendship groups may promote and reinforce social hierarchies.
- Low-status students may not be selected for groups.
- Balance may be needed between teacher-selected and student-selected groups.

Practical Activity

Ideas for Establishing Friendship Groups

Elementary School

★ The teacher discusses with the children that, as a special treat (because of the very successful way students have worked in groups previously), she or he is going to allow them to work with their friends. However, the teacher will need to choose the friends, thereby ensuring that low-status children, who may be overlooked, will be included. If emphasis is given to the importance of working together and using every members' talents, most students will accept other group members.

★ The teacher may need to consider alternating how groups are formed, depending on the activity. For example, it may be appropriate for some activities (i.e., those that last only a few sessions) to allow students to choose who they will work with, while for others it may be more appropriate for the teacher to choose group members, particularly if the task is complex and extends over a number of weeks. When students know they will have some opportunities to choose their groups, they are often more willing to accept groups where members are selected by the teacher.

★ Provide opportunities for students to work in groups where the teacher knows students have common interests and where friendships have developed (e.g., sport, reading, computer games). The teacher identifies these interests to the class and informs the children that they will be able to work with students who they know share these interests. For example, students who share an interest in the Harry Potter books may choose to work with classmates who also share this interest. While the task may involve students' reading different parts of a story, one group may decide to produce a diorama that depicts an aspect of it, while another may focus on a play that depicts an alternative idea to the one in the story. These can be fun activities that tap students' interests, they are highly motivating, and they provide group members with the opportunity of consolidating friendships.

Middle School

★ Teacher discusses a number of tasks (relevant to a theme) that students can work on in small groups. For example, tasks around a science theme of developing alternative energy sources may require students to work on identifying an alternative energy source (e.g., wind power, water, sunlight) and develop a model of a car or house that relies on this energy source to test out the viability of their energy source. Students are allowed to work with friends but are required to identify specific subtasks that they intend to complete in a given time. This requirement will ensure that the group continues to work productively together to meet the required goal.

★ Students can work with friends on a topic they have identified but, as above, must negotiate tasks and timelines with the class teacher after their initial meeting. Once again, this ensures that the group remains focused and on task.

★ Students can work with a friend but must also find two other members they have not worked with before to ensure that they are inclusive of all students. The task is set by the class teacher (to avoid conflict over choosing the topic) until members feel more comfortable with each other and are able to negotiate tasks among themselves.

High School

★ The teacher surveys the students to identify their interest areas. For example, these interests may include: sports, history, current events, movies, cars, and so on. Once these have been identified, the teacher may have to negotiate with the students to identify five or six common areas of interest. These interests will enable the teacher to identify group tasks that the students negotiate to complete. For example, under a common theme of "World Events Making History," students may choose to focus on key sporting events (e.g., the Olympics, specific athletes), historical events (e.g., the impact on African nations of the colonial past), current news events (e.g., recent initiative by peoples in the developing world to deal with the AIDS virus), movie releases (e.g., the issues around the production of the trilogy *Lord of the Rings*), and developments in the auto industry (e.g., the production of environmentally friendly new models of cars). Students agree to work with their friends on the selected group task.

(Continued)

(Continued)

> ★ Students identify interests from a list provided by the teacher. In order to keep the task manageable, this list may need to have a limited number of possible options. Students who indicate that they have an interest in a specific topic have their names placed in a box and are randomly selected for inclusion in a group. While this will often ensure that students have an opportunity of working with some of their friends (mainly because friends often share similar interests), it also ensures that students who may not be selected are included in a group. Adolescents will see this as a very fair way of allocating students to groups.
>
> ★ Both the teacher and students share responsibility for selecting students for inclusion in different groups. The teacher may precede selecting students by stating, "I know that John has some special interest in this topic and I've seen how well he's worked on it in the past, so I'd like him to work with this group and share some of his ideas." (This public acknowledgment of John's special interest and talent must be true.) In this way, John can move into the group with his status enhanced because of the public recognition provided by his teacher.

Status

Case Study 5.2

Enhancing Mandy's Low Status in Her Group

Mandy was a quiet 10-year-old, Grade 5 student who was always on the periphery of any group. She had changed schools frequently because her mother and partner (not Mandy's father) were transitional workers who moved to find employment or cheap housing, often living in trailer parks. This meant that Mandy's schooling was erratic as she moved from school to school and sometimes missed school for weeks on end until her family had been able to secure housing. Consequently, Mandy had fallen behind with her schooling and was experiencing difficulties with reading and math. She was also very shy around the students in her class, preferring to observe them as they played together rather than try to join in their games. Her teacher at her current school was very concerned about Mandy's reluctance to join in with the other children, so she decided to establish some cooperative groups in her class that would ensure Mandy had the opportunity work with others. Mandy was a great collector of items—comic strips, pictures, ribbons, shells—and her teacher decided to put this to use by ensuring that she had the role of resource manager in her team. The teacher made sure that the children understood that this was something Mandy could do by making the following comment: "I'm going to get Mandy to be the resource manager in this group because I know she's good at collecting things, and you'll need someone who can do that—collect the pictures and materials you'll need to make the diorama." Comments like this ensured that Mandy was initially accepted in the group, and ongoing monitoring of the group's activities helped the teacher ensure that all students, including Mandy, had opportunities to participate in the task and contribute their ideas.

In Case Study 5.2, the teacher has recognized that Mandy is regarded as a low-status student by her peers because of her academic difficulties and has intervened to ensure that she is accepted as someone with a special skill that will help the group as they work on constructing their diorama. After observing Mandy's behavior and noting that she is a good collector, the teacher has publicly acknowledged the importance of this skill. Moreover, by assigning Mandy the role of resource manager, she has indicated to the group that Mandy's special skill is important for the task at hand. In doing so, the teacher has fulfilled the criteria that Cohen (1998) believes is important for assigning competency to a student:

1. The evaluation must be public.

2. The valuation must be truthful and specific, referring to particular intellectual abilities or skills.

3. The abilities or skills of the low-status student must be made relevant to the group task. (p. 21)

Because Mandy is a low-status student, it is highly likely that she might not have participated in her small-group activity unless her teacher had made an effort to raise her status by assigning a particular competency to her. Low-status children are often less talkative in groups, have difficulty accessing resources, and may even be excluded by other group members. In contrast, high-status students are often more talkative, have no difficulty accessing resources, and are often very successful at getting the group to agree with their suggestions (Cohen, 1998). It is important that opportunities are created for low-status students to participate in groups, because research has consistently shown that those who talk more learn more (Cohen, Lotan, Scarloss, & Arellano, 1999).

By publicly stating that Mandy had a special skill that the group needed, her teacher created an expectation among other group members that Mandy would be someone they could value as they worked on completing their diorama. This was important because the group was working on a task that no member could complete alone, so it was critical that everyone, including Mandy, was able to contribute to its production. When students realize that they have valuable yet different skills or abilities that they can contribute and that they must interact if they are solve the problem at hand, differences in participation between high- and low-status students are likely to be reduced (Cohen, 1998).

Dealing with inequitable interactions among students during group work is a problem that must be addressed if low-status students are to fully participate in group activities. Cohen et al. (1990) proposed that there are a number of initiatives that teachers need to consider to address status issues for low-status children. These include the following:

- Training students in the interpersonal and small-group skills needed to promote cooperation in small-group settings. Learning to listen to others, providing opportunities for members to talk and share ideas, and assigning rotating roles to each member of the group will do much to solve the problem of access by low-status students to interaction.

- The curriculum materials need to be rich and stimulating and presented in such a way that they require different types of contributions from each group member. Cohen (1994) argues that when the task is open and discovery based so there is no single right answer, students are forced to interact about the process and discuss how to proceed, make decisions, and divide up both the task and how to manage the substantive content involved. In these circumstances, students tend to engage in more productive discussions as they work to resolve the problem at hand.

- Students need to understand that no single group member will be able to complete the task, because multiple abilities, talents, or skills are required. In this way, students learn that there are different ways to be "smart" and that all members have contributions to make.

- Teachers need to acknowledge publicly the contributions of low-status students. It's important that their contributions are genuine so that other students realize that they can provide a key component to completing the task and will interact with them.

The above suggestions will do much to enhance the standing of low-status children and ensure that they have more equitable access to the group's resources, including other students.

Multiple Intelligences

Howard Gardner's (1983) theory of *multiple intelligences* (MI) has challenged the notion of what intelligence is and how it can be identified. Gardner proposes that intelligence cannot be reduced to a single construct, but rather, individuals have different types of intelligences that they use in different contexts that help them to solve problems or create products that are valued by the group, whether it be the small group in the classroom or the larger cultural group within which they live. Unfortunately, schools have traditionally had a fairly myopic perspective on what intelligence is and have traditionally emphasized scholastic intelligence, focusing on developing students linguistic, logical-mathematical, and spatial abilities and often neglected other intelligent behaviors such as the musical, kinesthetic, naturalistic, intrapersonal, and interpersonal abilities that are also needed in the modern world (Gardner, 1999).

The theory of MI has had an enormous impact on education, not only helping to change teachers' thinking about students' talents but also helping to bring about changes in the formal curriculum in how teachers teach and how students learn (Cuban, 2004). As a consequence, teachers are now more likely to recognize that children's potential can be developed in different ways and that they need to create different opportunities in class for children to learn using different intelligences (Hickey, 2004).

Given that MI recognizes that children learn, process information about their world, and express their understandings in different ways, what are the principles and practices that underpin an MI classroom? Hoerr (2004) believes an MI classroom is identified in the following ways:

- Everyone has a different profile of intelligence; we are all smart in different ways.
- Teachers use all students' intelligences to help them learn.
- The classroom is child-centered.
- Teachers help students create meaning in a constructivist way.
- Personal intelligences are valued: Who you are is more important than what you know.
- Teachers create curriculum—lessons, units, themes.

- Teachers create assessment tools—projects, exhibitions, presentations (PEP)—which incorporate MI.
- Teachers work with colleagues in using MI, developing collegiality. (p. 47)

In addition, Green and Tanner (2005) recommend that the following also be considered when designing courses based on MI theory:

- Create complex asks that appeal to several intelligences at once.
- Aim to incorporate as many intelligences as possible within a task or a series of tasks.
- Establish tasks so that children are required to use different intelligences and not only the ones they are more comfortable using.

In classrooms, teachers can use MI as a basis for establishing group activities where students work on complex tasks that require them to use a number of different intelligences. For example, students may be expected to produce a group report in which they demonstrate that they have used not only their linguistic, logical-mathematical, and spatial intelligences but also their musical, kinesthetic, naturalistic, intrapersonal, and interpersonal intelligences. Initially, this requirement will be quite challenging for students who have relied on the more traditional intelligences and not been encouraged to explore those others that have the potential to extend and enrich their learning. If teachers ensure that students are taught about MI and how to identify their strengths, students are more likely to be prepared to work on activities that extend these strengths while simultaneously accept being challenged by those intelligences they have traditionally avoided. In addition, students learn to recognize strengths in others and often seek to have students with diverse intelligences included in their groups as a way of extending their own learning. In short, MI can be used as a basis for constructing groups where all students' strengths are acknowledged and valued.

Interest Groupings

Another popular way of grouping students is through their interests in particular topics or events such as drama, sport, music, books, hobbies, computer games, and so on. While teachers of elementary students will periodically form ad hoc groups around students' interests, adolescents are very responsive to these types of grouping arrangements, possibly because they tend to be able to work with others who have interests similar to their own, and this often enables them to develop more stable friendships over time. Moreover, because adolescents are particularly responsive to their peers, opportunities to work with them in formal or informal settings are often valued.

Teachers tend to form interest groups in class when students need to work together on specific projects or research topics. Interest groups may include students who are researching and using specific technologies to create an advertisement about a coming entertaining event. In these circumstances, students not only need to have an interest in the topic but are often required to have specific skills or abilities that they can contribute to the group. These skills or abilities may include an understanding of how to organize what needs to be done, conduct Web searches, use desktop publishing programs, understand how to use animation, and how to synthesize the parts to produce the advertisement.

Other interest groups may involve students' working in teams to produce a school musical or play. This type of group often involves teams within teams, where one team may be responsible for the lighting and stage production while others will represent the musicians, the actors and director, the wardrobe and costume management, and the sales and theater management teams. Students will often self-select into different teams on the basis of the contributions they perceive they can make so that someone with a flair for design may choose to be part of the wardrobe and costumes team while others may decide to contribute to the music team or the sales and theater management teams.

Typically, the interest groupings outlined above stay in place until the team has accomplished its goal, which may range from a period of a few weeks to some months. With elementary students, interest groups often last for only a session or a few sessions. While young students usually enjoy working with their friends, they often work better in groups that a have specific goal to achieve within a given time frame, usually a few weeks.

When establishing interest groups, teachers need to ensure that students understand the purpose of the group (i.e., what they are to achieve) as well as the group rules that need to operate to ensure that students manage their interpersonal relationships effectively. With elementary students, this will involve teachers' discussing with their students the rules they believe they will need to develop to be able to work together as a team; for high school students, this can be achieved through a process of collaborative negotiation. For large undertakings such as a theatrical production involving many students in multiple teams, the organizer (one or more teachers) will usually discuss expectations for the group at their initial meeting, with follow-up discussions occurring in the respective supporting teams (e.g., sales and theater management team). This gives these students the autonomy to develop their own group rules (e.g., we all arrive on time), which are often more relevant to their specific circumstances. Periodically, too, students need to be encouraged to reflect on how their team is working—what they've accomplished and what they may need to do as well as how they are managing their interpersonal relationships (see Chapter 6 for a more detailed review). These reflections are very important as they often allow groups to discuss issues that are of concern and resolve them before they get out of hand.

Surveying Students' Interests

The Interest Inventory (see Figure 5.1) is designed to assist teachers to identify students with common interests for group activities. The inventory taps students' interests across home, school, and community contexts. Although this inventory has been designed for elementary students, the questions can be adapted for young adolescents (Note: The Interest Inventory can be used as part of a teacher interview session with individual students, or students can write their individual responses to the questions).

Computer Technology Groupings

Students regularly use computers to network with others, search for information, prepare and present reports, and fulfill the demands required in many schools today. Children are generally introduced to computers as a tool that they can use in kindergarten, and as they move through the grades, they are taught how this tool can be used to access and process information, provide tutorials, integrate and use different multimedia technologies, and facilitate computer-mediated communication (Abrami, 2001). Students are using computer technology (CT) at unprecedented rates to facilitate learning in various subjects as well as to acquire CT knowledge and skills to meet the challenges of this rapidly changing technological age. In fact, there is great enthusiasm for integrating CT in education, as teachers have realized the potential it holds for assisting learning. This enthusiasm for CT has also presented teachers with a dilemma: mainly, how to optimize its use given that few classes have sufficient technological resources to enable all students to have individual access to computers when required.

Many teachers have dealt with limited access by grouping students around a computer console as they work on specific tasks, and while research indicates that students learn more effectively in small-group settings than when they

Interest Inventory

1. What do you like to do after class?

_____
_____
_____
_____
_____

2. What do you like to do on the weekends?

_____
_____
_____
_____
_____

3. Do you play any sports or have any hobbies? Can you tell me about them?

_____
_____
_____
_____
_____

4. Do you have any favorite movie stars or sports figures that you admire? Tell me about them and why you admire them.

_____
_____
_____
_____
_____

5. If you could have three wishes granted, what would they be? How would they make your life different?

_____
_____
_____
_____
_____

(Continued)

(Continued)

6. What are your favorite movies?

_____
_____
_____
_____
_____

7. How much do you like to read? (very much, quite a lot, not much, not at all)

_____
_____
_____
_____
_____

8. Have you read any books lately? If you have, can you tell me about them?

_____
_____
_____
_____
_____

9. What are some other things you read (newspapers, comics, magazines)?

_____
_____
_____
_____
_____

10. What do you like to do in class (projects, math, reading, science, computer studies)? Tell me about the activities you really like working on.

_____
_____
_____
_____
_____

Figure 5.1   Interest Inventory

work individually or in traditional whole-class settings on non–computer-based tasks (Sharan, 1990; Slavin, 1996), how this transfers to CT groups is less clear. Moreover, students often use a range of CT, from tutoring programs that are designed to help them learn basic information through to those that encourage students to investigate and explore topics. In addition, students learn to use programs that range from processing information to those that enable computer-mediated communication such as e-mail, computer conferencing, and computer networking. Given the ubiquitous use of CT and the plethora of programs available, questions are often raised about how to enhance student interaction and collaboration while they work together on computer-generated tasks.

In a meta-analysis of 122 studies in which students worked either in small groups with CT or individually with CT, Lou, Abrami, and d'Apollonia (2001) found that students who worked in small groups learned more, interacted more effectively, used more appropriate strategies with the task, persevered longer, had greater task success, and exhibited more positive attitudes for small-group work and toward their class peers than students who learned individually. Furthermore, students who worked in small groups generally produced better group products than individual products, and they also gained more individual knowledge than students learning with CT by themselves. Interestingly, Lou et al. (2001) found that students learned significantly more in their groups when they used tutorial or basic recall and practice programs than when they worked on exploratory or discovery-based tasks. Abrami (2001) proposed that these types of programs may allow students, particularly students from low socioeconomic areas, low-status students, and students with special learning needs, some control over the pace of instruction, so they can practice more difficult material without continually having to revise that which they have already mastered and that this helps to keep them motivated as they learn.

In an evaluation of a computer-assisted tutoring program for at-risk readers, Chambers, Abrami, McWhaw, and Therrien (2001) noted that when students perceive they can be active in regulating their own learning, they are often motivated to achieve more. Moreover, students learned more when these programs were used in subjects such as computer learning, social sciences, and social studies than in mathematics, science, and language arts, and they learned more in groups when they worked on closed tasks with immediate feedback than when they worked on open ones. This is not surprising because when feedback is immediate, students often learn faster, enjoy their classes more, and have more positive attitudes to computers (Abrami, 2001).

The results of Lou et al.'s (2001) meta-analysis led the authors to propose that the effects of small-group learning were significantly enhanced when students had previously worked in groups or had been trained to work in groups, cooperative learning strategies were employed to promote peer interaction, groups were small (i.e., two members), basic tutoring programs were used, and students were relatively low or relatively high in ability. Low-ability students benefit from receiving explanations that help them to correct any misunderstandings and to acquire appropriate learning strategies, while high-ability students benefit from giving explanations, which forces them to cognitively reorganize their own understandings and explain them in such a way that they can be more easily understood. In so doing, they often develop more elaborate cognitive understandings of the material than they held previously (Webb, 1991; Webb & Palincsar, 1996).

Given these findings, what are the implications for teachers who want to use CT in their classroom curricula as a tool to promote student dialogue and enhance learning? Abrami (2001) maintains that CT should not be used just to promote the acquisition of basic skills and information, although research indicates that students can learn effectively when it does (Chambers et al., 2001), but rather it should also be used to assist students to engage in the more meaningful construction of knowledge.

Activities such as student-initiated projects, explorative investigations, and problem-solving tasks where students work collaboratively with others to discuss ideas, challenge each other's perspective, and resolve differences are more likely to promote higher-order thinking and reasoning and the construction of new understandings and learning than tasks that require only basic recall and practice (Mercer, Wegerif, & Dawes, 1999).

Promoting Student Talk

In a study of CT and students' talk, Mercer, Fernandez, Dawes, Wegerif, and Sams (2003) noted that the software used needs to be designed to promote discussion (i.e., it does not include basic recall and drill activities) and students need to be taught the ground rules for exploratory talk.

Software design that was beneficial for promoting discussion in groups included the following features:

- Complex activities that require joint discussion and reflection
- Problems and choices that are embedded in a motivating narrative (i.e., story)
- A clear purpose for the activity that students understand
- On-screen prompts that remind participants to talk together and make predictions, proposals, and reasons clear

- Decision making that is reflective rather than rapid
- Responses that require simple keystrokes rather than extensive typing

The ground rules that promote exploratory talk in groups include the following:

- The group shares all relevant information.
- The group seeks to reach agreement.
- The group accepts responsibility for its decisions.
- Reasons for their responses are provided.
- Challenges are expected.
- Alternatives are discussed before a decision is made.
- Group members encourage each other to speak and share ideas.

When students work with CT that promotes discussion and they understand the rules for exploratory talk, Mercer et al. (2003) found that they exhibit more of the following features in their interactions with each other:

- They ask each other more task-focused questions.
- They provide more reasons for their statements.
- They consider other options before making a decision.
- They seek opinions from other group members.
- They seek to reach consensus as they work through different stages of the activity.

Case Study 5.3 provides an example of a cooperative, complex CT task for middle school students.

Case Study 5.3

Preparing a PowerPoint Presentation on Nicotine

The students in Grade 6 had been researching the effects of nicotine on the body as part of a unit of work on healthy living and healthy bodies. They had collated key information into 5–6 topic paragraphs that members of their group had composed together. The key points their teacher had asked them to research were

What is nicotine?

Analyze how nicotine affects your body.

Identify what the body does to process nicotine.

Identify other groups of people affected by nicotine exposure and analyze the consequences.

Explain why nicotine is a drug.

Find some interesting facts about nicotine use.

Today, the students are in the computer laboratory, and their task is to prepare a series of PowerPoint slides (no more than 6 slides) that can be used to convey the key findings from their research to other groups in their class. They have 45 minutes to discuss and prepare their slide presentation. Prior to commencing the activity, the teacher reminded the students of the ground rules for working together (sharing ideas, everyone contributes, every group member has an opportunity to use the computer, with each person typing out at least one slide, decisions are made by the group, and disagreements are resolved democratically). She also reminded them of the criteria that the class had previously negotiated that would be used to evaluate their presentations. The criteria required that they cover the key content points (listed above) as well as presentation points that were allocated to the PowerPoint display. These criteria included

Ensuring it was eye catching

Appropriate use of font size except when using headings

Appropriate use of pictures and diagrams

Appropriate use of sound effects

Effective use of colors

Logical sequence in the slide presentation

Appropriate background

In addition, other aspects that would be considered were

Correct spelling

Appropriate use of simple and complex sentences

Appropriate use of paragraphs

Correct punctuation usage

At the completion of the preparation period, each group gave a 10-minute PowerPoint presentation of its research on nicotine. Each presentation was followed by a short question-and-answer session to allow students to clarify any issues raised. This was followed by the teacher helping the class to critique the presentation on the basis of the criteria listed above. Students categorized their comments according to whether they believed the criteria were

Still developing

Were developed

Were highly developed

This feedback from their peers gave students the opportunity to reflect on each presentation and provide reasons to justify the comments they made. Because the feedback was constructive, the students in each group accepted it positively and commented on aspects of their presentation that they believed they would do differently next time.

The students in Case Study 5.3 worked in groups of three around a computer console. The teacher believed that this was an ideal group size because it ensured that the conversation would be multidirectional rather than unidirectional, as can occur when students work in pairs where one student may adopt the role of the tutor while the other becomes the tutee (Gillies & Ashman, 1998). Dialoguing was important because the task was complex (Cohen, 1994) and students had to be prepared to exchange ideas and information, discuss alternatives, and resolve differences and reach agreement in order to be able to complete it. Furthermore, by restricting the group to three members, all members had access to the keyboard; this was important because all were required to participate in composing the PowerPoint slides for their presentation. Further, the teacher had deliberately structured the groups so that each had students with a range of diverse talents, and while many students had overlapping talents such as special multimedia skills, visual design skills, and oral presentation skills, all students knew that they were expected to help each other to fulfill a variety of roles as they worked together.

Observations of the students as they worked in their groups confirmed that they were task-focused and their discussions were animated. Follow-up interviews with the students on their CT activity revealed that they enjoyed discussing their ideas, and they thought others in their groups did some "great things" because they knew how to incorporate different multimedia designs or sound bites into their slides and taught others how to do this. All reported that the task was highly motivating, and they were keen to do another one like it. When asked how they made decisions and resolved disagreements, most either said that they did not experience any conflict, or when they did they discussed it among themselves and "it worked out OK."

Practical Activity

Ideas for Establishing Computer Groupings

Elementary School

★ Students are going to design a Web page that conveys a key message about the dangers of too much exposure to the sun. The activity has been designed so that students are required to do some preliminary research on the importance of the sun in our lives (photosynthesis and its effect on plants and humans), the damage caused by the sun's rays on the human skin, particularly for Caucasians, and the adverse effects of skin melanomas (skin cancers).

★ Students work in groups of 3–4 students to develop an advertising logo for a cookie company they have become part owners of. This is a special cookie company because it can be owned only by children, who must guard its secrets from adults so the magic recipes are never divulged. The cookie company sells a variety of magical cookies but only children can taste the "magic" in them. To adults, they taste like ordinary cookies. The group's task is to develop a logo for these magical cookies conveying the scrumptiousness, delectableness, and succulence of the product to potential consumers through the integration of various multimedia. The logo will be judged on the extent it is able to convey the "magical qualities" by the incorporation of relevant design, text, visual imaging, video, and sound effects.

High School

The following task is complex and extends over two school terms. It involves a number of smaller subtasks that must be completed in order to complete the large task: designing a Web site for a client. Although the task was originally prepared for Grade 12 students, it is possible to pare it back so that younger high school students can do parts of it over varying periods of time.

Students are required to undertake the development of a Web site for their client, Fairyland. The students are to work in groups of three and provide a prototype that covers the following areas of the existing Fairyland site: home, rides, attractions, and guest information. One member of the group will take primary responsibility for the redesign of the home page and the rides page, another will take responsibility for the redesign of the attractions page, and the final member of the team will redesign the guest information page. Even though each member has a task he or she is primarily responsible for, it is expected that they will discuss the proposed redesign with each other before submitting all the component parts on a CD to the client. A final presentation to the class will be required from each group. Note: Each group is operating under the assumption that they are an organization delivering a product to the client, so the presentation of their work needs to reflect a professional attitude. The task consists of three parts:

Part A: Define and Plan a Solution to the Problem. This will involve a number of smaller tasks, including interviewing the client to determine his or her expectations for the redevelopment of the Fairyland site; detailing the aims and objectives of the project; identifying any modifications that may be needed to ensure the project is manageable; indicating the purpose of developing the Web site for the client; and providing a guesstimate of the expected costs of the project, detailing all work time allocated to it. Once this is completed, the group is to provide the client with a conceptualization of what the Web site will look like, a comprehensive description of the project, a storyboard that conceptually illustrates the nature of the intended Web site, a rationale for why the proposed Web format is better than other possible formats, a contract containing specific details of what the group will do to bring the project to fruition, and an invoice to be presented to the client for costs incurred. Members of each group are to discuss the above tasks, decide on how to proceed, consult regularly about their progress, and ensure that all group members are involved in the decisions that are made.

Part B: Implement and Test the Solution to the Problem. This involves a number of small tasks, including: creating the basic Web structure (the basis of the prototype that will be presented); designing the graphic elements that will be inserted into the site; designing the text elements that will be added to each page; designing or morphing the photographic elements that will be used; and developing the actual Web site by bringing together all the graphic, textual, and photographic

(Continued)

(Continued)

elements and incorporating them into the basic Web structure that the group designed earlier. In addition, the group needs to develop a detailed user's guide to the Web site. To ensure that the group has completed the implementation stage successfully, the Web site needs to be tested to make sure that any individual can use it without becoming confused. This will require that the group arranges for two individuals who are not familiar with the Web site to test it. This task will involve the group's developing a questionnaire that asks the testers to focus on each element of the site requiring testing. The testers need to provide feedback, and the group needs to demonstrate how that feedback has been incorporated into the finished product. Once again, members of each group are to discuss the tasks before deciding on how to proceed. This includes making sure that everyone is expected to contribute to the final product.

Part C: Evaluate the Solution. This involves the group's making judgments, supported by data and logical arguments, about the process of developing the Web site, the actual Web site, and the cost dimension of the project. This will involve evaluating the process (e.g., *How well do you feel you managed? What aspects did you complete successfully? How could you have improved your work?*) as well as the Web site itself (e.g., *How well does the finished product satisfy the aims and objectives established in the planning stage? What criteria can you use to judge the success of the Web site? Explain the positive aspects of your Web site and explain how it could be improved.*). In addition, the group will be required to evaluate the cost structure outlined at the start in relation to the final account prepared at the conclusion of the project.

BRINGING IT ALL TOGETHER: UNDERSTANDING THE RESEARCH

There is no doubt that students are more productive and learn more when they work cooperatively together in groups than when they work in whole-class settings (Sharan & Shaulov, 1990) or in unstructured groups (Gillies, 2003a, 2003b), and this includes students from different ethnic backgrounds and students with second-language needs (Shachar & Sharan, 1994). Moreover, the benefits attributed to cooperative learning experiences can be extended to students with multiple severe disabilities who successfully learned to acquire basic communication and motor skills in cooperative groups and were able to generalize these skills to follow-up sessions in different cooperative groups (Hunt, Staub, Alwell, & Goetz, 1994), as well as to students with learning disabilities who work cooperatively with peers (Saenz, Fuchs, & Fuchs, 2005). Furthermore, male students with learning disabilities were more likely to be accepted by high-, medium-, and low-status same-sex peers in school environments that have an inclusive and cooperative ethos than in schools where this ethos was not apparent (Plata & Trusty, 2005).

The apparent success of cooperative group work for students from kindergarten to college level and the key role interaction plays in the learning that occurs have helped focus attention on the types of grouping practices that facilitate student discussion. Identifying these grouping practices is crucial to understanding how they influence student interaction and learning.

In Chapter 4, I outlined the importance of helping interactions, such as giving explanations on students' learning during cooperative group work. The conditions that must exist for help giving to be effective included ensuring that it was sufficiently detailed, relevant to the student's need for help, and timely and the student requesting the help had the opportunity to apply it to the problem at hand (Webb & Mastergeorge, 2003). Establishing the conditions for helping to be effective are critical to understanding how students can be taught to provide assistance and help to each other as they participate in different small cooperative groups.

Teachers group students in different ways depending on circumstances, the children's attributes, and the type of outcome they want to achieve (i.e., improved status, improved cross-ethnic relationships, enhanced interactions). Although some research clearly indicates that certain types of grouping practices are more advantageous for particular students, research on other grouping practices is less clear and warrants further investigation. For example, research into ability groupings has indicated that low- and medium-ability students benefit from mixed-ability groupings while high-ability students generally work better with their high-ability peers although they are not disadvantaged by interacting with low-ability peers, and that high-ability students can benefit from reorganizing their own understandings in order to explain them in more easily understood ways to low-ability students (Lou et al., 1996; Webb, 1991; Webb & Palincsar, 1996). Hence, for the purpose of enhancing student interaction and promoting socialization and learning, the class teacher may choose to construct mixed-ability groups for one or both of these purposes (Johnson & Johnson, 2002).

Similarly, research indicates that students (especially adolescents) prefer to work in same-gender groups; however, it also indicates that the discourse in gender-balanced groups is likely to be more inclusive of all students (both males and females) than it is in gender-imbalanced groups. Teachers might therefore decide that this grouping practice may be more appropriate for the task at hand (Webb, 1991). Again, while gender-imbalanced groupings appear to have merits, the small number of studies that have examined gender groupings limits the recommendations that can be made.

Other types of groupings that teachers frequently use include friendship and interest groupings, and while these groupings can be highly motivating because students are either working with their friends or working with others who have similar interests, teachers report that they use them only for specific purposes (e.g., to produce a play) as they tend not to group students regularly on this basis. One of the problems with these types of groups is that they may reinforce status hierarchies that already exist, which tends to exclude low-status students (Cohen et al., 1999).

CT groupings are often formed for the purpose of completing a task where access to a computer console is required. While research indicates that group activities involving CT are often very motivating because students can be active in the learning process, group composition is rarely discussed apart from suggesting that groups should be limited to two or three students to ensure ready access to the keyboard and mouse.

CHAPTER SUMMARY

The research on grouping practices suggests

- Students learn more in mixed-ability groups of high-, medium-, and low-ability students.
- High-ability students' performances are not affected by working with low-ability peers.
- Students with diverse needs (i.e., second-language learners, those with learning difficulties or with disabilities) benefit from working in mixed-ability groups.
- Cross-ethnic relations and learning are enhanced in mixed-ability groups.
- Gender composition of groups influences interactions.
- Adolescents prefer to work in same-gender groups.
- Teachers use diverse strategies to group students, including friendship, status, multiple intelligences, interests, and computer technology groups.
- Low-status children benefit from structured cooperative learning activities.
- Teachers need to use their discretion when establishing friendship or interest groups in their classrooms.
- CT groupings are highly motivating for students.

ACTIVITIES

1. Interview two teachers who regularly use cooperative learning in their classrooms about their grouping practices. How do they group students? Do students self-select or does the teacher select students for different groups? How do they ensure all students are included? Do they notice any differences in the ways male and female students interact in groups and, if so, what are the differences? How do they deal with status problems in groups? When you have finished your interviews, construct a matrix of what the research has indicated about different grouping arrangements and see if you can match the information you've obtained from your interviews with what you have noted from the research. This activity will help you to make links between research and practice.

Matrix of Grouping Practices

Types of Groups	Teachers' Reports on What They Do When Grouping Students
Ability	
Gender	
Friendship	
Interest	
Computer technology	

2. Construct a list of status-busting strategies that teachers can use to ensure all students are able to contribute to groups. The following is an example of such a status-busting activity: Groups are each required to construct a geometric object; however, students in each group have been assigned one "handicap" that they must learn to manage. For example, one student may not be allowed to use his or her hands, while another is blindfolded and cannot see, and so on. In order to complete the activity, the students must talk to each other and provide directions to help those who cannot see work to construct the object. The purpose of the activity is not only to teach students that everyone can contribute, but to help them empathize with the difficulties some students confront in their daily lives. Students generally have fun as they work on constructing the object; however, teachers need to debrief the groups at the end to ensure that they have captured the purpose of the activity and to find out how it affected them.

SUGGESTIONS FOR FURTHER READING

Cohen, E., Lotan, R., Scarloss, B., & Arellano, A. (1999). Complex instruction: Equity in cooperative learning classrooms. *Theory Into Practice, 38,* 80–86.

Gillies, R., & Boyle, M. (2006). Ten Australian elementary teachers' discourse and reported pedagogical practices during cooperative learning. *Elementary School Journal, 106*(5), 429–451.

Mercer, N., Fernandez, M., Dawes, L., Wegerif, R., & Sams, C. (2003). Talk about texts at the computer: Using ICT to develop children's oral and literate abilities. *Reading Literacy and Language, 37,* 81–89.

Webb, N., Farivar, S., & Mastergeorge, A. (2002). Productive helping in cooperative groups. *Theory Into Practice, 41,* 13–20.

CHAPTER 6

Assessing Small-Group Learning

INTRODUCTION AND LEARNING OBJECTIVES

Assessment plays a key role in educational accountability. Being able to assess the outcomes of students' learning is very important, and probably more so for such pedagogical practices as cooperative learning where responsibility for learning is devolved to the group and where teachers act as facilitators of learning rather than instructors of knowledge. With this approach to learning, teachers need to be able to assess how students are managing the learning process (process learning) as well as what they are achieving (outcomes of learning) if they are to make changes to how they teach and how students learn. This is particularly important given the accountability requirements of the No Child Left Behind (NCLB) Act of 2001 that requires schools to close the gap between high- and low-performing students not only overall but also between minority and nonminority students and between disadvantaged students and their more advantaged peers (Kim & Sunderman, 2005; see also discussion in Chapter 1 of this volume). While the research on the academic and social benefits of cooperative learning is unequivocal for students, generally, and specifically for those in minority groups such as second-language learners, the ethnically diverse, and students with special learning needs (Cohen, 1994; Johnson & Johnson, 2002; Putnam, Markovchick, Johnson, & Johnson, 1996; Sharan, 1990; Slavin & Cooper, 1999), effective assessment practices require that these benefits be documented so teachers can communicate them to parents, students, and reporting authorities. Moreover, by doing so, teachers are able to reflect on their own teaching practices and determine what they may need to adjust or change to promote improvement in students' learning. This is important because research clearly indicates that teachers become committed to new practices after they have actively engaged in using them in their classrooms and seeing the changes in students' achievements for themselves (Guskey, 2002; Warfield, Wood, & Lehman, 2005). The purpose of this chapter is to present an overview of different assessment practices and the types of rubrics that can be used to assess learning, as well as examples of rubrics used to assess different higher-order thinking and problem-solving skills that students demonstrate.

When You Have Finished This Chapter You Will Know:

- The difference between formative (process) and summative (outcomes) assessments
- How different types of formative and summative assessments can be used to inform the teaching and learning process
- How to design different rubrics to assess the processes and outcomes of learning
- The importance of conducting authentic assessments
- How to design rubrics to assess higher-order thinking and problem-solving skills

---

Case Study 6.1

Teachers' Reports on How They Assess Small-Group Learning

I: Can you tell me a bit about how you assess students' learning during small-group work?

T1:   I use a variety of checks to monitor how they're working. I do a lot of my work informally where I cruise around the room and keep an eye on what's happening in each group. I can tell at a glance who's contributing and who's loafing. Sometimes I'll get them to do specific tasks or I'll give them different colored pens so I can see each person's contribution. I find the informal checking that I do really helps me to get a handle on what's going on.

I: What about you, Dani?

T2:   I have some checklists that I've developed like, who's contributing, who's helping others, and so on to give me a way of monitoring what's happening. I encourage the students to work together with everyone having a chance to present ideas, work and so on, so I like to see that happening when they're working together. I also have checklists that I give the students—every now and then so they can evaluate themselves. When they do this, we spend time in class debriefing each other so we can hear what's happening and what others are doing.

T3:   I've used both those approaches (referring to the comments by T1 & T2). I also think it's important to keep a tight handle on what they're actually learning as they go along so I have little checks that I do on their learning. Sometimes, I'll check on where they're up to—as a bit of a check on their progress with the task. . . . When they finish, I always get them to give a group presentation to the class so we can all see what they've accomplished. It's pretty hard to hide then because each person has to present a piece of the work, so they've got to know it.

T1:   Yes, I agree. I do a lot of the things that have been mentioned and I also do things a bit more formally. For example, when they do their group presentation, I give them a *rubric* of what they're going to be evaluated on. We go over this before they start so they know what's expected. The sorts of things I look for include making sure they've addressed the topic . . . clear presentation of all the content and the presentation itself has to be interesting and designed to capture the interest of others. So for a PowerPoint display, I'd be looking at the visual presentation and what they did to capture my interest.

T2:   One of the best ideas I read about was to get the class to provide the group with feedback on their presentation—how interesting it was, did they cover all the key areas, did everyone contribute, and so on. The kids like doing this, and I've found that provided they have clear guidelines on how they are to provide feedback . . . so it doesn't become destructive, they manage it OK and the groups seem to listen to what their peers have to say.

Note: I = Interviewer; T = Teacher

In Case Study 6.1, the teachers report that they use a number of different approaches to assessing students' work during their small-group learning activities. For example, the first teacher (T1) uses different informal approaches to check on her students' learning (Turn 2), while the other two teachers (T2 & T3) report using more formal checklists or procedures to help students evaluate their learning (Turns 3 & 4). Interestingly, T1 indicates that she also presents her students with a rubric that outlines what they are going to be evaluated on (Turn 5), while T2 provides her students with opportunities to give constructive feedback to their peers (Turn 6). As can be seen from the above discussion with the interviewer, the teachers are using a variety of approaches to assess both how their students are learning and what they have achieved.

Formative Assessment

The informal approaches adopted by T1 often allow teachers to obtain some quick feedback on how students are managing the learning process so changes can readily be made to task requirements or additional scaffolding can be provided if students appear to be experiencing difficulties. This is in contrast to the more formal approach adopted by T2, where she is using checklists either to keep a record of who is contributing to the group or to encourage her students to evaluate themselves. Both these approaches are acceptable and are designed to provide information on how students are managing their learning. The informal approach used by T1 and the more formal ones adopted by T2 are generally referred to as *formative assessments* because they are designed to provide information that informs the ongoing teaching and learning process to ensure its effectiveness and to ascertain whether other approaches should be adopted or whether expectations for the task should be changed (McInerney & McInerney, 1998).

There are many different types of formative assessments that can be used to provide information on students' learning, from those that consider how students interact, the types of discourse they use to facilitate understanding and learning, through to those that tap students' perceptions of how they are learning, and so on. These assessments generally require teachers to be observant and move around the room so they can listen to the discussions occurring in groups and when appropriate intervene to challenge students' perceptions or scaffold their understandings. Both actions require teachers to be active in the learning process to ensure that misconceptions are corrected or developing understandings are consolidated.

Curriculum-Based Assessments

Another type of formative assessment is *curriculum-based assessment* (CBA). This approach uses a variety of probes or stimulus questions to gauge students' understandings or progress at some point during their participation in the curriculum. Paris and Hoffman (2004), in a review of the different types of reading assessments teachers use from kindergarten through third grade, found that they ranged across observations, anecdotal evidence, informal inventories, and work samples as the main source of evidence for students' reading achievement and progress. Interestingly, although teachers had access to some very sophisticated standardized reading tests, most regarded informal measures or formative assessments that they design, select, and embed in the curriculum as more useful for teachers, students, and parents than commercial instruments. Paris and Hoffman argue that because a single reading assessment cannot capture the variety of skills and developmental levels of children in most K–3 classes, teachers use multiple assessments and choose those that fit their purposes.

Graves, Plasencia-Peinado, Deno, and Johnson (2005) used a series of curriculum-based measures of reading (randomly selected first-grade reading passages that had been standardized to ensure equal levels of readability) and a list of nonsense words to measure the oral reading fluency of a group of English learners in Grade 1 and found that all students (high, medium, and low readers) were able to demonstrate improvements on both measures. These findings were consistent with findings from other studies examining the growth in oral reading of first-grade students who are not English learners. Graves et al. argued that the curriculum-based measures used in this study provide valuable information to first-grade teachers on the progress of English learners. Moreover, the authors argued early use of these curriculum-based progress measures can signal the need for intense preventative intervention that can assist teachers in avoiding the erroneous placement of some English learners in special education.

Similarly, Weissenberger and Espin (2005), in an evaluation of curriculum-based measures (students were required to write two stories in response to a sentence prompt) used to assess students' writing proficiency for Grades 4, 8, and 10, found moderate to strong positive correlations between the curriculum-based measures used and the standardized Wisconsin Knowledge and Concepts Examinations (WKCE) scores for language arts and writing assessment, providing evidence of the validity of the curriculum-based measures they used. Furthermore, the alternative-form reliability correlations of the two writing samples (i.e., the writing samples were compared) were high, suggesting that teachers can have confidence in the stability of these curriculum-based measures. These findings led the authors to propose that these curriculum-based writing measures can be used to assess the developing writing skills of students at the elementary, middle, and high school levels.

Curriculum-based assessments have also been used successfully in mathematics. In a study that investigated the extent to which teachers' use of different instructional practices related to improved performance in mathematics for

Grade 10 students, McCaffrey et al. (2001) found that the use of *reform practices*, as opposed to traditional practices, were positively related to achievement gains for students. The reform practices that the authors identified included the following:

- Students worked in small groups.
- Students used manipulatives in solving problems. Students were encouraged to consider alternative methods for solving problems.
- Students were required to explain reasons for their answers.
- Students worked on solving real-world problems.
- Students worked in small groups on extended mathematics investigations of projects.
- Students made formal presentations to the class of their group's project.
- Students wrote reflections on what they learned from their experiences.
- Students were tested using open-ended responses requiring them to provide descriptions and explanations.
- Students were required to complete performance tasks both individually and in groups.

These reform practices were in contrast to the traditional practices for teaching mathematics where teachers predominantly explained problems to the class and students worked from textbooks or worksheets (often individually) to practice mathematics facts, rules, or formulas. In these classrooms, tests were predominantly short answer, true or false, or fill in the blanks.

In short, McCaffrey et al. (2001) demonstrated that when student assessment practices are curriculum based and are linked to teaching practices that are student-centered and inquiry based, students obtain higher achievement gains as measured on traditional standardized tests than peers who are taught by traditional practices. The authors argued that the results should alleviate teachers' concerns that reform-based teaching will adversely affect students' performances on standardized tests, because that did not happen in this study.

Peer Assessment

A further type of formative assessment may involve peer assessment where students are asked to consider the level, value, or quality of a product produced by their peers. This type of assessment appears to be most helpful if it provides rich and detailed qualitative feedback about strengths and aspects that need to be improved rather than a mark or a grade. Topping, Smith, Swanson, and

Elliot (2000) used a formative peer assessment process to provide feedback to postgraduate university students on the quality of the academic reports they had compiled as a requirement of their educational psychology training program. Students were paired so that each acted as assessor and assessee to the other and were provided with the criteria staff had previously used to assess the academic reports they were evaluating. The results indicated that there was a balance between positive and negative statements between staff and peer assessments, and although only half of the detailed formative assessment statements made showed some degree of correspondence between staff and peers, Topping et al. (2000) concluded the reliability and validity of this type of assessment appeared adequate. Moreover, the overlap in detail between staff and peer assessment suggested that peer assessments add value to the feedback provided to students. In turn, students reported that although the process of providing formative feedback to their peers was time-consuming, intellectually challenging, and socially discomforting, it was effective in improving the quality of their own subsequent written work and it helped them to develop other transferable skills that would generalize to their own future writing. It appeared that the peer assessment process prompted self-assessment among many of the students, and this coupled with the obvious pressure to spend time scrutinizing and clarifying the assessment criteria contributed to a greater understanding of effective ways to learn new content, the importance of structure and organization, and the reader's perspective in receiving a written report.

Computer-Supported Peer Assessment

Formative peer assessment can also be conducted in a computer-supported collaborative (CSCL) environment. Prins, Sluijsmans, Kirschner, and Strijbos (2005) report on such a study where students, enrolled in an online virtual seminar series, worked in multidisciplinary teams investigating sustainable development and enlargement of the European Union. As part of the seminar series, students were required to discuss the assessment criteria they had been given and adjust it to their group's needs, assess a draft of their own report and a fellow group's report using the assessment criteria, and, finally, write a reply to a fellow group indicating how they had revised their report according to the feedback they had received. The formative assessment criteria the students used as a template (which they were able to adjust to their group's needs) included both content-related criteria (e.g., application of result, quality of language used, links to different knowledge bases, summary) and process-related criteria (e.g., planning research, planning individual tasks, cooperation within the group). Results showed that students' attitude to peer assessment was positive and many felt quite comfortable about providing feedback to students they had never met. Prins et al. noted, however, that the quality of the assessment reports was low, with more negative statements rather than positive ones, probably because the majority of students did not apply the provided criteria and feedback rules. This resulted in some students' having difficulty accepting critical feedback, although they also indicated that peer feedback was valuable for the revision of their report. These findings led Prins and colleagues to suggest that students not only needed rules for providing formative feedback but they also needed more support or explicit rules for receiving or accepting feedback and coping with it.

Weinberger, Ertl, Fischer, and Mandl (2005) used both epistemic and social scripts to support students' dialoguing in computer-supported collaborative learning. *Epistemic scripts* specify and help sequence knowledge construction activities. They are designed to guide learners toward specific aspects of the task and toward specific task-orientated activities, while social scripts are designed to help students learn how to elicit information from each other during collaborative learning. Palincsar and Herrenkohl (2002) used an epistemic script to guide the audience's feedback to the group on the presentation of their explanations about the scientific phenomena they had been investigating. The *cognitive roles* different members of the audience adopted required some to provide feedback on the group's presentation on the clarity of the relationships between the predictions and the theories; others were responsible for ascertaining clarity of the summary of the findings, and others were responsible for determining if the reporter discussed the relationships among the group's predictions, theory, and findings. Palincsar and Herrenkohl reported that the use of these cognitive roles and the associated tools (scripts) for providing feedback promoted student dialogue, advanced students' theorizing, influenced their thinking, and promoted conceptual understanding.

The epistemic script students used in the Weinberger et al. (2005) study involved students' discussing a series of case problems that was presented online as text and jointly preparing an analysis of each. In order to facilitate the learning process, students were provided with a series of prompts or questions that suggested they apply specific theoretical concepts to the problem cases. In addition, students were provided with social scripts that aimed to foster critical negotiation and to discourage quick decisions and arriving at a false consensus. Hence, each student was assigned two roles; one as an analyst of one of the cases discussed, and the other as a constructive critic on the remaining cases. Both these roles were supported by online social script prompts. Interestingly, Weinberger et al. found that the epistemic script actually impeded the individual acquisition of knowledge whereas the social script facilitated it. In a second study where students worked online in pairs and teleconferenced about the task they were assigned, the results once again showed that students using the epistemic script learned less than those without it, while the social script enhanced learning. Weinberger et al. concluded that in both studies, the epistemic scripts appeared to hinder the individual acquisition of knowledge if students were not sufficiently motivated to engage in joint elaborative discussions of the learning task. In contrast, social scripts appear to change the interaction pattern and motivate learners to critique the contributions of the learning partners more strongly; as a consequence, they acquire more individual knowledge than learners who do not have this type of support. These findings prompted Weinberger et al. to suggest that careful consideration needs to be given to the type of epistemic scripts that are used in virtual environments and how they can be used to foster elaboration of the group task.

Given the above findings, what are the implications for teachers who need to be able to assess how students learn and what they achieve as they work cooperatively? The following summarizes the research on formative assessments:

- Process learning involves monitoring how students are managing to learn in their groups.
- Formative assessments can involve both informal and formal approaches to assessing the learning process.
- Informal formative assessments may include observations, *anecdotal records*, and work samples.
- Formal formative assessments may include checklists, inventories, and progress reports.
- Curriculum-based assessments have high validity as they are designed to match closely what students are learning in the curriculum.
- Peer assessments are most helpful if they provide rich and detailed qualitative feedback.
- Peers learn from being able to assess their own and other's work.
- Computer-supported peer assessment presents difficulties unless peers are prepared to engage with the task and receive training in how to provide feedback.
- Epistemic and social scripts can be used to guide students' learning and feedback during computer-supported learning; however, social scripts are more successful at promoting learning, possibly because they may support interaction of learners, which, in turn, appears to facilitate individual knowledge acquisition and learning.

Conducting Formative Assessments of Small-Group Learning

Elementary School

★ Teacher self-reflections on student learning. Teachers will often ask the following types of formative evaluation questions as they monitor groups: How well are the students working together? What are they learning? What can they do? What do they need to know? How are they providing feedback to each other? What else might facilitate their learning?

★ Team word webbing and how to assess the group's efforts. Students are provided with different color pens for this task. The topic for discussion is written in the center of a large piece of butcher paper. The students take turns contributing their ideas to the web, focusing on key ideas and supporting elements. The completed web enables the teacher to have a ready tool for assessing the group's functioning, and because individual members have contributed their ideas in color, it is easy to identify each student's contribution. Requirements can be established for each of the component parts so that students may be required to identify a minimum of three or four key ideas (preparation, camping, social, activities) and a similar number of supporting elements (food, clothes, pets, camp equipment). It is possible to construct a rubric that acts as a checklist for the students and a tool for the teacher to evaluate the group's productivity.

Word Webbing

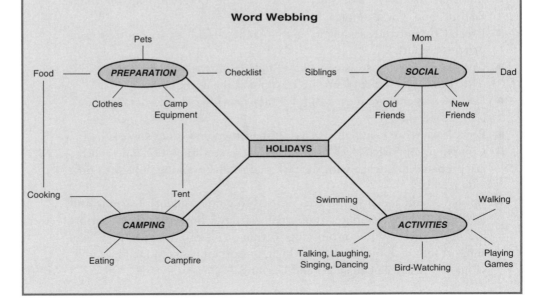

★ Student reflections on their learning. The following Know-Want-Learned (KWL) is designed to help structure the group's planning so students can clearly identify what they need to learn in the context of what they currently know and what they want/need to learn. This exercise is very helpful in getting students to make links between current knowledge and future needs to know.

Know: *What do we know?*	*Want:* *What do we want to know?*	*Learned:* *What have we learned?*

★ Strategic Questioning (King, 1999). The following questions are designed to help students focus on the task so they can plan, monitor, and evaluate their progress. The questions can be constructed as a rubric so that children have the questions down the left side and their responses on the right, or they can be given the questions on prompt sheets or cards:

Planning:

- What is the problem?
- What are we trying to do here?
- What do we know about the problem so far?
- How can this help us?
- What is our plan?
- Is there another way to do this?
- What should we do next?

Monitoring:

- Are we using the best plan?
- Do we need a different plan or strategy?
- Has our goal changed?
- Are we on the right track?

(Continued)

(Continued)

Evaluating:

- What worked?
- What didn't work?
- What would we do differently next time?

★ Group's action plan. This action plan is designed to help students plan the task, including who will do what and by when. The evaluation section is to enable students to keep a record of where they are and what they have achieved.

Group's Action Plan
Goal: Our goal is:

_____

_____

_____

_____

_____

_____

★ Student reflections on how their group handled the process of learning. The following two surveys are designed to tap student' perceptions of how their groups worked.

Task	Subtasks	Who Does What?	Time	Evaluation		
				Finished	Not Finished	Not Attempted
Comments:						

(Continued)

(Continued)

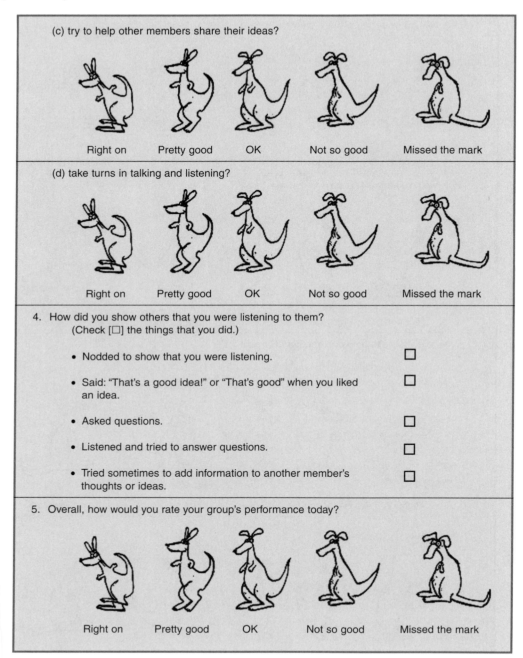

(c) try to help other members share their ideas?

Right on   Pretty good   OK   Not so good   Missed the mark

(d) take turns in talking and listening?

Right on   Pretty good   OK   Not so good   Missed the mark

4. How did you show others that you were listening to them?
   (Check [□] the things that you did.)

   • Nodded to show that you were listening.   □

   • Said: "That's a good idea!" or "That's good" when you liked
     an idea.   □

   • Asked questions.   □

   • Listened and tried to answer questions.   □

   • Tried sometimes to add information to another member's
     thoughts or ideas.   □

5. Overall, how would you rate your group's performance today?

Right on   Pretty good   OK   Not so good   Missed the mark

Thoughts About Group Work Questionnaire

Read each statement below. Rate your response from 1 (almost never happens) to 5 (almost always happens)

1. Group members give each other time to talk and make suggestions.	1	2	3	4	5
2. Group members treat each other nicely.	1	2	3	4	5
3. The ideas of others are important.	1	2	3	4	5
4. Group members often use the ideas of others.	1	2	3	4	5
5. Group members offer help to each other when it is needed.	1	2	3	4	5
6. Group members seek help from each other before asking the teacher.	1	2	3	4	5
7. Group members feel free to talk and make suggestions.	1	2	3	4	5
8. Decisions are made by the group.	1	2	3	4	5
9. Group members do the best they can.	1	2	3	4	5

Middle School and High School

★ Ways of assessing process-related criteria for a project. The following rubric is an adaptation of one used by Prins et al. (2005) to assess the learning process during an online virtual seminar series. Students use the rubric to reflect on their group's learning process.

Process-Related Criteria	Above Average	Average	Below Average
Planning	Work was spread out over the time of the project.	Most of the work was done at the end.	One or more of the deadlines were not met.
Individual tasks	The division of labor was fair.	The division of labor was fair but not every student had a reasonable load.	The division of labor was not clear.

(Continued)

(Continued)

Process-Related Criteria	Above Average	Average	Below Average
Cooperation	The discussion boards were used, so decisions are traceable.	Decisions were made, but not every group member participated in the decision.	The group did not work as a group, so decisions were not discussed.
Participation	Each group member contributed to the online discussions and the final report.	Not every group member participated equally to the online discussions and the group report.	Not every group member participated equally, and input into the report differs strongly.
Respond to feedback	The team dealt with comments given by other team members and staff.	The team dealt with the comments received in a way that fits with the rest of the report.	The team did not deal with the comments they received.

★ Teacher reflections on how the students are learning in their groups often involve asking the following types of questions: How are the students managing the task? Have they identified the component tasks and planned their schedule to completion? How are they dealing with diverse ideas and opinions? Are they able to work independently as a group or do I need to monitor and intervene when needed? Does everyone have opportunities to express opinions and contribute? How are they utilizing their resources, both personnel and material?

★ Samples of the group's planning and small-task sheets will also provide the teacher with ongoing anecdotal information on how the students are managing the learning process.

★ Students' perceptions of how they cooperated in their group.

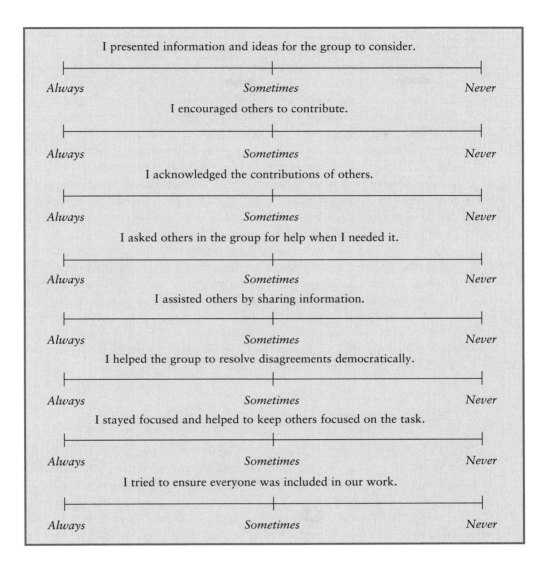

I presented information and ideas for the group to consider.

Always   Sometimes   Never

I encouraged others to contribute.

Always   Sometimes   Never

I acknowledged the contributions of others.

Always   Sometimes   Never

I asked others in the group for help when I needed it.

Always   Sometimes   Never

I assisted others by sharing information.

Always   Sometimes   Never

I helped the group to resolve disagreements democratically.

Always   Sometimes   Never

I stayed focused and helped to keep others focused on the task.

Always   Sometimes   Never

I tried to ensure everyone was included in our work.

Always   Sometimes   Never

Summative Assessment

A *summative assessment* is designed to measure what students have learned or have accomplished at the end of a period of instruction. In small-group learning, summative assessment provides information on what the group has accomplished by working together on the task; it may include such assessments as a group presentation, a group assignment, or the presentation of a group product. Summative assessments rarely involve the administration of standardized tests simply because such tests are not usually considered to be valid measures of what students have learned from such an experience. Most summative assessments that are used to measure the outcomes of group learning are criterion referenced and are designed by class teachers to see if students have achieved a predetermined goal, based on specific learning experiences from their curriculum. In group work, criterion-referenced assessments can include curriculum-based measures (discussed previously) and a variety of authentic assessments such as the development of a portfolio of information or ideas, the presentation of a multimedia display, the demonstration of specific skills or outcomes (e.g., presentation of a play), and so on. In addition, teachers may decide to develop a scoring matrix to assess whether the component part of the criteria has been met and if so, how adequately. The scoring matrix may also be weighted so that consideration is given to the processes of learning (discussed previously) as well as to the achievements obtained. In this way, teachers are able to gain some well-documented, highly valid information on the achievements of the group. This is particularly important given the need to be able to demonstrate students' achievements in practices such as cooperative learning where teachers act to facilitate learning and students are expected to be self-directed and active as learners in the construction of knowledge (Hackmann & Schmitt, 1997).

Criterion-Referenced Assessments

In criterion-referenced assessments, achievement goals are clearly specified in a set of criteria so that students understand what they are expected to accomplish. The criteria are usually based on expectations in the different syllabi for students' achievements for specific core learning outcomes and the associated knowledge, processes, and attitudes needed to understand key concepts that have been identified as critical to these core learning areas. Hence, students are assessed on whether they have met the required criteria or not, although many teachers prefer to refer to a criterion as developing (not quite fully developed), developed, or highly developed to provide them with the diagnostic information they need when they are determining what additional learning experiences students may require in order to be able to determine that the criterion is developed.

Teachers often prefer to conduct criterion-referenced assessments because they provide information on what students can or cannot do, which can be very helpful in communicating with parents about a student's progress.

Moreover, as many educational objectives are written in performance terms, the criterion-referenced approach appears more suitable for measuring the achievement of these performance objectives (McInerney & McInerney, 1998). In addition, criterion-referenced assessments can be very useful in helping students to understand what they have accomplished and what else they may need to accomplish in a specific subject or core area.

Authentic Assessments

Another type of criterion-referenced assessment is an *authentic assessment*. Authentic assessments are designed to measure student learning in a real-life context against specific performance criteria. According to Woolfolk (1998), authentic assessments have the following characteristics:

- Involve real-life tasks
- Are contextualized
- Are intellectually challenging
- Involve student's own research
- Assess student's higher-order thinking
- Are engaging and educational
- Require collaboration with others
- Are criterion referenced
- Include student self-reflections
- Use a multifaceted approach to evaluation
- Are compatible with schoolwide aims
- Allow for different student learning styles
- Aim to support and help student learning as necessary

Herrington and Oliver (2000) proposed that authentic assessments need to occur in authentic learning environments if they are to have veracity, integrity, and fidelity. Their argument is that these types of assessments need to reflect the types of problem situations students are likely to encounter in real-life learning environments where problems are generally complex and ill-defined and there are no set procedures to follow. Moreover, in order to solve these problems, students need to have access to a range and diversity of materials that will allow them to explore topics in depth and to apply sustained thinking to their resolution, have access to the critical insights of others (this usually occurs when students work collaboratively), and present their findings as both oral and written reports to their peers. The authentic assessment that was discussed was based on the results of the investigation the students conducted and was assessed against specified performance criteria that had previously been discussed with them. Herrington and Oliver believe that this type of assessment has high validity and reliability as it is based on the task that the students have completed. Moreover, as the assessment is seamlessly integrated with the task, there is no need for follow-up testing, because the oral and written presentation provides teachers and peers with multiple indicators of the learning that has occurred.

Building on Herrington and Oliver's (2000) work, Gulikers, Bastiaens, and Kirschner (2004) developed a five-dimensional framework for authentic assessment that included (a) the assessment task, (b) the physical context, (c) the social context, (d) the assessment form, and (e) the assessment criteria. According to Gulikers et al., the authentic task, on which authentic assessment is based, is generally complex, ill-structured, and involves multiple solutions, similar to Cohen's (1994) definition of a complex learning task that has no definitive answers or clear-cut solutions. It must be located in a real-life context and collaboration with others must be required to work it out. Moreover, as Herrington and Oliver have stated, the learning task needs to resemble the assessment task, and students need to understand how they are going to be assessed as this will guide their learning. While this five-dimensional framework was developed in the context of professional practice for college students training to be nurses, Gulikers et al. proposed that, overall, it provides a good description of the dimensions and elements that should be taken into account in an authentic assessment.

Using Authentic Assessments in Different Contexts

Darling-Hammond and Snyder (2000) discussed the use of authentic assessments in preservice teacher education programs that were designed to help novice teachers move from an intellectual understanding of issues to the enactment of practice. The authors argue that without an appreciation of the intense and dynamic realities of classroom life and for the multidimensional problems and possibilities posed by different students, it is difficult for those with sound theoretical knowledge to apply what they know in practice. Moreover, authentic assessments not only better reflect the complexity of teaching and provide valid data about competencies, they also help teachers improve the caliber of their work.

Based upon emerging research and their own experiences, Darling-Hammond and Snyder (2000) identified four aspects that make up an authentic assessment of teaching. These include assessments that

- sample the actual knowledge, skills, and dispositions desired of teachers as they are used in teaching and learning contexts
- integrate multiple types of knowledge and skills as they are used in practice
- use multiple sources of evidence collected from different situations and over time
- are evaluated by individuals with recognized expertise in the field against accepted performance criteria

The types of authentic learning that capture the aspects identified above are case studies, portfolios or examples of practice, exhibitions of performance, and problem-based inquiries.

Case Studies

While Darling-Hammond and Snyder (2000) argue that no single type of authentic assessment represents the totality of teaching, each does assess important aspects of teaching that enable novice teachers to integrate different areas of learning and to apply them in different ways. For example, *cases* or *case studies* allow for the investigation of particular issues through theories, principles, and practices as they occur in the real world. A case study of a child with behavioral difficulties may involve an exploration of theories of child development and learning, an investigation of classroom context and curriculum, and an explication of management strategies employed by the class teacher. Opportunities to reflect on the information obtained in the light of feedback from mentors and peers often lead to a greater understanding of how different knowledge and theories can be better integrated and applied in classroom situations with students who manifest behavioral difficulties. In other words, novice teachers often learn to arrive at more meaningful understandings of what factors may be contributing to the difficulties students are experiencing when they have had the opportunity to undertake real-life investigations that involve the analysis of multiple sources of information and their application to the problem at hand and to receive feedback from others with expertise in the field.

Although the research above refers to case studies in the context of helping teachers to learn more about the students they teach, case studies can also be used in classrooms to help students gain a better understanding of the real-life experiences of individuals who have made various contributions to humanity and the sciences. For example, students may develop a greater appreciation of the political contributions that Abraham Lincoln made through a case study of his life. This type of case study would provide students with the opportunity to study features of the economy during Lincoln's presidency, the historical significance of different events, the sociodemographic makeup of the community, and so on. Such a case study would provide students with opportunities to develop a rich and in-depth knowledge and understanding of this president, an appreciation that might not occur if they were left to read about him in a text.

Portfolios

A second type of authentic learning proposed by Darling-Hammond and Snyder (2000) involves the use of *portfolios*. Portfolios are collections of exemplars of teachers' practices from multiple sources. They may include various curriculum documents such as lesson plans; units of work; and samples of students' work such as DVDs, CDs, and other multimedia presentations as well as samples of their written work. They may include detailed descriptions of specific lessons; analyses of students' work; and teachers' timetables, logs, or journals as well as feedback obtained from their own teaching practice or reflections on it. In addition, various class and school policy documents and procedures for working with students with diverse learning and adjustment needs are often included. In this sense, portfolios allow novice teachers to collect and assemble a rich variety of documents relevant to a range of teaching practices that can help to inform their own developing pedagogical skills. Novice teachers are often required to submit teaching portfolios to demonstrate their learning and involvement with specific cases or classroom experiences. Moreover, as part of the assessment process, they are often required to write reflections on these experiences: what they have learned and the insights they have gained both from the practical experience they have had and the background research they have undertaken. Opportunities to share these reflections with supervising teachers or peers often lead to additional insights and learning as novice teachers learn to justify decisions, actions, and interpretations in the light of the information they have presented and the feedback they have received from experienced practitioners in real-life contexts.

In classroom situations, teachers will often use portfolios to collect examples of students' work over a period of time. Portfolios can be assembled by teachers on students, or students can construct their own portfolios. Either way, they are designed to be an ongoing record of work students have attempted or completed and as such can provide insights into progress. They can be used to facilitate communication with parents, students, and other teachers so that successes can be celebrated and difficulties can be identified and strategies developed to help overcome them (Gillespie, Ford, Gillespie, & Leavell, 1996).

Micklo (1997) used mathematics portfolios with elementary students and found that when students understood the purpose of a portfolio, it became a tool to help students learn to monitor their own learning by setting goals for themselves and checking their progress toward reaching them. Moreover, Micklo argued such portfolios provide insights into students' abilities to communicate mathematically, to solve problems, to demonstrate mathematical reasoning, and to make connections between different concepts and relationships in mathematics. This enables teachers to make more appropriate decisions about an instructional program based upon students' knowledge and capabilities.

Exhibitions of Performance

A third type of authentic assessment involves exhibitions of performance (Darling-Hammond & Snyder, 2000). In preservice teacher training programs, exhibitions of performance allow teachers to demonstrate particular competencies in ways that simulate teaching contexts or events. These exhibitions can draw upon video observations, case study analyses, observations of simulated events, lesson plans, or group activities to demonstrate what teachers do when solving particular problems. The advantage of exhibitions is that performances can be evaluated in relation to prescribed standards of practice that have been previously discussed. Moreover, when novice teachers have to demonstrate competencies through performance, it sharpens their awareness of the knowledge and skills they must integrate in order to meet required standards. Similarly, students who are required to give a performance in a specific field (i.e., music, drama) must also learn to integrate their knowledge and skills if they are to demonstrate their competencies.

Problem-Based Inquiries

The final type of authentic assessment referred to by Darling-Hammond and Snyder (2000) involves the establishment of *problem-based inquiries*. With problem-based inquiries, teachers design and conduct investigations into issues arising from their work. For example, an investigation into the apparent high rates of truancy in a high school may lead investigators to form hypotheses about the causes of the absenteeism as well as possible ways of resolving it. This may require them to consider relevant research on engagement–disengagement and motivation to learn in adolescents as well as an examination of current data on rates of absenteeism in the school and compare them with previous years' records or absenteeism rates in similar neighborhood schools. Furthermore, as part of the inquiry, the investigators may need to interview students, parents, and school personnel to ascertain their perceptions of the problem and potential solutions. In this sense, the inquiry has to be very detailed and comprehensive and it must include all stakeholders as well as all available information that can be used to inform the investigation. Investigators have a responsibility to be able to analyze and synthesize the available data and provide evidence for the conclusions they have drawn so they can propose suggestions that may help to solve the problem. The sharing and critiquing of the research that follows can help to transform teaching as investigators and teachers collaborate to work on the problem. Darling-Hammond and Snyder maintain that having novice teachers engage in this type of inquiry can help prepare them both as consumers of research and producers of knowledge. Moreover, it can give them the tools to make sense of their practice and help them to think systematically and analytically about the problems they confront.

Problem-Based Learning Using Formative and Summative Assessments

Zimitat and Miflin (2003) report on the development and application of a four-step assessment task (4SAT) that was used to gather both formative and summative assessment information on medical students engaged in problem-based learning. The impetus for the instrument was to align assessment with the philosophy and process of the problem-based learning (PBL) curriculum that aims to help students better explore clinical cases, engage in more effective hypothetico-deductive reasoning processes about the presenting problem, share their findings with their peers, and probe and challenge each other's understanding as they further refine their hypotheses and gather additional information.

Students worked initially on the problem case by themselves, identifying key features and formulating potential hypotheses (Step 1), before working with their group members to share their analyses and hypotheses. With the presentation of new clinical data by the tutor, students were forced to reconsider their hypotheses and discuss possible scenarios before submitting a written summary of their deliberations and their learning objectives and tasks for the week. A list of the top 10 learning issues identified by the different groups was then collated and e-mailed through to students, which Zimitat and Miflin believe made the learning genuinely reflective of students' learning needs (Step 2). It was during this step that information was collected on both the learning product (written report and learning issues) the students had generated from their discussions and the group process.

The group's written response was assessed according to the extent they were able to identify key presenting symptoms, formulate hypotheses, utilize prior knowledge, justify the need for further information, reconsider hypotheses in the light of new information, and develop learning issues related to the case. The group process was assessed according to whether group members participated in the discussion, maintained a supportive and nonjudgmental learning environment, considered the ideas of others, recognized and resolved conflicts and disagreements, negotiated members' tasks, and reviewed the group's progress with the case.

During Step 3, students were encouraged to work collaboratively together on their learning tasks and independent study and to share resources. Step 4 consisted of a written examination based on the top 10 learning issues identified by the groups in Step 2. Case scenarios were constructed (similar to Step 1), and students were expected to generate hypotheses, interpret data, and answer a variety of questions based on these cases.

Zimitat and Miflin (2003) propose that the advantage of the 4SAT was that it mirrored the PBL process; students were therefore tested on the learning issues that the groups had discussed and examined. As such, the 4SAT was an integrated assessment tool that provided both formative and summative information on the learning that had occurred and the group processes involved. Moreover, it had high face validity (it appeared to measures what it is supposed to measure, as it was closely linked to the curriculum), and an analysis of its psychometric properties indicated that it is moderately correlated to other summative assessment instruments used to test students' basic and clinical science skills in medicine. Furthermore, as the 4SAT was criterion referenced, students had clear guidelines on what they had to do to achieve specific goals in the PBL curriculum.

Classroom teachers can use problem-based inquiries not only to extend students' learning and foster their interest in a topic, but also to gauge the extent to which students are constructing understandings in their groups. The advantage of this approach to assessment is that it is closely linked to problem issues that students have been investigating, so the assessment is a valid reflection of what the children have learned.

Key Points on Summative Assessments and Their Purposes

- Summative assessments are designed to measure outcomes of learning.
- Most summative assessments for group learning are criterion referenced.

- Criterion-referenced assessments specify clear criteria for achieving the goal.
- Teachers often prefer to use criterion-referenced assessments to communicate with teachers and students and to set learning goals.
- Summative assessments can involve authentic assessments.
- Authentic assessments are criterion-referenced assessments.
- Authentic assessments are designed to measure progress.
- Authentic assessments involve real-life tasks.
- Authentic tasks can include cases, portfolios, performances, and problem-based inquiries.
- Authentic assessments can be used to measure progress in different learning contexts.

Practical Activity

Conducting Summative Assessments of Small-Group Learning

Elementary School

★ Criteria to assess group's PowerPoint presentation on the drug nicotine

Criteria	Still Developing	Developed	Highly Developed
PowerPoint presentation:	Sometimes uses the following design features: • Eye catching • Same size font except when in headings • Appropriate picture • Appropriate use of sound effects • Effective use of colors • Includes transition • Similar background	Usually uses the following design features: • Eye catching • Same size font except when in headings • Appropriate picture • Appropriate use of sound effects • Effective use of colors • Includes transition • Similar background	Consistently uses the following design features: • Eye catching • Same size font except when in headings • Appropriate picture • Appropriate use of sound effects • Effective use of colors • Includes transition • Similar background

Criteria	Still Developing	Developed	Highly Developed
Describes nicotine	Unable to write one or two sentences describing nicotine	Writes a paragraph describing nicotine	Writes a paragraph or more describing and comparing it to alcohol
Analyzes how nicotine affects the body	Unable to write one or two sentences on how nicotine affects the body	Writes a paragraph on how nicotine affects the body	Writes a paragraph or more on how nicotine affects the body and compares it to alcohol
Identifies what the body does to process nicotine	Does not identify what the body does to process nicotine	Writes a paragraph and identifies what the body does to process the nicotine	Writes a paragraph or two and identifies what the body does to process nicotine and compares it to alcohol
Identifies other groups of people affected by nicotine exposure and analyzes the consequences	Does not identify other groups of people affected by nicotine exposure and does not analyze the consequences for these groups	Writes a paragraph to identify other groups of people affected by nicotine exposure and analyzes the consequences for these groups	Writes a paragraph or two to identify other groups of people affected by nicotine exposure and analyzes the consequences for these groups
Explains why nicotine is a drug	Does not explain why nicotine is a drug	Writes a paragraph to explain why nicotine is a drug	Writes a paragraph or two to explain why nicotine is a drug
Identifies some interesting facts about nicotine use	Does not identify interesting facts about nicotine use	Writes a paragraph on interesting facts about nicotine use	Writes a paragraph or two on interesting facts about nicotine use
Language:	• Spells most familiar words accurately as well as some new/topic-specific words	• Spells most familiar words and new/topic-specific words accurately	• Spelling is nearly error free

(Continued)

(Continued)

Criteria	Still Developing	Developed	Highly Developed
	• Sentence structure: mostly simple sentences • Paragraphing: attempts to group sentences containing related information into paragraphs • Punctuation contains some common punctuation	• Sentence structure: mostly simple sentences with some complex sentences • Paragraphing: generally groups sentences containing related information into paragraphs • Punctuation: consistent use of most common punctuation	• Sentence structure: demonstrates control of simple, complex, and compound sentences • Paragraphing: consistently groups sentences containing related information into paragraphs • Punctuation: error free and appropriate punctuation
Student comments:			
Teacher comments:			
Level of support: Check appropriate comment	Lots of teachers help	Some teacher help	Very little teacher help

★ Group has been asked to discuss a problem (e.g., getting rid of plastic bags because of the difficulties with disposal) and write a report on their proposed solution(s). The following questions have been given to the group to help stimulate their discussion on the topic:

What do I know about the problem?

Why is it worth solving?

How will solving it help us?

What are the minuses of solving this problem?

How do I feel about this problem?

What are some ways of solving this problem?

How could the solution be put into practice?

The criteria to evaluate the information presented in the report are listed below:

Criteria	Example of Criteria	Stimulus Questions	Score
1. Knowledge review	Able to recall three basic facts relevant to the topic	What do I know about the problem?	
2. Comprehension	Able to understand the need to solve/deal with the problem using two cause-effect relationships or a plus and minus of the problem	Why is this worth solving? How does it help us? What are the minuses of solving this problem? What are some ways of solving this problem?	
3. Connecting	Able to demonstrate at least one more complex understanding of cause and effect or make links between thoughts and feelings or connect ideas	How do I feel about this problem?	
4. Application-extending knowledge	Able to demonstrate how to apply known information to possible practice	How could the solution be put into practice?	
5. Thinking about thinking	Able to generate additional information relevant to the problem based on connecting ideas and constructing new knowledge or idea or generating question to seek more information	Are there any other questions I need to ask to help with this problem?	

Scoring: 1 = acceptable response; 0 = unacceptable response.

(Continued)

(Continued)

★ Students have been asked to think about a problem and depict their thinking in the following way:

Problem: What are some ways of solving the water shortage problem in city X?					
Suggested solution 1:		Suggested solution 2:		Suggested solution 3:	
List Consequences + and −		List Consequences + and −		List Consequences + and −	
+	−	+	−	+	−

Best solution:

Reason it's the best solution:

Create a slogan, design a logo, or design a poster for your group that communicates the main message arising from your best solution.

The criteria for evaluating the group's response to the problem are presented below:

Level	Criteria	Score
1. Suggested solutions	Able to identify two possible solutions to the problem	
2. Consequences	Able to identify at least one consequence for each solution	
3. Best solution and reason	Able to identify the best solution and provide at least one reason. The reason needs to be well argued so it shows cause and effect for at least two different groups (people, animals, industry).	
4. Thinking about thinking	Able to communicate the main message through a logo or poster. Message needs to be well reasoned and not basic recall of detail; successfully combines various thinking abilities.	

Scoring: 1 = acceptable response; 0 = unacceptable response.

★ The group has been asked to develop a television advertisement to promote a product of their own choosing. Below are the criteria used to assess the television advertisement:

Criteria	Self-Assessment					Teacher Assessment				
Slogan, jingle	1	2	3	4	5	1	2	3	4	5
Logo										
Packaging										
Pricing										
Persuasive techniques used										
Target audience, appropriate use of language										
Critique										
Storyline sequencing										
Performance										
Overall success of the advertisement										
Scoring: 1: Low; 5: High Group members: Comments:										

Middle School and High School

★ Ways of assessing content-related criteria for a project. The following rubric is an adaptation of one used by Prins et al. (2005) to assess the learning that occurred from a group project that was the outcome of an online virtual seminar series.

★ The group's task is to investigate an alternative fuel source and write a report providing information on their chosen alternative fuel and justifying their choice. As part of the report, students must explain how their energy source works and its advantages and disadvantages, as well as the implications of this alternative energy source being the sole provider of energy in today's society. Possible choices of energy include: hydroelectric, nuclear, biomass, tidal, solar, wind, ocean thermal, wave, geothermal.

(Continued)

(Continued)

Content-Related Criteria	Above Average	Average	Below Average
Topic under discussion is made operational	Students give a definition used in their report and suggest practical tools to measure their solutions.	Students give a definition but do not suggest practical tools to measure their solutions.	Students do not give a definition and do not suggest practical tools to measure their solutions.
The different aspects of the topic are used in coherence	The different aspects of the topic are balanced, and coherent arguments are given priority.	Not all aspects of the topic are used, but when they are, they are balanced and coherent.	The different aspects of the topic are not balanced or coherent.
Consistency in content and awareness of gaps in knowledge	The content of the report is cogent and consistent. Insight is given into gaps in knowledge.	The content of the report is cogent and consisten. Gaps in knowledge are not recognized.	The content of the report is not cogent or consistent. Gaps in knowledge are not recognized.
Integration of disciplinary contributions (sources of knowledge)	The different disciplines are integrated in each chapter of the report, not just at the end.	The different disciplines are integrated only at the end of the report.	The different disciplines are not integrated.
Relationship between problem definition, analysis, and solution	The report is scientifically written. Questions are answered, and recommendations are logical.	The report is scientifically written. Not all questions are answered.	The report is not well written scientifically. Not all questions are answered. Recommendations do not flow logically.
Creativity	Different understandings and knowledge are linked to each other in a creative way. Recommendations are provocative and sharp.	Different understandings and knowledge are linked to each other in a creative way.	No new insights are provided because different knowledge and understandings are not linked.
Summary	A two- or three-page summary is added containing: background research, target group, recommendations, and possible ways to implement solution. The summary is sharp and provocative.	Summary is lacking one of the following: background research, target group, recommendations, and possible ways to implement solution. The summary leaves room for interpretation.	Summary is lacking two or more of the following: background research, target group, recommendations, and possible ways to implement solution. The summary leaves room for interpretation or no summary is added.

Criteria	Highly Developed	Well Developed	Satisfactory
Knowledge and understanding	Comprehensively explains concepts and interrelationships	Explains concepts and interrelationships	Adequately explains concepts and interrelationships
	Uses a wide variety of sources to obtain information	Uses a substantial variety of sources to obtain information	Some evidence of variety of sources to obtain information
	Extensive use of key terms and concepts	Good use of key terms and concepts	Adequate use of key terms and concepts
	Comprehensive use of scientific concepts to explain processes and changes that occur	Good use of scientific concepts to explain processes and changes that occur	Adequate use of scientific concepts to explain processes and changes that occur
Investigating	Collects wide variety of relevant and reliable quantitative and qualitative data	Collects a variety of relevant and reliable quantitative and qualitative data	Collects a range of quantitative and qualitative data
	Comprehensively identifies and analyzes patterns of similarities and differences	Identifies and analyzes patterns of similarities and differences	Adequately identifies and analyzes patterns of similarities and differences
Communicating	Excellent use of written genre to explain terms and meaning	Good use of written genre to clarify terms and meaning	Adequate use of written genre to clarify terms and meaning

BRINGING IT ALL TOGETHER: UNDERSTANDING THE RESEARCH

There is no doubt that there has been increasing pressure on schools as a consequence of the high-stakes testing regime for teachers to "teach to the test" or to spend inordinate amounts of time and energy preparing students for the *standardized testing* that occurs (Posner, 2004). Given that the funding for schools and school districts depends on the numbers of students who can meet required proficiency standards overall and within major subgroups within a school (i.e., economically disadvantaged, major racial and ethnic minorities, students with disabilities, and students with limited English proficiency), it is not surprising that a great deal of attention is devoted to ensuring students meet the required standards (Kim & Sunderman, 2005).

Moreover, given that schools that fail to demonstrate adequate yearly progress (AYP) for 2 consecutive years are identified as "in need of improvement" (Kim & Sunderman, 2005, p. 3) and subject to a series of sanctions that increase in intensity the longer a school remains delinquent, teachers are undoubtedly feeling strongly pressured as they teach. When this happens, some teachers question the value of other types of nonstandardized tests, such as criterion-referenced formative and summative assessments, that often take time for the teacher to develop and generally do not provide students with experience in responding to the types of multiple-choice and short answer questions that generally appear on standardized tests. In contrast, other teachers often express concern over the relevance of standardized testing when it ignores the process of teaching and learning that occurs in classrooms, arguing that it does not provide them with the guidance they need to be able to improve how they teach (Stiggins, 2002).

In an effort to investigate both these concerns, Black and Wiliam (1998a) conducted a synthesis of the results of evidence on formative assessments published in more than 250 articles from a number of different countries and concluded unequivocally that formative assessments do raise students' achievements and that these findings hold for students from kindergarten to university undergraduates and across different subject areas. Furthermore, formative assessment was more beneficial for low achievers because it helped to close the achievement gap while raising achievement for all students overall. Black and Wiliam (1998b) attributed this improvement to the frequent use of feedback, which helped students to understand what they needed to do to achieve or to be successful. When students are involved in the assessment process, they not only learn what they must do but also how to monitor their own learning more closely, and this enhances their cognitive and metacognitive thinking. Furthermore, when formative assessments are conducted in a culture of success and the belief that all students can succeed, students are more likely to persevere with their tasks than they would otherwise.

The success, however, of formative assessments is also dependent on the type of task students are given, the emphasis given to the procedural aspects of knowledge acquisition, the quality of the discourse between teachers and students and students with each other, and the ongoing adjustments that are made to teaching to accommodate changes in students' learning (Black & Wiliam, 1998a).

There is no doubt that the task students are given on which the formative assessment is based needs to be novel and varied, intellectually challenging, and meaningful if students are going to be motivated by it. It also needs to provide students with opportunities to focus on how to solve the problem rather than just declare what they know about it, and this usually occurs when students are provided with opportunities to discuss their ideas with their peers and receive feedback from them. Students are remarkably honest about the feedback they provide about both themselves and each other. When they have been taught how to provide feedback in a socially acceptable manner, many students are receptive to the opinions of their peers as these are an important complement to self-feedback and they will learn from it (Black, Harrison, Lee, Marshall, & Wiliam, 2004; Black & Wiliam, 1998a).

Teacher discourse is also very important, particularly when it is used to challenge students' thinking and scaffold their learning. Probing students to think about issues and encouraging them to consider alternative positions is likely to promote more self-reflection and higher-level thinking than engaging them in *initiation-response-feedback (IRF) exchanges* where teachers typically ask closed questions to which students often already know the answer (Rojas-Drummond & Mercer, 2003). Moreover, when teachers engage in discourse that promotes thinking and scaffolds learning, students' own thinking becomes influenced by these communication exchanges and they begin to model them in their interactions with each other. It seems that the responses expected in this type of discourse appear to create an expectation in recipients to reconcile their understandings with those of others, clarify misunderstandings, and provide justifications that others will accept as well reasoned and valid. Furthermore, this situation, coupled with the security of the small group, appears to provide a psychological environment that motivates students to be more willing to reconcile contradictions between themselves and others, try out their ideas, and work to construct new understandings (Gillies, 2004b).

Other ways in which students can learn from formative assessments include having students develop a scoring rubric that focuses their attention on the criteria required to produce a quality product (Black et al., 2004). This helps to make explicit the expectations for meeting the criteria or achieving a quality outcome. Moreover, engaging students in peer-assessment and self-assessment encourages students to be active in their learning, prepared to acknowledge their mistakes, and responsible for monitoring when they are learning and when they are not.

Feedback is very important for students' learning. In a comprehensive review of studies on feedback to students, Kluger and DeNisi (1996) found that feedback improved performance in the majority of these studies. Feedback that focuses on what needs to be done is more helpful than the awarding of a mark or a grade. Furthermore, students are often prepared to accept the feedback they receive when they understand its purpose and how it can be used to help them overcome difficulties they may be experiencing. Feedback that focuses on what needs to be done can encourage students to believe they can improve. Such feedback can enhance learning as students are motivated to invest in the effort required (Black et al., 2004).

While there is strong evidence that the use of formative assessments or assessment for learning leads to higher quality learning and enhanced learning outcomes, the effects of this type of assessment on summative assessment outcomes is less clear because of the limited research on this topic. Wiliam, Lee, Harrison, and Black (2004), in a study of the use of formative assessments with high school students, found that when teachers made time to develop and use formative assessments there was strong evidence of tangible benefits in terms of students' achievements on mandated standardized tests. Similarly, Engel, Pulley, and Rybinski (2003), in a study of the use of authentic assessment activities in the curriculum for students in Grades 2 and 4, found that these activities helped students to do well on standardized tests. The authors argued that performance tasks involving hands-on activities that were completed before the standardized tests enabled students to apply those skills to the standardized assessment. Moreover, Black et al. proposed that it is possible to improve classroom teaching practice and hence students' learning when summative assessments are used for formative purposes. This happens when students

- Engage in reflective reviews of the work they have completed to allow them to study more effectively
- Set questions and practice responses to gain a deeper understanding of the assessment process
- Use peer- and self-assessment to help them better understand what they need to do

Assessment is so important that Stiggins (2005) argues that students need to be inside the assessment process so they understand what they have to achieve and the scaffolding that will support them as they learn. When this happens, students can see themselves grow as they learn to monitor their progress, feel in control of their learning, and believe that success is possible if they keep trying. Moreover, Stiggins maintains when these practices are consistently carried out in classrooms, they have been consistently linked to gains on high-stakes testing, with the largest gains made by low achievers.

CHAPTER SUMMARY

The research on assessing small-group learning suggests

- Formative and summative assessments can be used to assess student learning in small groups.
- Students learn more when these assessments are criterion referenced.
- Criterion-referenced assessments are designed to help students understand what they must do to achieve a specific outcome.
- Formative assessments do raise standards of achievement overall.
- Formative assessments are more beneficial for low achievers.
- Changes in teaching practice need to occur as a consequence of feedback students receive from formative assessments.
- Formative assessments lead to tangible benefits on summative assessments such as standardized achievement tests.
- Students benefit when summative assessments are used for formative purposes or to help students understand what they need to know and how they can learn.
- Students benefit from both formative and summative assessments when teachers use the information to make changes in their teaching.

ACTIVITIES

1. Discuss with students your expectations for the completion of a small-group activity/project they are about to undertake. Work with the students to develop a rubric that reflects both the group process and the performance criteria required. Negotiate with the students levels of demonstrated performance, such as: beginning, developing, accomplished, and exemplary. Spend time at the completion of the group activity/ project to discuss how the students perceived they met the various criteria for both the process of learning and the performance achieved.

2. Help students to construct a journal of their learning experiences. Provide guidelines for what they might like to include in their journal. For example, information on what they have learned from a specific experience, what they may still need to do to accomplish a special goal, and so on. Make time to have an individual conference with each student to discuss his or her perceptions of his or her progress and what goals the student might like to develop as a consequence.

3. Discuss with the class how they can provide feedback to a group of students at the completion of their presentation. Suggestions may include having members focus on discussing clarity of the presentation, links established between points/issues raised, quality of the background research, presentation of thesis/key points, and so on. Clear performance criteria need to be established so all groups understand the assessment process. Feedback can be used for both formative and summative purposes. It may be advisable to help students construct a rubric of the criteria they will use to assess the group's performance so all students are aware of the criteria that are going to be applied to their presentation. The advantage of using a formalized rubric is that it focuses on the group's presentation and not the individuals within the group.

4. Interview two teachers about how they assess cooperative group work. Focus on both formative and summative assessments and try to ascertain how these assessments are conducted. For example, are these assessments embedded in a group activity or task? What types of tasks do they use? How do they assess the process and outcome of these group tasks? How do they provide feedback to the group? Does anyone else provide feedback? Check to see if the teachers are satisfied with this approach to assessment. If they are, investigate the strengths. If not, ask them what they would like to do differently next time they give feedback to a group. These are just some of the questions that can be asked. Collate your information and discuss the similarities and differences with your study group. What have you learned about teachers' attitudes to assessment as a consequence? Reflect on how you believe the information you have collected and discussed will inform your own approach to assessment.

SUGGESTIONS FOR FURTHER READING

Black, P., Harrison, C., Lee, C., Marshall, B., & Wiliam, D. (2004). Working inside the black box: Assessment for learning in the classroom. *Phi Delta Kappan, 86*(1), 8.

Stiggins, R. (2002). Assessment crisis: The absence of assessment FOR learning. *Phi Delta Kappan, 83*(10), 758.

Stiggins, R. (2005). From formative assessment to assessment FOR learning: A path to success in standards-based schools. *Phi Delta Kappan, 87*(4), 324–330.

CHAPTER 7

Teachers' Responsibilities in Establishing Cooperative Learning

INTRODUCTION AND LEARNING OBJECTIVES

The research on effective schools or schools that make a difference in students' outcomes clearly acknowledges the key role teachers play in implementing effective pedagogical practices to maximize students' learning (Rutter & Maughn, 2002; Sammons, Hillman, & Mortimore, 1995). This includes ensuring that students work in supportive learning environments where teachers set clear expectations for achievement, provide opportunities for a diverse range of learning experiences, and actively monitor students' progress. There is no doubt that students' learning is maximized when they work in classrooms where teachers know their pedagogy and are able to motivate students. This is no more clearly illustrated than in the paper "Valued Segregated School for African American Children in the South, 1935–1969: A Review of Common Themes and Characteristics" by Vanessa Walker (2000), who, in a best synthesis of the literature on segregated schools that were valued by their communities, identifies the characteristics of exemplary teachers who taught in these schools. Given that many of these segregated schools were poorly resourced, they were remarkably successful with the educational programs they provided for their students. The success of these schools can certainly be attributed in part to the responsibilities teachers accepted to ensure that their students received the best education available at that time.

The exemplary teachers in these segregated schools were characterized by the high expectations they set for their students; their refusal to lower standards; and their insistence that students learn their work, even if this meant that they stayed after school until this was achieved. These teachers built personal relationships with their students; they interacted with them before and after class and outside the school, provided extracurricular tutoring sessions, visited homes and churches in the community, and provided guidance to students about their life and community responsibilities. In short, they acted both as teachers and moral guides to the students in their care.

Interestingly, in a time when professional development was not readily available, many of these teachers undertook extensive professional development to stay informed of educational changes that could benefit their students. In many cases, they participated in summer schools, traveling widely to develop their professional skills. When they returned, they ensured that they reported what they learned to the school community so that others could remain abreast of current educational developments.

Walker (2000) also reports that many of these teachers had a clear understanding of the philosophies of child development and teaching and how students could be motivated to believe they could achieve, and that they made sure they communicated these beliefs to their students. In turn, the students were inspired by their teachers and they worked hard not to let them down, with many consistently attributing their success and self-confidence to these teachers.

The *attributes* of *exemplary teachers* identified by Walker (2000) are supported by Dolezal, Welsh, Pressley, and Vincent (2003), who found that teachers who were highly successful at motivating student engagement created warm, caring environments that encouraged students to take risks, think deeply, and challenge their abilities. Students' strengths and potential for growth were emphasized; teachers created opportunities to promote students' work by ensuring it was displayed in the classroom, and they acknowledged and validated students' achievements. Moreover, the activities the students were assigned were exciting and cognitively challenging, and students were encouraged to work together in groups to generate solutions to the problem at hand.

Ayres, Sawyer, and Dinham (2004) used a combination of teachers' interviews and classroom observations to identify the factors associated with effective teaching and found that teacher qualities such as friendliness, approachability, sense of humor, knowledge of content area, repertoire of teaching strategies, passion for their subjects, and willingness to try different things were important attributes of successful teachers. In addition, a willingness to create positive classroom learning environments where students were encouraged to work with others and accept responsibility for their own learning and were challenged to think were other important attributes of effective teachers.

In short, effective teachers create learning environments that are conducive to learning, set high expectations for students' work and communicate those expectations to them, challenge students' thinking and understanding through the problem-solving activities they set, and monitor and evaluate their progress. In addition, these teachers have good teacher-student relationships, encourage student collaboration, and communicate their belief that students can succeed.

The purpose of this chapter is to review the key role teachers play in establishing cooperative learning in their classrooms to create learning environments that are inclusive of all students, including those with diverse learning and adjustment needs. It will achieve this by providing examples of how teachers establish expectations for cooperative group work with students, encourage appropriate small-group behaviors that facilitate learning, choose topics for discussion, and monitor and evaluate students' progress.

When You Have Finished This Chapter You Will Know How Teachers Can:

- Establish a cooperative learning environment that is inclusive of all students
- Negotiate expectations for small-group behaviors
- Develop those communication skills that facilitate small-group discussion
- Develop appropriate helping behaviors
- Choose tasks for small-group discussion
- Monitor students' progress and evaluate outcomes

Case Study 7.1

A High School Teacher's Experience With Cooperative Learning

I: John, you've been using cooperative learning in this Grade 8 class now for the last six months. Can you tell me what your experiences have been?

T: Interesting. It took a while to set things up with this class. I have about four or five students who get very restless and weren't responding well to the more traditional classes. They needed to have more opportunities to work on projects that motivated them and gave them opportunities to learn in ways that suited their different learning styles.

I: So how did you set the whole thing [cooperative learning] in motion?

T: I just decided to have a heart-to-heart with them one day and said that we were going to do some group work where they'd have opportunities to work on different projects. Once I told them what the projects were and what it all meant, they pricked up their ears and became quite interested. I think the tasks I described were highly motivational—you know, making puff mobiles out of paper, pins, and LifeSavers and then racing them. They thought these sorts of activities sounded great.

I: So you motivated them with interesting activities, but how did you set up your groups and get them to understand they needed to work cooperatively?

T: That was a challenge, but we worked it out over time. I basically put it to them that if they wanted to work in small groups to complete these activities, they needed to agree on some rules for group behaviors.

I: How did they react to "rules for group behaviors"?

T: Well, I put it to them in a very matter-of-fact way. I wasn't demanding. I kept telling them that we needed to negotiate some rules that everyone agreed on.

I: So how did you negotiate the rules?

T: I got them to work with a partner to think of some rules that they thought the groups might need if everyone was going to be able to get on and do what they needed to without being distracted by others. Then I got them to discuss their rules with another pair—so they were in groups of four. From there, it was quite easy, as each group contributed one rule that they thought was important. I wrote them up on the whiteboard and then the whole class discussed the essential four or five rules that they thought were important.

I: I notice the students are working well in their groups. They seem to be focused, and it looks as though everyone's involved. How did you make sure students had a clear understanding of what you were expecting?

T: OK, it took time. I used to have to discuss the rules and my expectations at the beginning of each group work session. They (students) were pretty good. Sometimes they'd forget or different ones would get a bit agitated, but basically they settled into the routine and just got on with what they had to do.

I: What did you do once they go working in their groups?

T: Ah! I had to keep moving around them and checking that they understood what they were doing. It also acted as a bit of a break on any misbehavior because they knew I'd pull them up if I had to. They liked me to see what they were doing, and I'd quiz them to make sure they could see the purpose behind what they're doing. The puff mobiles, for example; they used the principles of physics on force and motion to get them moving. They worked out the size of the sail they needed to have and the force of the puff they needed to get it to move and then they measured the distance covered in five seconds and plotted that on their computers against the performances of the others (other groups).

I: There's a lot of work in that activity. What did you notice about the groups as they worked on that one?

T: Well, there was a lot of discussion. They had to agree on how to construct the mobile, and this required them to think about what they knew about getting something like this to move, the type of sail they'd need, its size, the wheels and how they needed be attached to the chassis. This took a bit of time as they decided on the design and the production.

I: How did the girls respond to this type of activity, because it seems to be one that boys might be more interested in?

T: No, they were fine. They got in there, like the boys, and focused on how to make it work. In fact, I think they had as great a time as anyone else.

I: They talked and contributed?

T: Yes. They discussed their ideas and everyone listened. Sometimes they (groups) worked it out (what to do) and sometimes they took a vote. There wasn't any squabbling.

I: What did you do at the end of the activity?

T: Well, after they'd completed their race and plotting each contender's times and distance, we spent time debriefing each other to get them to see how what they had learned linked up with other information that they knew but hadn't made any connections with.

Note: I = Interviewer, T = Teacher

———————————— ❧ ————————————

In the interview above, John displays many of the characteristics of an effective teacher outlined in the introduction to this chapter. He realized that some of his students were not responding to the more traditional classes and needed an alternative way of being able to engage with learning. He understood how important it was to capture students' interests, so he set up activities that were very "hands on" but at the same were designed to be purposeful and challenging. He also realized how important it was to get the students to agree on some rules that they were to abide by during their group activities. Rather than impose a set of rules on them, he arranged for the students to work together to identify some rules they thought were important and shared those with the whole class, and then, through discussion and negotiation, he helped the students identify a common set of group rules that would guide their behaviors. Having adolescents develop their own set of rules often ensures that they are more likely to adhere to them than they would if the rules were imposed. Moreover, adolescents often like to experience a sense of autonomy, and negotiating their own rules enables this to happen.

By establishing their group rules, students demonstrated that they knew the expectations that existed for their behavior and learning. They understood that they were to work together, share ideas, promote each other's learning, and resolve any conflicts that arose. In so doing, John ensured that many of the key elements that are critical for successful cooperative learning were in place (Johnson & Johnson, 1990). Moreover, he not only actively monitored each group's progress, but he challenged their thinking and scaffolded their learning—key teacher behaviors for promoting students' thinking and learning during small-group activities (Gillies, 2004a).

Once the students in John's class understood what they were expected to do and how they were expected to behave, they settled into their group activities, sharing their ideas and working on resolving their tasks. The tasks were designed so they were open and discovery based with no obvious clear-cut solutions. Cohen (1994) observed that with these types of tasks students have to share ideas, problem-solving strategies, materials, and skills as the group's success depends on members' willingness to engage in task-related interaction on the problem at hand. In John's class, the students were motivated by the tasks, which they saw as challenging, and this, with the realization that they were interdependently linked together, ensured that everyone contributed, including students with diverse needs.

Given the success that John has experienced with cooperative learning, questions naturally arise about teachers' responsibilities when establishing this pedagogical practice in their classroom. For example, John identified a need for an alternative way of helping his students to learn and in so doing he focused on creating a cooperative environment where students were given more responsibility for their own learning, worked on tasks that were context specific and relevant, and were expected to cooperate and help each other.

Creating a Cooperative Learning Environment

It is important for teachers who are going to introduce cooperative learning into their classrooms that they spend time creating the environment that will be conducive to this type of learning. This includes helping students understand that they will be expected to work together and contribute to the group goal, share ideas and resources, facilitate each other's learning, and resolve conflicts democratically. Often these behaviors need to be discussed in class before the students begin their group work so they have a clear understanding of how they are expected to behave.

Students will also need to understand that the way they learn will change and that they will be expected to play a more active role in their learning by working on problems that require them to think through solutions that may not be readily apparent. This may involve them in searching for information themselves and working with their peers to solve problems, reason, and think critically as they seek to resolve dilemmas and construct new understandings. Teachers will no longer dispense knowledge and information but will facilitate students' learning by monitoring their progress, encouraging their efforts, challenging their understandings, and scaffolding their learning.

Student-Centered Learning

Pentecost and James (2000) report on how they created a *student-centered learning* environment when they implemented a guided reading program in a college chemistry class by requiring students to seek out answers for themselves rather than have their teachers tell them what they were. The guided reading program consisted of a series of questions and problems that students answered while reading the text. The questions ranged from being straightforward answers found in the text, through to higher-order questions that challenged students' thinking and often required them to seek out other sources of information. The results showed that students in the guided reading program were active in their small-group tutorials, sharing their ideas and challenging the perspectives of others, with many, in turn, commenting on how this approach to learning helped them to gain a clearer understanding of the concepts they were learning. Others noted that it helped them to be more organized so they read the material prior to class, something that many had not done previously because they had relied on formal teacher instruction to tell them what to do.

Similarly, Brush and Saye (2001) report on how a student-centered learning environment was used to help two Grade 11 history classes use different cognitive and *metacognitive scaffolds* with hypermedia supported learning to explore specific topics from a set of multimedia content resources and tools. The students worked in four-person groups around a computer console to research their topic and summarize key information. The results showed that the hypermedia-embedded scaffolds were used prolifically by the student groups. Moreover, many of the groups used the hyperlinks within the interactive essays (one type of multimedia resource) to explore the database, as opposed to just using the menu of documents available. In this way, students were attempting to create links between information in the database, demonstrating they were active participants in the construction of their own knowledge during these multimedia group activities.

Finally, Smeets and Mooij (2001) report on a study that was conducted in 25 schools that investigated, first, how information and communication technology (ICT) was employed in these classrooms, and second, the characteristics of learning environments and teacher behavior that were the main contributors to student-centered learning. Students worked in pairs or small groups for the majority of their ICT work, and teachers used a variety of content and tasks, such as simulations, problem-solving activities, word processing, games, and drill and practice exercises, to stimulate students' learning. Although the authors noted that only a minority of the ICT lessons they observed were regarded as innovative where ICT was integrated in student-centered learning environments, they did note that in these environments students were stimulated to be active learners and higher-order thinking was fostered. Moreover, teachers in many of these classes were observed acting as coaches or facilitators of students' learning rather than dispensers of knowledge.

In summary, each of the studies outlined above that established student-centered learning environments highlighted the key role that students play in being active in the construction of their own learning. Learning was also specific to a situation and involved hands-on activities with students accepting more responsibility for their learning. Moreover, in all cases, interaction with others in small-group settings was involved. Kock, Sleegers, and Voeten (2004) refer to this type of learning as new learning as opposed to more traditional or old learning, where learning is essentially transmitted from the teacher to the student through lectures or directions. In contrast, the term new learning generally is "used to refer to new learning outcomes, new kinds of learning processes, and new instructional methods both wanted by society, and currently stressed in psychological and educational research" (Simons, Van der Linden, & Duffy, 2000, p. vii). This type of learning is based on a body of research that clearly demonstrates that learning is interactive (Gillies, 2003a, 2004b), situated in a context that is meaningful to the individual (Brown, Collins, & Duguid, 1988), constructive (Webb, Troper, & Fall, 1995), self-regulated (DeJong, 1995), and a reflective process (Johnson & Johnson, 1990). When these aspects of new learning are integrated, the learning environment becomes very powerful and students can be helped to achieve high-quality knowledge goals, problem-solving skills, transfer of knowledge skills, and self-directed learning skills, all of which are important goals of student-centered learning environments (Konings, Brand-Gruwel, & Merrienboer, 2005).

Negotiate Expectations for Small-Group Behaviors

If groups are to be interdependent and their members are to work cooperatively together, it is important that expectations for behavior are negotiated before group activities are begun. In the interview with John reported earlier (see Case Study 7.1, Turn 6), he stated, "I basically put it to them that if they wanted to work in small groups to complete these activities, they needed to agree on some rules for group behaviors." When the interviewer inquired about how the students reacted, he responded, "I kept telling them that we needed to negotiate some rules that everyone agreed on" (see Turn 8). Being able to negotiate rules rather than impose them on students is very important because it communicates to the students that they can make decisions about their learning circumstances and their decisions are valued by their teacher. Moreover, when teachers negotiate with students, they model behaviors such as active listening, reflecting meaning (i.e., restating key ideas to confirm their meaning), tentatively suggesting ideas, and summarizing main points that are important for students to use in their own interactions with their peers (Gillies, 2004b; Ivey & Bradford Ivey, 2003). Gillies and Boyle (2005, 2006) found that when teachers model these types of verbal behaviors with students during small-group work, students will model them in their interactions with each other. Furthermore, learning how to negotiate in situ, as occurs when teachers and students actively work together to generate a list of rules on which they agree, is more meaningful to students' understanding than just discussing them.

Webb and Farivar (1994) outline an example of a three-part social skills training program that they taught to a cohort of seventh-grade students to help them work effectively in small groups on mathematical tasks. The first part of the program was designed to build trust and understanding among classroom peers so they would become more familiar with each other and more comfortable working together. Students learned each others' names, found out details about their interests and aspirations, and entered information on students on their group charts. Members of the class then circulated around the room, trying to link students' names to the characteristics listed on the charts. These types of activities are often referred to as icebreakers and are designed to help students feel relaxed and at ease with each other in an environment that is non-threatening and supportive of students' endeavors.

The second part of the program involved the teachers' discussing the norms for group behavior with students, identifying appropriate behaviors and summarizing them on charts. Behaviors that were identified as being important if groups were to work successfully included listening to others when they speak, not putting others down, using soft voices so they do not distract others, and allowing everyone to contribute to the group. In addition, Webb and Farivar report that students also made charts of the social skills to use, including making sure students checked information for understanding, shared ideas and information, encouraged others, and discussed difficulties. Students also filled out group processing sheets to help them reflect on whether they demonstrated these skills during their group activities. Furthermore, to help build a sense of group cohesion, each small group chose a name and created a group sign.

The final part of the program involved teaching students the skills associated with learning how to help each other while working together. To focus on specific helping skills, the teacher introduced charts of the different helping skills students needed to use when they sought help from or gave help to others. The skills the teachers focused on were: learning to ask clear and precise questions, providing detailed responses rather than just the answer, and asking other students to describe how they solved a problem. These skills were discussed with the students, and the students, in turn, practiced these skills as they worked in their groups on novel mathematical problems. In addition, the students completed checklists of these helping behaviors after group work to reflect on which ones their group used and where they needed to improve.

In summary, Webb and Farivar (1994) detail a comprehensive three-part approach to teaching basic social and communications skills to students in preparation for their small-group work. Teaching students to engage in exploratory talk with others has been supported by Mercer (1996), who found that the steps involved helping students to dialogue more effectively together, and Gillies (2003a) and Gillies and Ashman (1998) have consistently found that students need to be taught the interpersonal and small-group skills needed to facilitate appropriate social and helping behaviors during group work.

Developing Communication Skills for Group Discussion

In Chapter 4, I discussed those strategies that can be taught to students to enhance their small-group discussions. One strategy included providing students with opportunities to learn specific scripts such as reciprocal teaching, where students are taught how to interrogate a passage using such strategies as predicting, clarifying, questioning, and summarizing to develop comprehension and understandings (Palincsar & Herrenkohl, 1999). Other strategies to help students communicate more effectively with each other included peer tutoring or peer learning, where students adopt specific roles (i.e., tutor or tutee) and have clear procedures for interacting together (Topping, 2005) to develop specific skills (e.g., automaticity with number recall). O'Donnell's

(1999) scripted cooperation is a form of collaborative peer tutoring where students alternate between being the listener and the recaller as they work in dyads to acquire information and to promote each other's understanding. Learning is facilitated when each partner adopts the role of the recaller where he or she summarizes the information while the listener seeks clarification on any information that is unclear. O'Donnell maintains that this often promotes a state of cognitive dissonance as students seek to reevaluate their understandings in the light of this new information, clarify misunderstandings, and justify their perspectives. The cognitive processes that emerge often help students learn the information better.

In a study that used scripted cooperation where students alternatively took the role of teacher (recaller) and learner (listener), O'Donnell and Dansereau (2000) found that the "teachers" consistently outperformed the learners on measures of recall and organization of information. The authors argued that this may have happened because "teachers" were given very specific guidelines on how to present the material and the communication tools they could use to facilitate understanding (e.g., knowledge maps or outlines of the material to be learned). It appeared that the explicit instructions students were given on how to teach probably stimulated their own reorganization of the information, which assisted their learning.

Similarly, in a study of student interactions during partner reading (a scripted cooperative learning strategy) in 12 second-grade classrooms, Meisinger, Schwanenflugel, Bradley, and Stahl (2004) found that basic partner reading script instruction was associated with better social cooperation and high-quality interactions during partner reading sessions, which enhanced the development of fluent reading skills.

Boxtel, van der Linden, Roelofs, and Erkens (2002) describe how high school students interacted during a physics class when they were required to coconstruct a *concept map* using a given set of electricity concepts such as voltage, energy, current strength, and resistance and to connect related concepts. The authors found that the requirement that students work together to produce a concept map demonstrating these relationships stimulated talk about the topic as they sought clarification from each other, worked to resolve disagreements, and coconstructed common understandings. The discussion stimulated by this talk led the authors to conclude that when students work on a common task where there are no predetermined answers, they are forced to work together to create a shared understanding of the task, the concepts, the procedures, and the strategies to use. In so doing, they use language for thinking and reasoning that helps them to gain greater conceptual clarity of the material they discuss. The authors concluded that it was both the design of the task and the requirement that students work together that stimulated students' interactions and enhanced learning.

Similarly, Chinn, O'Donnell, and Jinks (2000) found that students' discourse was enhanced when they were required to discuss reasons for their conclusions. In this study, the students learned to conduct experiments with electrical circuits and to generate conclusions from those experiments. The authors found that when students were required to provide reasons for their conclusions, as opposed to those students who were required only to indicate whether a conclusion was OK or not OK, they engaged in more complex argumentation with each other. In so doing, they learned to support or rebut each other's reasons and evidence, and this was positively related to improvement in students' abilities to write their own conclusions. The authors argued that the results demonstrate the importance of peer discourse and the structure of that discourse as a mediator of what students learn from peer interactions.

In short, the studies outlined above clearly demonstrate that students' discourse can be enhanced when one of the following is required:

- Students are given specific scripts on how they are to interact with each other (O'Donnell & Dansereau, 2000)
- Students are required to produce a common task where they have to interact to find a solution to the problem (Boxtel et al., 2002)
- Students are expected to provide reasons for their conclusions (Chinn et al., 2000)

These studies highlight the importance of teachers' ensuring that students are given explicit instruction in the roles, tasks, and thinking activities they are to undertake together.

Specific Metacognitive Skills That Promote Discourse

Although the studies outlined above clearly demonstrated the mediating role discourse plays in the construction of knowledge and learning, much of the learning that occurs is at the more basic comprehension level (e.g., reciprocal teaching, scripted cooperation). Certainly this type of learning is important; it has been shown to lead to greater understanding of the task and to enhance learning. In order to move beyond the comprehension discourse patterns, however, King (1999) developed the ASK to THINK-TEL WHY guided peer tutoring model to address the cognitive and metacognitive aspects of learning that other models of peer tutoring often neglect. This model is based on the knowledge construction pattern of discourse where students learn to ask questions that prompt their partners to make links or connections between different ideas or information. The responses that are generated often contribute to newly constructed knowledge that can extend the discussion or provoke the generation of additional questions that lead to further knowledge creation. The ASK to THINK-TEL WHY model of peer tutoring utilizes five different types of questions that partners use to scaffold learning from comprehension checking to connecting information through to building new knowledge and monitoring thinking (see Chapter 4 for examples of the types of questions students are taught to ask).

When implementing this model in the classroom, teachers need to ensure that students who act as tutors (students alternate between tutor and tutee roles) learn to ask the questions in sequence so that they begin with review questions, followed by thinking, probing, and hint questions, as appropriate, through to thinking-about-thinking questions. The sequence is important because it follows the three phases that are introduced: questions that help students to assess and consolidate prior knowledge, build new knowledge, and monitor their thinking processes (King, 1999).

Because the ASK to THINK-TEL WHY guided peer tutoring model requires that students not only follow the questioning sequence but that tutors only ask questions and do not explain or give answers to their partner, teachers need to ensure that students have had explicit training in the sequence of steps needed to implement this model. In addition, tutors must also be trained in the interpersonal skills that facilitate communication within the tutoring dyad. King (1999) identifies these skills as listening attentively, providing thinking time (i.e., pausing after asking a question), learning to give accurate feedback to a response from the tutee, and giving encouragement. Tutees, in turn, also need to be taught how to respond. This includes learning to explain rather than describe so that they link ideas within the material to prior knowledge. This involves learning to provide reasons, such as telling why or how the material is different as opposed to describing it. King maintains that this requirement challenges tutees to *paraphrase* the material in their own words, which generally demonstrates real understanding, as opposed to repeating it verbatim, often with little depth of understanding.

When the ASK to THINK-TEL WHY guided peer tutoring model is implemented correctly, students learn that they are linked interdependently together, as the question asked by the tutor is dependent on the previous response made by the tutee, which, in turn, determines the type of question that is consequently asked. This questioning and answering interaction continues with both the tutor and tutee jointly scaffolding their learning to progressively higher levels. The higher-order learning that occurs involves students' being able to generate relationships and link them with previous learning experiences, make inferences, and draw *generalizations* to construct new knowledge. In so doing, students clearly demonstrate their capacity to think cognitively and metacognitively about the material under discussion.

In short, when implementing the ASK to THINK-TEL WHY guided peer tutoring model to enhance student discourse, teachers need to ensure students understand these points:

- How to sequence the questions, beginning with comprehension questions through to cognitive and then to metacognitive thinking questions.
- The tutor's role is to ask questions only and not to explain.
- The tutee's role is to explain and not to describe answers.
- Both tutor and tutee are interdependent, depending on each other for what and how they learn as they scaffold and guide each other's responses.

The Teacher's Role in Promoting Mediated Learning

While the peer tutoring scripts discussed above are designed for students to use as they interact in their groups, Gillies (2004a) trained teachers to use specific communication skills to facilitate students' thinking and learning during cooperative group work. The specific skills that the teachers were taught to challenge students' thinking and scaffold their learning included the following:

- Probing and clarifying (e.g., Can you tell me more about what you're intending to do here?)
- Acknowledging and validating (e.g., I can see you've worked really hard to find out how these items are related. I wonder what you could do now to identify a common way of categorizing them?)
- Confronting discrepancies and clarifying options (e.g., I wonder how you can include . . . when you've already mentioned . . . ?)
- Tentatively offering suggestions (e.g., I wonder if you've considered doing it this way?)

Gillies (2004a) found that when teachers are trained to use these types of communication skills, they engage in more mediated learning behaviors or verbal behaviors designed to promote learning, they ask more questions, and they use fewer disciplinary comments than teachers who have not been trained to use these skills as they interact with students during cooperative group work.

The mediated learning behaviors that the teachers used included paraphrasing information to assist understanding, prompting to help elicit ideas, using open questions in a tentative manner to promote thought about an issue the student is focused on, and mediating or scaffolding learning among students to facilitate discussion.

The following are examples of the mediated learning comments that one teacher made during her interactions with a small group in her classroom that was working on identifying different energy sources: "*I can see that you've been working to gather information from different sources to help you with the project* (This was a validation of students' efforts to gather different resources for their project.) . . . *I wonder if you can determine the proportion of energy that comes from water power?*" (This tentative question was designed to focus students' attention on how they might seek the answer they need from the information sources they are using.) "*Now can I check out . . . how is water power turned into energy?*" (The students are challenged to make the link in the stages of energy development.)

Interestingly, the students' responses to each other in their groups mirrored many of the mediated learning behaviors their teachers used as they interacted with students during their group work activities. For example, they probed each other's opinion (e.g., "*So what do you think about that? Do you think we should use it?*"), acknowledged each other's points (e.g., "*We could use those. That's a good idea.*"), and attempted to link new information to previous understandings (e.g., "*Were there any other features? What about that one? Can it fit in here?*"). Moreover, they did this in a context that was inquiring and task oriented yet open and supportive of other ideas.

It appeared that when teachers use the mediated learning behaviors (outlined above), they model not only how to engage in problem-solving discourse or thinking about thinking but also how to participate in developing a shared understanding of the task at hand. Moreover, students, in turn, model many of the verbal behaviors they have seen demonstrated in their interactions with each other.

Gillies (2004a) argued that although teachers have the capacity to create opportunities for students to dialogue together when they establish cooperative learning activities in their classrooms, these activities alone are not sufficient to promote intellectually sophisticated talk. Teachers also need to be explicit in the thinking skills they teach if students are to use those skills in their own discourse. This involves teachers' demonstrating the skills that challenge, probe, and confront anomalies in students' thinking and learning. When this happens, students often model these discourses in their interactions with each other and in so doing learn new ways of reasoning and thinking.

In summary, it is clear from the studies reviewed in this section that teachers have the capacity to facilitate and enhance students' discourse during cooperative group work when one of the following conditions exists:

- Students are taught specific dialogic scripts to help them learn to interrogate information (i.e., reciprocal teaching)
- Students learn to adopt specific roles that have different procedures for interacting together (i.e., scripted cooperation)
- Tasks are structured so students are required to interact as they problem-solve together
- Students are taught how to sequence cognitive and metacognitive questions to help scaffold each other's learning to higher levels (i.e., ASK to THINK-TEL WHY guided peer tutoring model)

Developing Appropriate Helping Behaviors

In a number of studies that examined students' helping behaviors as they worked together in groups, Webb (1991, 1992) found that it was the explanations they gave to each other that were related to achievement gains, whereas help that was not elaborated (i.e., short response) did not contribute to achievement. It is believed that when students provide help to each other, they are often forced to reexamine their own understandings, fill in gaps in their own learning, and explain the material in such a way that they often learn it better than they would have by themselves (Wittrock, 1990). It should be noted that giving help that is not elaborated does not involve as much cognitive restructuring and is not related to achievement gains for the helper or the recipient.

Students who receive help from others can also benefit from the help given provided the explanations they receive are sufficiently detailed to allow them to correct their misunderstandings, and it is offered at a time when they are able to use that help (Webb et al., 1995). In contrast, when students receive less than an explanation, it has been found to be negatively related to, or not related to, achievement gains.

There is no doubt that students benefit from giving elaborated help such as explanations during cooperative group work. Gillies and Ashman (1996, 1998) found that when students had been trained to work cooperatively together, and this included training in how to provide help to each other, they gave more detailed help and assistance to their peers and they obtained higher learning outcomes than students who worked in untrained cooperative groups. Interestingly, Ross (1995), in a study of the effects of receiving feedback on Grade 7 students' helping behaviors during cooperative learning, noted that when they were given feedback on how to give and receive help, it enhanced their helping behaviors, and, in particular, their skill at asking for and giving help. Consequently, students learned to request good quality explanations, and these requests became more persistent, precise, and appropriately directed from the feedback they received.

Although Gillies and Ashman (1996, 1998) and Ross (1995) reported a relationship between cooperation and giving explanations during cooperative group work, these studies did not examine the circumstance under which explanations emerged or the quality of the help-giving relationship that was observed, apart from stating that students who worked cooperatively gave more explanations to each other. This is a concern because Webb and Mastergeorge (2003) argue that explanations are useful only if they are relevant to the recipient's need for help, timely, correct, and of sufficient detail to enable the recipient to correct his or her misunderstanding. In other words, the explanations given need to be suitable to the student's need for help at that point in time.

In addition, Webb and Mastergeorge (2003) found that in order for students to maximize their chances of receiving explanations that are relevant and sufficiently detailed, students need to learn to ask precise questions that communicate what they do not understand. Help seekers must continue to ask for help until they receive the help they need and then they must apply that help to the problem at hand, because it is only when students are actively engaged in interpreting and using the help received that they will develop new understandings and learning. Furthermore, students who provide help not only have a responsibility to ensure that recipients have the opportunity to apply that help but must continue to monitor recipients' attempts until they are satisfied that the help given has been understood.

In order to assist students to learn how to seek help and from whom, Webb, Nemer, Kersting, Ing, and Forrest (2004) propose that teachers need to ensure that students are taught the following steps:

1. Recognize that help is needed to solve the problem.

2. Decide to get help from another group member.

3. Choose a group member to ask for help.

4. Ask clear and precise questions.

5. Keep asking for help and clarification until the answer is understood.

It is suggested that teachers of elementary students may need to discuss and demonstrate these help-seeking behaviors so students understand how they can be used. Moreover, emphasizing how to seek help highlights the importance of obtaining quality help.

Learning how to seek help is important, but students also need to be responsive to their peers and to give help, especially if they perceive others need that help and they can provide it. Webb et al. (2004) suggest that teachers need to ensure that students are taught the following steps if they are to be effective helpers:

1. Be aware of others students' needs and when they may require help.

2. Encourage other students to ask for help if they need it.

3. Provide help if other students asks for help.

4. Listen carefully to other students.

5. Provide explanations and not just the answer.

6. Watch how the help given is used.

7. Provide feedback on how the problem was solved.

8. Always check for understanding and provide additional help if it is needed.

9. Acknowledge the effort the student put into solving the problem.

In short, Webb et al. (2004) are suggesting that seeking help and providing help necessitate a great deal of thought and planning on the part of the student, and the skills required to be successful need to be explicitly taught. Teaching also involves providing students with the opportunity to apply these behaviors in their groups and with the opportunity to reflect on how they were used. Reflection may also involve students' responding to checklists adapted from the help-seeking and help-giving behaviors listed above. Both activities are designed to increase students' awareness of the skills their groups used and what they need to do to improve.

Given the training needed to help students learn to seek and provide help, questions naturally arise as to how successful students are at applying these steps. Webb et al. (2004), in a study of the help-seeking and help-giving behaviors of six Grade 7 classes, found that students who had been trained to seek and provide high-quality help not only learned to ask more specific questions that focused on the type of help they needed, but they also received higher quality help during cooperative group work than their peers who were not trained. Moreover, Webb et al. found that students who asked a greater number of specific questions obtained higher posttest scores, students who obtained high-level help performed better on the posttest, and students who were successful at applying the help they received to the problem at hand obtained higher posttest scores. In short, Webb et al. argued that training students to seek and provide high-quality help enhances their capacity to seek and provide help and this has a positive effect on their achievement.

Choosing Tasks for Small-Group Discussions

There is no doubt that different tasks affect the way students interact in groups. For example, when students are required to work on *well-structured tasks* where there are set answers such as computational assignments or those involving basic recall or understanding of information, student interactions are minimal as they are required only to exchange information and explanations or to request assistance. Cohen (1994) suggested that these types of tasks involve low levels of cooperation because students do not need to discuss how to proceed as a group or negotiate meaning.

In contrast, high-level cooperative tasks require students to interact and discuss how to proceed, including how to make decisions, allocate tasks, and manage the substantive content. With these types of tasks, Cohen (1994) argues the task is often more open and discovery based, with no set procedures to follow or solutions to find. In other words, these tasks tend to be ill structured, and in group situations where interaction is vital to productivity, it could be expected that students would engage in more productive discourse as they worked to solve the problem at hand.

In choosing group tasks, teachers need to be mindful of the effect they have on students' discourse. For example, if students work on well-structured tasks where the potential for student dialogue may be limited, teachers may need to provide students with scripts or question cues (e.g., ASK to THINK-TEL WHY guided peer tutoring model) to help them scaffold each other's learning or to provide them with the help they need to seek to obtain high-quality information (Webb et al., 2004).

With *ill-structured tasks* or more open tasks, students need to exchange ideas and information if they are to come up with creative solutions to their assignments or discover underlying principles. With these types of tasks, achievement depends on the frequency of task-related interactions. Moreover, Cohen and her colleagues (Cohen, 1994; Cohen, Lotan, Scarloss, & Arellano, 1999) have consistently found that simple measures of the frequency of task-related interactions are related to follow-up gains on computational and mathematical concepts and applications as well as on content-referenced tests. In short, it is the frequency of students' talking and working together in a task-related manner that has been found to be positively correlated with follow-up achievement gains.

Although it is difficult to understand how simple task-related interactions contribute to learning, one explanation may be found in Bales's (1970) process interaction analysis, in which he demonstrated that when students seek suggestions, opinions, or information from others, they generally attract five responses per question or request. Consequently, increasing the amount of information considered during discussions should increase the likelihood that group members will include more information as they seek to solve the problem, and this increased amount of information is believed to be related to learning gains.

In more recent work, Cohen, Lotan, Abram, Scarloss, and Schultz (2002) provided sixth-grade students with specific guidelines as to what makes an exemplary group product and investigated the effect the guidelines had on group discourse and the quality of the final product. The study involved five teachers, three of whom practiced using the evaluation guidelines during skill-building exercises with their students prior to implementing the group activities. In the two comparison classrooms, students participated in general skill-building activities designed to improve the quality of group discussion. The results showed that in classrooms that used the evaluation guidelines, students had a significantly higher rate of evaluating their group product in their discussions than groups without the guidelines. In terms of classroom talk, the groups with the evaluation guidelines used more questions, statements, opinions, and reflections to evaluate the accuracy, relevance, and appropriateness of their group products than groups that had not been trained to use the evaluation guidelines. Cohen et al. concluded that evaluation guidelines stimulated group discussion and this, in turn, helped produce a better quality group product. Moreover, it also contributed to students' obtaining higher individual learning gains in follow-up achievement tests.

In summary, it appears that teachers need to be aware of the effect different tasks have on student discourse during small-group activities. Moreover, it is clear that if teachers want students to generate high-level discourse, they will need to teach the skills that promote the development of high-level interactions.

Monitoring Students' Progress and Evaluating Outcomes

It is important that teachers monitor students' progress as they work cooperatively together to ensure they are able to deal with the assigned tasks, provide feedback when needed, and be prepared to challenge their thinking and learning. Emmer and Gerwels (2002), in a study of 18 elementary school teachers' practices and lesson characteristics during cooperative learning, found that teachers who implemented more successful cooperative lessons built in higher levels of group or individual accountability, spent more time monitoring students' work in their groups, provided more relevant feedback, and made more use of manipulative materials than teachers who had less successful cooperative lessons. These findings led the authors to recommend that students are likely to have more successful small-group experiences when teachers regularly check students' progress, review their group interaction skills, and monitor group progress and task completion. Moreover, when difficulties arise, teachers need to be prepared to provide feedback and redirection to groups to help them solve problems at hand.

Similarly, Gillies and Boyle (2006), in a study of 10 elementary teachers' discourse and reported pedagogical practices during cooperative learning, found that not only was it important for teachers to set expectations for students' group behaviors, teach the social skills students needed to deal with disagreements in groups, and establish group structures so students understood what was required both from each other and the task, but it was also important to train students to think both cognitively and metacognitively if they were to promote high-level processing and thinking in their students.

In short Emmer and Gerwels (2002) and Gillies and Boyle (2006) believe that teachers actively need to monitor and review students' progress during cooperative group work. This includes the following:

- Setting expectations for students' behaviors
- Establishing task interdependence
- Teaching students to think cognitively and metacognitively
- Providing feedback to groups when they experience problems
- Being prepared to provide redirection when students experience difficulties they cannot solve

Case Study 7.2

Developing Criteria for Assessing Group Outcomes in Sixth Grade

T: OK. Before we start our group work, I want you to see if you can think of what expectations you have for how you are going evaluate how your group worked on developing the design that you have to come up with today. What sort of feedback do you want the rest of the class to give you about the product you produce? So think about that carefully before I get you to give me some ideas.

(Students have been participating in different cooperative small-group experiences as part of their general school curriculum and are aware of the need to develop criteria for how well they worked together, but they have not previously developed criteria about the product they produce. The task the groups have been given is to create a freestanding design, using the materials they have been given, that incorporates some of the mathematical principles they have been learning. This task represents the culmination of a unit of geometry they have completed). OK. Who has an idea? *(T. directs her comment to the whole class)*

S: We need to say how they may have used different colors to give different effects.

T: Yep. That's fine. Can anyone else think of criteria that you'd like the class to comment on?

S: We could look at how creative their ideas were?

T: What do you mean by that, Dylan?

S: Well, I mean. We could see if they had any unusual designs that nobody else had. Like some of those jazzy geometric shapes we saw the other day. The ones that gave different illusions.

T: OK. That gives us an idea of what you mean. Can anyone else think along those lines and come up with some additional criteria you think are important for this activity? OK. How about you spend a few minutes in your groups brainstorming the criteria you think are important for this task. *(Students then proceeded to work in their groups for about 10–15 minutes to identify the criteria. Teacher moved around the groups, listening to their discussions, contributing suggestions when needed, and acknowledging and validating students' ideas as they worked on compiling their lists. The whole-class discussion resumes with the teacher having written some of the students' ideas on the whiteboard)*

T: OK. Let's see what we have here. You've suggested that you'd like your group product to be evaluated for creativity, imagination with using different materials, unusual use of different materials, practical usefulness (i.e., can it be used somewhere and not just be used as an artistic design), explanations about how the design was created, and the extent to which students used mathematical principles in developing their design. Is there anything else that you think should be included?

S: No. *(Students comment that they are satisfied with the list that has been developed)*

T: OK. Now we have the criteria on which your product is going to be evaluated, but how will you do that? How will you determine if the criteria have been met and at what level?

S: We could say it's satisfactory or not?

T: How do you others feel about that? *(T. directs question to the whole class)*

S: No. I don't reckon that's enough. I think we need to say something like it's "satisfactory" or "good" because that gives a bit of an idea about whether it's just OK or it's better than OK.

T: Sure. Is there any way we could combine Josh's (student) comment about it being "satisfactory or not" with Tamara's [student] comment that "it's satisfactory or good"?

S: We could have three options . . . like satisfactory, not satisfactory, and good.

T: Does anyone have anything to say about that suggestion?

S: I think that we could say something like: on the way, satisfactory, and good.

T: Any other ideas?

S: How about saying: on the way, well thought out, and good.

T: I like the way you're giving some thought to explaining the criteria and how they were met at three levels. This makes it clearer rather than just acceptable or not acceptable. I wonder if you were receiving the feedback, what you would you like to hear? Would you understand what was meant or would you like the feedback to be a little clearer?

S: I think it's (*referring to the terms, on the way, well though out, and good*) OK. (*Students concurred that they understood what was meant*)

T: OK. Let's see how these criteria look on a matrix with on the way, well developed, and good. (*Teacher drew matrix on the board and then asked students to consider whether it was possible to evaluate all the criteria using the matrix*)

Note: T = Teacher, S = Student

In the scenario above, the teacher gets the students to consider how their group product can be assessed. By doing this, she's trying to get the students to identify the key components of the task and then consider how they could be meaningfully evaluated so that the students receiving feedback can understand what they did well and what could be improved. While the students have been used to constructing rubrics that focus on the processes of learning (i.e., contributing ideas, sharing materials, helping others), they have not previously constructed one that focused on evaluating the product outcome. This is quite a challenging task for the students because they are required to think about the different aspects of the task that they will need to consider when they are constructing their freestanding design and then determine how these aspects, in turn, will be evaluated. This is clearly an exercise in getting students to think metacognitively about the assessment rubric they are constructing. Certainly, Emmer and Gerwels (2002) and Gillies and Boyle (2006) reported that teachers believed that it was important to challenge students' thinking if they were to promote high-level understanding and learning in their students. The above scenario, where the teacher had students identify the criteria to evaluate their product and then construct a rubric to measure those criteria, is an illustration of how to promote high-level understanding and thinking in students.

CHAPTER SUMMARY

The research on teachers' responsibilities in establishing cooperative learning suggests

- Teachers need to create learning environments that are inclusive of all students.
- Teachers need to establish student-centered learning environments that involve interactive, meaningful, constructive, and reflective processes.
- Teachers actively need to teach students how to interact socially in groups.
- Teachers can facilitate students' dialoguing with others by helping them to use different scripts, adopt different group roles, or requiring them to complete tasks where they need to interact to solve the problem.
- Teachers need to be prepared to challenge students' thinking and scaffold their learning so they learn to think more cognitively and metacognitively about problem issues.
- Teachers can facilitate thinking in their students (e.g., asking probing questions, confronting discrepancies in students' reasoning) when they use specific communication skills that challenge students' thinking and scaffold their learning.
- Teachers must actively monitor students' progress, provide feedback and redirections as appropriate, and be prepared to review students' achievements as a consequence of their small-group experience.

ACTIVITIES

1. Reflect on your own years as a student (elementary, middle, and high school) to see if you can identify a teacher whom you regarded as an excellent teacher. Write down the characteristics of this excellent teacher. Share them with others in your group to see if there are characteristics that you have in common. How does your group's list compare with the research outlined earlier in this chapter on effective and exemplary teachers?

2. Arrange to visit a classroom (elementary, middle, or high school) and ask the students to identify the characteristics of a good teacher. This can be quite a challenging activity for students, who will need "to think outside the box" for this activity. Compare their ideas with those outlined earlier in the chapter on effective and exemplary teachers.

3. Construct a list of what you would look for if you were monitoring students' progress during cooperative learning. Such lists not only help teachers to identify how students are progressing and what they are learning, but also help teachers to review and reflect on their own effectiveness. In a sense, they serve as checks for what is working well and what still needs to be achieved.

4. You have been asked to give a short talk to a group of fellow teachers on the responsibilities teachers have in establishing cooperative learning in their classrooms. I wonder what key points you would highlight and why? How would you deal with teachers who wanted to maintain a more traditional or transmission style of instruction?

5. Remembering that tasks that are open and discovery based are more likely to promote discourse among group members than ones that require specific solutions or procedures to follow, visit one of the following Web sites to see if you can identify three or four tasks that would be suitable for your students (i.e., elementary, middle, or high school). What are the characteristics of these tasks? How do you think students will respond to them? What benefits do you believe students might derive from these tasks?

http://www.henry.k12.tn.us/teachersworkshop/cooplearn/lessons.html

http://www.atozteacherstuff.com/pages/1875.shtml

SUGGESTIONS FOR FURTHER READING

Cohen, E., Lotan, R., Abram, P., Scarloss, B., & Schultz, S. (2002). Can groups learn? *Teachers College Record, 104*, 1045–1068.

Emmer, E., & Gerwels, M. (2002). Cooperative learning in elementary classrooms: Teaching practices and lesson characteristics. *Elementary School Journal, 103*, 75–92.

Gillies, R., & Boyle, M. (2006). Ten Australian elementary teachers' discourse and reported pedagogical practices during cooperative learning. *Elementary Journal, 106*(5), 429–451.

Webb, N., & Mastergeorge, A. (2003). Promoting effective helping in peer-directed groups. *International Journal of Educational Research, 39*, 73–97.

CHAPTER 8

Future Developments in Using Small Groups

INTRODUCTION AND LEARNING OBJECTIVES

Some questions that teachers frequently ask are, "Can schools improve?" "Can they reform?" I suspect that these questions naturally arise with each wave of change that teachers see introduced that is designed to herald the arrival of the next panacea for raising students' standards of achievement. The pressure from government policy, parent and community groups, corporate interests, technology changes, and so on have helped to make schools more vulnerable to seeking a quick solution to current problems (Hunt, 2005). Over the years, pressures to change have resulted in schools' spending large amounts of money on technology, teachers, professional development, books, information kits, instructional aids, and buildings, often with no documented evidence that these resources have in any way enhanced students' learning outcomes (Christensen, Aaron, & Clark, 2005). It is because of the disappointing results obtained from allocating huge financial resources to improving schools with few or no discernable benefits that the momentum has developed to identify educational initiatives that work, that warrant the investment.

There is no doubt that any attempt at change has to be systemic or school-wide if there is to be effective and lasting improvement. Furthermore, if school reform is to succeed, schools need to reach out into the communities and build positive relationships with parents and other stakeholder groups so that reform initiatives are jointly developed and supported (Fullan, 1998).

A review by Sammons, Hillman, and Mortimore (1995) of the characteristics of effective schools or schools that make a difference in students' outcomes identifies 11 factors of effective schools:

1. Professional leadership by the school principal

2. Shared vision and goals by the staff

3. A school ethos that is conducive to learning

4. Classroom teaching practices that emphasize academic achievement

5. Purposeful and well-structured lessons

6. High expectations for student achievement

7. Positive reinforcement of appropriate behavior

8. Frequent monitoring of the performance of students

9. Recognition of students' rights and responsibilities

10. Promotion of home and school partnerships

11. Continuing professional development

Interestingly, Taylor, Pressley, and Pearson (2000), in a review of five large-scale studies on effective, moderate- to high-poverty elementary schools, found that they report strikingly similar factors that support and extend the earlier research (e.g., Sammons et al., 1995) on the characteristics of effective schools. The factors Taylor et al. found that contributed to high achievement in high-poverty schools included the following:

1. A focus on putting students first to improve student learning

2. Strong leadership by the principal

3. Strong collaboration among teachers

4. Consistent use of student data to improve learning

5. A focus on professional development and innovation

6. Strong links to parents

These findings led Taylor et al. to conclude that

Effective schools are typically characterized as learning, collaborative communities in which staff assume a shared responsibility for all students' learning, monitor progress as a way of planning instruction for groups and individuals, help one another and learn more about the art and science of teaching, and reach out to families they serve. (p. 12)

In a synthesis of school effectiveness findings from 1979 to 2002, Rutter and Maughan (2002) identified the common school features that promote student progress. These include the following:

1. Contextual variables such as adequate resourcing and community support

2. Innovative school organization and management

3. School ethos that promotes learning in a positive school environment

4. Regular monitoring of students' performance across a range of domains

5. Emphasis on efficient organization of classroom lessons

6. Good pedagogical practices

In short, the above studies report surprisingly convergent results on the characteristics of effective schools. Moreover, these results indicate that students' achievements can be influenced by the characteristics of the school environment, and that students from high-poverty areas can succeed if school personnel and the community are prepared to help their schools become effective schools.

Comprehensive School Reform (CSR)

Findings from the effective schools literature helped to provide the impetus for the *Comprehensive School Reform Program* initiative. This initiative, which began in 1998, has become an important component of the No Child Left Behind (NCLB) Act, as it is seen as a way of helping schools raise students' levels of achievement.

CSR programs target high-poverty and low-achieving schools with the intention of helping them implement reforms that are grounded in scientifically based research and effective practices (Comprehensive School Reform Program, 2004). CSR programs are designed to foster coherent schoolwide improvements rather than piecemeal, fragmented approaches to reform to help students meet state academic achievement standards (*About CSR*, 2004).

The 11 mandated components of a CSR program that represent a comprehensive and scientifically based approach to school reform include (see *About CSR,* 2004) the following:

1. The use of proven methods for student learning, teaching, and school management, which includes programs that have demonstrated to be successful through either well-grounded research or practice

2. The integration of instruction, assessment, classroom management, professional development, parental involvement, and school management

3. The employment of ongoing, high-quality professional development for staff

4. The establishment of measurable goals and benchmarks for student achievement and benchmarks for achieving those goals

5. Whole-staff support for school reform

6. The provision of support for staff through shared leadership and responsibility for reform efforts

7. The meaningful involvement of parents and the local community in planning and evaluating school improvement initiatives

8. The participation of an external partner with experience and expertise in schoolwide reform and improvement

9. The annual evaluation of the strategies for the implementation of school reform and for student achievement results

10. The identification of an available state or private resource to support and sustain the school's comprehensive reform efforts

11. The requirement that the program employed must either be grounded on scientifically based research or that there is strong evidence that the program will significantly improve the academic achievements of participating students

The impetus to use CSR programs in high-poverty schools has gathered momentum in the past few years as it has become apparent that at-risk students are better served by schoolwide reforms than by pull-out remedial programs (Felner, Jackson, Kasak, & Mulhall, 1997). In addition, the provision of hundreds of millions of dollars to support the cost of implementing externally developed school reform models, the growing research base that demonstrates success for some externally developed school restructuring efforts, and the focus by the New American Schools Development Corporation (NAS) on identifying reform models that could be scaled up to schools nationally has led to the continuing expansion of externally developed CSR models (Borman, Hewes, Overman, & Brown, 2003). However, although CSR models are continuing to be implemented, Borman et al. noted that there was an absence of research on the overall, long-term effects of these models on schools. This information is critical as it can be used to help schools distinguish more successful models from less successful models or models that have no effect.

In an attempt to investigate the effects of different CSR models on school outcomes, Borman et al. (2003) conducted a meta-analysis of 29 studies that had used different CSR models. Of the 29 CSR models that were included in the analysis, the authors concluded that only 3 models—Direct Instruction (Becker & Carnine, 1980), the School Development Program (Comer, 2005), and Success for All (Slavin, 2004a)—had accumulated enough evidence to demonstrate that they can improve test scores. Interestingly, when CSR schools were compared to other Title 1 schools that provide pull-out support programs and other resources for their at-risk students, the average CSR school still outperformed 55% of Title 1 schools, clearly indicating that CSR programs provide value-added effects.

Good, Burross, and Mccaslin (2005) reported on the effects of CSR programs that were implemented in 24 schools and compared them to 24 matched control schools over 6 consecutive school years in Arizona. The authors investigated the longitudinal effects of the programs over time (e.g., do students' scores improve from third grade to fourth grade to fifth grade, etc.?) as well as the cross-sectional effects (e.g., do fourth graders in 1999 outperform fourth graders in 1998?) to determine whether students as a group become more competent the longer they stay in CSR schools. The results showed that students in the CSR schools made distinct progress over the period of the study; however, when compared to non–CSR schools, the progress was not significant. Both CSR schools and non–CSR schools made progress. The authors argued that because Arizona is a high-stakes testing state, this may have motivated schools generally to ensure that their students progressed, making the effects of the CSR program not as obvious as they might have been.

In a national randomized study of Success for All (a comprehensive reading reform model) that was conducted in 41 elementary schools, Borman et al. (2005) report students in the Success for All schools obtained significantly higher scores on the word attack subtest than their peers in the schools where Success for All was not implemented. The magnitude of the difference was approximately one quarter of a standard deviation or nearly 3 months of additional learning on individual word attack test scores. (It should be noted that

that students did not score significantly higher on the other three subtest scores of the Revised Woodcock Reading Mastery Tests: letter identification, word identification, and passage comprehension.) The authors argued that the pattern of first-year treatment effects (i.e., word attack skills emerge first) was consistent with previous experimental work on the Success for All program, the Success for All program theory, and more general research and theory on the development of young children' emergent literacy skills, which indicates that the phonetic and structural analysis skills tapped by the word attack test help students develop more advanced comprehension and reading skills.

In short, the research clearly indicates that there are CSR models that do work and that have a positive effect on at-risk students' achievements in high-poverty schools. This is not to say that these interventions can eliminate the effects of low socioeconomic status and transform low-income students into high-income students, but rather that the research (Borman et al., 2003; Good et al., 2005) does indicate that schools can make a difference in enhancing students' achievements within the constraints of home and community resources.

When You Have Finished This Chapter You Will Know:

- The implications of *comprehensive school reform programs* for democratic and learner-centered schooling practices
- The importance of involving students in negotiating opportunities for learning
- The impact of computer technology on small-group learning
- The implications for designing classrooms of the future
- The importance of teamwork and communication

Case Study 8.1

Two Middle School Teachers' Experiences With a Comprehensive School Reform Program

I: Your school has been using this CSR program now for the last three years. Can you tell me a little about how it got going and what you've noticed?

T1: Sure. We did some fairly extensive investigations before we settled on the model we now have because we wanted to make sure it was right for our school. We've got a lot of kids from poor backgrounds who really experience a lot of hardship—poverty at home, often only one parent, or high parent unemployment. These kids don't have books and resources that other kids from more affluent areas have so we wanted to make sure that whatever we tried was going to be the best for our kids.

T2: Yes, I'd agree. There's a lot of poverty here—emotional, material, spiritual—you name it, we've got it. These kids don't have a great deal going for them, apart from what happens here at school. The school is really their anchor. This is their only stable environment.

I: So what did you see about this program that attracted you to it?

T1: I was impressed the way the developers stressed that they were going to build on what we were already doing—things that we'd found worked. It was kinda nice to have them affirm what we already had in place. But I probably liked the structure the program provided. I could see that if we had a consistent approach across the grades with what we did, the kids would be better for it.

T2: I liked the professional development we had—that was needed. I wouldn't have felt comfortable without it and the ongoing support we received from the team. That was important too.

T1: Yep. The PD was good and the materials and resources were excellent—very good for motivating the kids. I personally like the reading program—it really grabs my kids.

T2: I think training one of us . . . you know, Maree . . . that's helped. She's obviously willing to stick with it and she keeps us updated on any PD we might need and because she's a very good teacher and she gets in there and does the work herself. She's got a lot of credibility with the staff and they accept her role as the facilitator.

I: Is there anything else about the program that stands out for you?

T2: Yep. I like the flexible grouping arrangements. We used to have tracking, mainly so we could focus our resources on the lowest track—special teachers, aides, books, and so on. I never really understood the importance of cooperative learning and how to get the groups going so I was really surprised to see how you do it. My kids like it and they're getting better at getting into their groups. It used to be chaotic, but they're learning.

T1: What I think is important is the way we monitor their progress—through the curriculum, in their groups, by themselves, in class. We got some excellent ideas from the program on how to monitor what they learn and how they learn. I think it's made me very conscious of their progress. As I walk around the room, I'm always ticking over checks in my head about what certain ones (students) are doing.

I: What do you think are the benefits to date from the program?

T2:   I think the way we're (staff) all committed to the program, that's made a difference to staff. We all know what's happening and we talk about it and work out how we deal with problems—not like previously when we only worked with our grade colleagues.

T1:   We've been keeping results from the testing and the kids are making progress. We've still got our knocks and bumps to sort out but most staff will say they can see an improvement. Of course, we have the hard cases (students), but we're working on them.

I: How do the kids line up for the state testing?

T2:   Not bad. They're holding their own with other schools like this. We've got records that go back since we started and we can see small improvements—not great, but they're there.

T1:   Don't forget, we were warned by the developers that it may take time but I think it's on the way. The kids have a much more positive attitude to school. They can see that we're trying to involve them more in learning. We give them opportunities to talk about their work with each other and work out how they're going to meet goals. We obviously have goals we expect them to achieve but we negotiate them with them so they can see we're being consultative. This is important because these kids make their own decisions about their lives outside school so let's let them make some decisions in school.

Note: I = Interviewer, T = Teacher

In the interview above, the teachers identify many of the elements that Slavin (1999) maintains are critical for the success of comprehensive school reform programs. These include having a well-structured approach that can be consistently implemented across the grades; and although it is not clear whether the program emphasized research-based strategies, it is clear from what Teacher 1 had to say that it was certainly based on good practice—"things that we'd found worked" (Turn 5).

Professional development is another very important element, especially if teachers are to use those strategies that promote effective instruction. It is apparent from Teacher 2 that she would not have felt comfortable using the program unless she had received this type of support. In addition, the role of the facilitator, a member of the staff, is important for the smooth running of the program as she not only keeps her colleagues updated about professional development but in many schools acts as a peer coach to help en-skill other teachers.

Flexible grouping arrangements are also very important for the success of many comprehensive school reform programs, particularly as the programs often emphasize cooperative learning activities that are designed to be cognitively challenging and highly motivational and where students have opportunities to interact with their peers on problem-based learning activities. Engaging in partner and small-group reading activities, finding problem solutions in narratives, summarizing main points in a story, and engaging in collaborative writing activities are just some of the activities students can undertake during cooperative learning where they may be required to complete specific tasks or fulfill certain roles as part of their contribution to their group. Having students work successfully in small groups is obviously a challenge for many teachers and no less so than for Teacher 2; yet with training in the small-group and interpersonal skills needed to promote cooperation, students learn how to manage their interactions and discussions with each other.

Monitoring students' progress is another very important element of CSR programs. As Teacher 1 indicated, it is an ongoing process that involves monitoring students' progress "through the curriculum, in their groups, by themselves, in class" (Turn 11). In fact, this is something that effective or successful teachers regularly do because it helps them to determine where and when to make adjustments to how and what they teach (Allington, Johnson, & Day, 2002). Continuous monitoring enables teachers to identify those who are struggling, provide scaffolding to assist understanding, or ensure that additional assistance is forthcoming if one-on-one tutoring or help is required.

Having school staff committed to the program is critical if it is to be successfully implemented. In many instances, CSR programs will not be implemented unless more than 80% of staff has indicated they are prepared to support implementation. Slavin (2004a) maintains that high levels of support are essential, because when schools make the decision to be involved with Success for All, they are choosing a particular model of reading instruction, a particular use of Title 1 and special education resources, and particular within-school support structures. Certainly, Teacher 2 identified staff commitment as one of the benefits of the program: "We all know what's happening and we talk about it and we work out how we deal with problems" (Turn 13).

Finally, the program (discussed in Case Study 8.1) clearly tries to promote opportunities for students to be involved in negotiating aspects of what they learn. This is very important for young adolescents, who often feel the need to exercise some autonomy over their own learning. In more traditional schools, however, the freedom these students need is often denied because of how the curriculum and the classroom routines are structured. In CSR schools, the program is often designed so that students are able to engage in a variety of ways of working from large class groups through to working in different small groups to working by oneself. In this regard, the program is student centered, allowing teachers to adapt their pedagogical practices to ensure that how and what students learn is determined by their learning needs. Furthermore, because small-group work and individual work usually require students to negotiate specific learning goals with their teachers, students often feel they have more autonomy over their own learning. When young adolescents believe they have more control over what and how they learn, Gillies (2003a) found they have a stronger perception of their cooperative group experiences as being more enjoyable and more motivating than the perceptions of their peers who do not work cooperatively together.

The Implications of CSR Programs for Democratic and Learner-Centered Teaching Practices

There is no doubt that comprehensive school reform programs are going to have an effect on how school staff teach, particularly as more research-based evidence becomes available on how to structure students' learning so teaching, classroom management, and assessment are more aligned and integrated, with a focus on helping students to meet state achievement standards. This does not mean that learner-centered programs are to be discarded—definitely not. The research that is emerging is based on trying to understand how students learn and how they can be motivated to learn so that they will benefit from the reforms that are proposed. Well-founded evidence is designed ultimately to benefit children by helping teachers to do a better job with the students they serve (Slavin, 2004b). Experienced teachers and researchers know that any reforms, if they are to be successful, have to be designed to engage students' interests, challenge their curiosity, and provide them with the skills they need to be able to succeed.

How does this happen? How do teachers manage to reconnect students who have disengaged from learning or students who are not particularly motivated to do more than is needed? McCombs (2001) argues that educational models that reconnect youth and adults need to be person-centered while also providing challenging learning experiences that prepare children and youth to be knowledge producers, knowledge users, and socially responsible citizens.

Person-centered approaches to teaching and learning focus on the personal and interpersonal relationships, beliefs, and perceptions that are affected or supported by the educational system as a whole. Such approaches project hope to students, convince them of their worth and ability to succeed, and respect students and honor their perspectives (McCombs, 2001). Teachers demonstrate these values when they model appropriate interpersonal relationships with their students and ensure that students, in turn, have opportunities to participate in learning environments that are engaging and encourage creativity, invention, and imagination. Such environments provide opportunities for students to interact with others, share ideas, and negotiate their learning goals. Moreover, in learner-centered environments teachers include students in the decision-making process about how and what they learn; value each learner's unique perspective; respect and accommodate diversity in learners' backgrounds, interests, abilities, and experiences; and acknowledge learners as cocreators and partners in the learning and teaching process.

Although there are many ways in which teachers can provide opportunities for students to be actively involved in the learning process, one well-recognized way is through cooperative learning where students have opportunities to negotiate group tasks and goals, work collaboratively together to share and discuss information, challenge each other's perspectives and understandings, resolve differences, and, in so doing, construct new understandings and knowledge. As a teaching pedagogy, cooperative learning capitalizes on adolescents' desires to engage with their peers, exercise more autonomy over their learning, and express their desires to achieve (Slavin, 1996). In fact, it has been argued that cooperative learning experiences are crucial to engaging students in learning and preventing and alleviating many of the social problems experienced by children, adolescents, and young adults (Johnson, Johnson, & Stanne, 2000).

In summary, there is no doubt that there are some CSR programs that do work, that do promote students' achievement gains. They do this by implementing different research-based, learner-centered practices that have been demonstrated to be successful with helping to motivate students' learning. Included in these practices are person-centered approaches to teaching and learning that focus on building strong interpersonal relationships in classrooms among teachers and students so students are able to act responsibly, autonomously, and creatively during the learning process.

Student Participation in Negotiating Opportunities for Learning

McCombs (2001) investigated teachers' beliefs and perceptions of their practices and students' perceptions of their teachers' practices and found that teachers who are more learner centered are more successful in engaging all students in an effective learning process. Interestingly, these teachers are more effective themselves as learners and they are happier with their jobs than teachers who are less learner centered. Furthermore, teachers who are more learner centered are more likely to reflect on their practices, particularly if there are discrepancies between their own and their students' perceptions of their practices, and to help them identify ways in which they might change so they can be more effective in how they teach. In short, these teachers are reflective practitioners who regularly critique their teaching practices with the intention of adopting and promoting more effective pedagogical practices in their classrooms.

Learner-centered teachers view each student as unique and capable of learning, have a perspective that focuses on the learner, understand how students learn, and respect and accept the student's point of view. McCombs (2001) found that students' desires to learn, master the environment, and develop and mature in positive ways were therefore enhanced. For example, young children are motivated to learn and achieve when teachers

- Establish a positive classroom environment
- Adapt instruction to individual differences
- Facilitate students' learning and thinking skills

In addition to the above, middle and high school students are also motivated to learn and achieve when teachers honor their voices and provide opportunities for individual choice and challenge. This is not unexpected, given that most adolescents like to feel that what they do is meaningful and that they have some control over how and what they learn.

There is no doubt that students are more motivated when they are provided with opportunities to be actively involved in their own learning. Moreover, effective teachers ensure that they create learning environments that provide opportunities for students to work in situations that are positive and supportive of their personal, social, and academic needs.

Practical Activity

Helping Schools Establish Positive Learning Environments

Elementary School

★ Demonstrate respect for each other. Teach children to understand that if they want to be treated with respect as individuals, they need to treat others likewise. This includes teaching children to respect the cultural, ethnic, and learning diversity among their peers.

★ Demonstrate care and concern for all individuals. Children can be taught how to empathize with others by having teachers model these behaviors in their interactions with them. In addition, providing opportunities for young children to care for a classroom pet is a wonderful way to help children learn how important it is to take care of other living things and, by implication, classroom peers and family members.

★ Demonstrate appropriate interpersonal behaviors. When teachers take time to ask children how their weekend went or to find out more about their favorite baseball or football players, they interact at an interpersonal level that not only shows interest in the children but also demonstrates care and concern for their well-being. Children are very receptive to these types of interactions and will adopt them when they interact with their peers or family members.

★ Encourage children to try. It is very important that children understand that they can attempt tasks or have a go at them without having to worry about being rebuked for not doing them correctly. Children will continue to work on tasks that may initially appear to be too difficult if their teachers establish an understanding in the classroom that "we all try." Comments such as, "I can see you're really trying to work that problem out—that shows me you're a good trier," help to encourage children in their efforts.

★ Articulate the importance of having a safe working environment. Ensuring that children understand that they do not bring any harmful objects such as weapons or drugs to school is very important for helping them to understand that the environment they work in has to be safe for everyone. Moreover, if they know of anyone who has any of these banned or harmful objects, they must tell their teacher so that these can be removed—safety being the priority.

★ Bullying is not tolerated. Ensure that children understand that bullying others is not acceptable and that when it occurs, perpetrators will be sanctioned. Train students in strategies for dealing with bullies, including those strategies that promote personal resilience. For example, teaching children to use such self-affirming statements as, "I'm strong and I can cope with this" helps them to think positively about themselves rather than being intimidated by bullies' threats.

★ Establish peers support groups where children can enjoy the company of other children who may have similar interests or where children can go if they require mediation to resolve difficulties with their peers. Many schools have established peer mediation teams of older students who help children to resolve difficulties and settle disputes themselves.

(Continued)

(Continued)

Middle School and High School

With adolescents, it is important to negotiate appropriate codes of behavior to help create a safe working environment so that students understand the following:

★ All actions must be safe and aboveboard. This includes ensuring that no weapons or drugs or other harmful substances are brought into schools. When this does happen, students need to understand that they have an obligation to ensure the safety of themselves and their peers by reporting such information.

★ Bullying is not tolerated and bullies will be sanctioned. Provide students with strategies for dealing with bullies, including the use of self-affirming statements to promote personal resilience, peer support networks, and avenues to report the abuse to school personnel.

★ Provide opportunities for students to have their voices or choices heard. This may include establishing a classroom council where all students have the right to raise issues with the class group. It may include opportunities for students to drop in to see you during break time to discuss personal issues or negotiate alternative submission dates for assignments. In short, teachers need to be creative about providing opportunities that let students make their wishes known or express their opinions.

★ Provide opportunities for students to work on intellectually challenging tasks where they can test their ideas and receive feedback from their peers. Adapting the working environment so students have opportunities to move around to different work stations that have different tasks and different technologies is one way to challenge students and motive their interests. Establishing expectations that they have to report back to the class group is another way to ensure that students complete required tasks.

The Impact of Computer Technology on Small-Group Learning

In Chapter 5, I discussed the use of computer technology groupings and the benefits that accrue to students when they have the opportunity of work with their peers on a range of tasks from basic tutorial activities through to more complex problem-solving programs that stimulate higher-order thinking and learning and involve students' working in groups of three or four members. Classes where these types of groupings are practiced are often learner-centered environments where students work together on tasks that are developed in response to their specific learning needs. In these classes, students are expected to be actively involved in the construction of knowledge and to accept responsibility for their own learning. In addition, teachers act as facilitators of learning rather than dispensers of knowledge as occurs in more traditional classrooms where teaching is often more direct and students are less active in the learning process.

Information computer technology (ICT) can play a significant role in the development of learner-centered learning environments where computers serve as tools for helping students to access multiple sources of information to build knowledge and understandings. ICT encourages students' cooperation and reflection on the information obtained while simultaneously providing teachers with opportunities to adapt the learning content and tasks to meet the diverse needs of students. Moreover, innovative and creative teachers will interweave these technologies in a variety of ways into their teaching programs to ensure the best outcomes for their students (Smeets & Mooij, 2001).

Given that teachers are the crucial factor in the process of introducing ICT, questions naturally arise as to whether teachers take these technologies on board. If they do, do they embed them in their curriculum as part of their teaching pedagogy? What issues do teachers face when implementing an ICT program that is designed to be student centered?

Pedersen and Liu (2003) conducted a study among 15 middle-years science teachers to identify key issues in the implementation of a computer-based program designed to support student-centered learning and to examine teachers' beliefs about these issues. The computer-based program presented students with a complex science problem that required them to undertake investigations of the various planets and large moons in our solar system and to match different alien species to a new home world. The program offered several challenges to students, including how best to gather required data using different instruments, given that an inappropriate design would result in malfunctions or in a failure to obtain the needed information. Other problems embedded in the program included the need for students to convert between the different temperature scales, identify substances from their spectrograms, and interpret data. The authors argued that the complexity of the problem and the numerous small challenges students had to deal with encouraged them to seek support from their peers as they worked on resolving the issues at hand.

Data for the study were collected from teacher interviews and classroom observations of the implementation of the computer-based science program. The findings showed that while the teachers recognized the importance of student-centered learning, their understanding of this term varied from considering the interests and needs of the students and then providing instruction based on those interests and needs (i.e., high student-centered approach) through to presenting a topic that students were required to learn about and then allowing them to investigate different aspects of the topic that were of interest (i.e., low student-centered approach). In effect, teachers had somewhat varied understandings of what student-centered learning entailed.

Although teachers' interpretations of student-centered learning varied, most saw their role as being a facilitator of learning where they often asked questions to gauge students' thinking and to encourage reflection. They also saw student collaboration as being very important because it helped students learn to develop the social skills necessary for working with others. Only two teachers mentioned the importance of better problem solving through social reasoning and enhanced communication. All teachers expressed the belief that they thought it was important to grade students' performances during this activity because that helped to motivate students to do their best work and this, in turn, helped students to learn more.

A further issue that teachers identified as important was the impact of curriculum standards and standardized tests on the types of activities teachers use with their classes. For example, while many teachers believed that computer-based programs such as the science one they had implemented in their classes are effective in helping students to develop problem-solving skills, most believed that they may not be effective in helping students to learn the factual knowledge that is often required on standardized tests. Teachers did note, however, that if the current standardized tests were to focus more on problem solving and less on factual recall, they would be more likely to engage in student-based learning activities in the future. The teachers noted that the computer-based science program they implemented in their classrooms was rich in its use of media, and they believed this enhanced its presentation and made it highly attractive and intrinsically motivating to students.

Based on the findings that emerged, Pedersen and Liu (2003) concluded that teachers are more likely to use student-centered computer programs if the design of such programs is consistent with their beliefs about how students learn. For example, teachers' understanding of student-centered learning differed, and this can lead to misconceptions about how programs should be used. It was also clear that many of the teachers did not recognize the full potential for collaboration during enquiry learning, particularly as a tool to enhance discourse, problem solving, and learning. Professional development that helped teachers to discuss their experiences and link different strategies and practices to a theory of how learning occurs within this type of environment would help teachers to connect theory and practice more effectively and to figure out ways to apply their theoretical beliefs within the complex environment of the classroom.

In summary, computer technology can enable teachers to adapt learning content and tasks to the diverse needs and abilities of students so that learning is more student centered and less teacher directed. When this happens, students assume more autonomy for their learning while teachers act as facilitators rather than directors of it. Although teachers acknowledged the importance of establishing student-centered learning environments, they often did not fully understand the important role discussion plays in social reasoning and the construction of learning, nor did they understand that it is not always necessary to grade students to motive their efforts. In student-centered classrooms, students are often motivated by the challenge the task poses and the autonomy they exercise over their own learning as they work together in small groups on the problem at hand. These findings have implications for how teachers can be assisted to embed ICT programs into small-group learning in classrooms.

The Implications for Designing Classrooms of the Future

Sometimes to be able to understand the future one has to look at the past to see what it reveals. This is certainly the case with trying to adopt a futuristic perspective on classroom design that includes the learning and teaching processes that will be employed in such classrooms, given the growing recognition that such classrooms need to be student centered, with students being more actively involved in their own learning.

Classrooms are complex and dynamic organizations involving a number of different dimensions—organization for learning, interactions among teachers and students, students' attitudes and behaviors, and the curriculum—all of which interact so that changes in one dimension will affect changes in other dimensions. It is important to understand this interdependence because as developments occur in one dimension, they are likely to affect how students and teachers behave in others and so on.

To understand the interplay that occurs among these dimensions, Hertz-Lazarowitz (1992) proposed a model of classroom behaviors called the Six Mirrors of the Classroom. This model provides a conceptual framework for understanding how each of the dimensions is interrelated and reflected in each of the others, like a mirror. The relationships can range from being highly coordinated so things run smoothly through to being poorly coordinated where there is disjunction and discord. When the relationships between the different dimensions are highly coordinated and running smoothly, students are more active academically and socially and this results in higher levels of thinking. In contrast, when the relationships between the different dimensions are not synchronized, students are more likely to be less active both academically and socially, and this has implications for what and how they learn.

To understand the Six Mirrors of the Classroom model that Hertz-Lazarowitz (1992) proposes, it is necessary to examine each of the different dimensions separately to determine how each interacts with the others and the effect each has on the total classroom environment. The dimensions to be examined are as follows:

1. The physical organization of the classroom

2. The learning task

3. The teacher's instructional behavior

4. The teacher's communicative behavior

5. The students' academic behaviors

6. The students' social behaviors

1. The Physical Organization of the Classroom

Classroom organization varies depending on whether teachers are working with whole-class groups through to whether students are working in a series of small groups that are highly integrated with students working on complex problem-solving tasks independent of the teacher. In between these two different types of classroom organizational structures, students have opportunities to work in dyads on tutorial-type tasks, or in small groups where there are low levels of cooperation (often groups that are formed in an ad hoc way), through to being able to work in groups where there are high levels of cooperation.

Certainly, having students work in groups where there are high levels of cooperation and where groups are well integrated into the classroom organization is ideal because learning under these conditions is student centered and requires students to be interactive and constructive during learning. This type of small-group structure is more beneficial for student learning than whole-class teaching or small-group learning where there are low levels of cooperation (Gillies & Ashman, 1998). In addition, Almog and Hertz-Lazarowitz (1999) argue that well-integrated small groups that are functioning simultaneously fit the high-technology learning environment where the coordination and collection of multiple sources of information and the sharing of that information across networked computers enables the dynamic presentation of information and products involved in learning projects. In short, the physical organization of the classroom has an effect on how groups function during cooperative learning.

2. The Learning Task

Classroom tasks range from those that focus on basic recall of information through to highly complex tasks that require students to share their expertise when trying to resolve them. Learning tasks can be completed individually through to those that are broken up and worked on simultaneously at different levels in an integrated way. For example, a science topic on the solar system can be divided up so that each member studies one planet and then reports back to the group on what he or she has found (horizontal level) or, alternatively, all group members can study the solar system, noting similarities and differences among the planets (vertical level). When these two approaches are combined (horizontal and vertical), the groups are working at an integrated level where all members are required to think critically and reason constructively to develop theories or hypotheses regarding the identified similarities and differences.

Tasks that are integrated are often complex and open-ended, requiring students to discuss information and share resources; hence there is a high level of cooperation among group members. With this type of task, where there are no set answers and the problem is open and discovery based, students must share their resources (i.e., information, knowledge, and ideas) and task-related interactions are vital to productivity (Cohen, 1994). Interestingly, research has consistently shown that it is the frequency of students' task-related interactions that is related to achievement gains on follow-up content-referenced tests and conceptual development in mathematics (Cohen, Lotan, & Leechor, 1989). Similarly, Gillies (2004b) and Gillies and Ashman (1998) have consistently found that task-related interactions, such as providing directions and help to peer group members, enhance learning among students in elementary and high school settings. Research clearly indicates that student interactions are affected by the type of task they undertake during cooperative learning.

3. The Teacher's Instructional Behavior

Teachers use a range of instructional behaviors, depending on the setting in which they are operating and the type of activity they are teaching. For example, when teachers are directing students prior to the start of an activity or providing feedback at the culmination of an activity, they may choose to do that as part of a whole-class activity. At other times, however, and particularly when they are working with individual groups of students, they may decide to act as a group facilitator or as the guide on the side rather than the sage on the stage. In other words, teachers' instructional behavior is very much influenced by the type of activity they are involved in with their students.

Interestingly, in a study that investigated the different verbal behaviors of teachers in whole-class and small-group settings, Herzt-Lazarowitz and Shachar (1990) found that the structure of the classroom affected the ways teachers interacted with their students. For example, when teachers implement cooperative learning in contrast to whole-class instruction, they increase their positive instructional behaviors so they are more encouraging of students' efforts and facilitating of students' discussions, and they drastically reduce negative instructional behaviors such as disciplining students, interrupting students' verbalizations, and hurrying students when they work. The difference in the discourses was so marked that the authors concluded that when teachers implement cooperative learning where they interact with small groups as opposed to large ones, they become involved in a complex process of linguistic change as well. Their language becomes more personal and intimate and less authoritarian as they reach out to their students. Given that classrooms of the future are likely to involve students' spending more time working on tasks in small groups around different multimedia, it is heartening to know that this very structure may help to moderate the ways teachers interact with their students. This is very important, given that Gillies and Boyle (2006) reported that students model the verbal behaviors their teachers demonstrate and they use these behaviors in their interactions with each other.

4. The Teacher's Communicative Behavior

In many ways, the teacher's behavior as an instructor is related to his or her behavior as a communicator or organizer of communication networks in the classroom. Hertz-Lazarowitz (1992) proposes that these networks can range from *unilateral communications* where teachers talk directly to students through to bilateral and multilateral systems of communication existing on several levels. These levels can include teachers' interacting with an individual, small group, whole class, and finally, as facilitators of communication among and between groups. The impetus to build and promote these communication networks rests with teachers, but given the expectation that students are expected to be actively involved in their own learning, wise teachers are likely to continually act to facilitate these networks to encourage open patterns of communication among students and the sharing of both personnel and material resources.

There is no doubt that teachers will become increasingly immersed with students as partners in learning in which multidisciplinary teaching will become commonplace as teachers share their expertise and skills more widely with both students and their teaching colleagues (Almog & Hertz-Lazarowitz, 1999). This way of working will be particularly important as it will have implications for how teachers communicate with students and how students, in turn, learn during cooperative learning.

5. The Students' Academic Behaviors

Students' academic behaviors in classrooms range from the simple and passive where they listen to teachers talk but do not interact, through to highly interactive behaviors as students work on complex tasks that require evaluative and creative academic skills. There is a wealth of research available that attests to the fact that students' problem-solving and reasoning skills are enhanced when they have opportunities to work with others on open and discovery-based tasks where they are required to share ideas, justify suggestions, and resolve differences to arrive at a solution to the problem at hand (Rojas-Drummond & Mercer, 2003). The interaction that results helps students to sharpen their perspectives and focus their thinking, which, in turn, often helps them to gain a clearer understanding of the problem than they had previously. In effect, students learn new ways of talking and thinking when they engage with others on complex problem-solving tasks. Yet to be able to interact effectively with others, students need to have the social skills that will facilitate such interactions.

6. The Students' Social Behaviors

The social behaviors that students demonstrate are critically important for successful interactions with others. When students' social skills are well developed, they learn to listen to what others have to say, share materials and ideas, deal with differences through discussion, and resolve conflicts amicably. Students rarely demonstrate all these skills and often have to be taught those social behaviors that are required when they are interacting with others, whether in a whole-class setting or in smaller groups in the classroom. With younger children, teachers will need to teach these behaviors in explicit ways so that young children understand not only how to use them but also the effect these behaviors are likely to have on others. With adolescents, teachers will often negotiate the types of behaviors that are expected from class members if they are to work successfully together.

Establishing a code of behavior prior to an activity has the advantage of helping students to remember to monitor and self-regulate their behaviors. Furthermore, drawing attention to an infraction of the code lets the student know that it is his or her behavior that is inappropriate and not the student's worth as an individual that is being sanctioned. This is particularly important with adolescents, who can often feel quite vulnerable to criticism that they perceive as personal.

In summary, Hertz-Lazarowitz (1992) proposed that the physical organization of the classroom, the learning task, teachers' instructional and communicative behaviors, and students' academic and social behaviors are highly related and interdependent dimensions in that changes in one dimension affect what happens in other dimensions. It is important to understand this connectivity, because as expectations are placed on schools to ensure that they are more student centered in the programs they offer and students are more actively involved in their own learning, changes are likely to occur in how classrooms of the future are structured, particularly given that such learning environments are likely to be more open and have flexible grouping arrangements that enable students to move among small groups to work on different types of tasks.

Students are also more likely to be using a wider variety of resources, both technological and human, as they work on negotiated tasks. This means that teachers are going to be required to look at teaching from a more multidisciplinary perspective because they are not going to be a "font of all knowledge" but rather partners in helping students to construct knowledge and understanding from their learning experiences. In turn, students are going to be more involved with their peers, at both an academic and a social level, as they work together on group-based tasks.

The Importance of Teamwork and Communication

Given that students are going to be spending more time working collaboratively together in classrooms of the future, it will be important that they understand the importance of teamwork and good communication. In Chapter 2, I discussed the key components of successful cooperative groups, which included ensuring that interdependence was established within the groups so that students understood that they were linked in such a way that if the group was to achieve its goal, then every member had likewise to achieve his or hers. When students understand that their goals are interdependent, they will map onto this understanding a state of psychological interdependence; it is this state that contributes to a sense of group cohesion and identity (Slavin, 1996). Once students have developed this sense of "group," they will be more willing to listen to what others have to say, promote each other's learning, and pull together as a team.

Certainly, being able to work together as a team is critical for the success of cooperative learning. Teamwork and cooperation are dependent upon students' being able to demonstrate those interpersonal and small-group skills that are essential for building relationships among members. In fact, there are a number of studies that demonstrate that children work better and achieve higher learning outcomes when they have been trained in the social skills needed to manage group behaviors (Gillies, 2003a; Gillies & Ashman, 1996, 1998). Moreover, students are more likely to be accepted as friends when they demonstrate care and concern for others, a willingness to help others succeed, and a commitment to completing group tasks (Johnson & Johnson, 1989). Interestingly, in a recent meta-analysis of the effects of cooperative learning on students in middle school, Roseth, Johnson, Johnson, and Fang (2006) found that there was such a strong positive relationship between interpersonal attraction or friendship and academic achievement that they recommended that teachers who want to increase students' academic achievements need to ensure that each student has a friend. Friendship is a very powerful determinant of academic achievement, and teachers will need to structure group experiences that enable students to build those social relationships that help to develop mutual respect.

CHAPTER SUMMARY

The research on future developments in using small-group learning suggests

- Comprehensive school reform movements support the use of small-group learning as a pedagogical practice that promotes learning.
- Teachers need to participate in ongoing professional development to keep abreast of research-based learner centered practices that work.
- Learning and teaching will become more student centered as students work in flexible grouping arrangements in the future.
- Technology will be interwoven into teaching programs to enable students to access information from multiple sources, engage in problem solving together, and collaborate to create new knowledge and understandings.
- Students will be expected to assume more autonomy as learners while teachers act as facilitators during the learning process.
- Classrooms of the future will be better integrated as the effects of different dimensions (i.e., the physical organization, the learning task, teachers' instructional and communicative behaviors, and students' academic and social behaviors) on students' learning are more clearly understood.
- Teachers will become partners with students in the learning process.
- Teachers will need to be more multiskilled and multidisciplinary as they are required to use multiple resources and to have a wider understanding of different discipline bases that inform teaching and learning.
- Students will need to be able to work in teams and have well-developed communicative skills.
- Friendship is a powerful determinant of academic success.

ACTIVITIES

1. Arrange to visit a science-technology center to investigate changing technologies and their predicted effects on the way people will manage their daily lives in the future. See if you can identify how these changes will affect students and schools. Construct a matrix of current and future developments to present to your group for discussion.

2. Interview an experienced teacher and discuss the following aspects of the changing classroom environment. See if he or she can identify changes that have occurred over the past 10 years and how they have affected his or her teaching.

3. Reflect on your own experience as a student to see if you can identify how teaching has changed over that period of time. You may like to consider the following in your reflections: professional training, teaching style, physical facilities, student composition, curriculum expectations, community expectations, and more.

Changing Classroom Environment Checklist	*Changes Observed*	*Comments*
1. The physical organization of the classroom		
2. The different types of learning tasks		
3. The teachers' instructional behaviors		
4. The teacher's communicative behaviors		
5. Students' academic behaviors		
6. Students' social behaviors		

SUGGESTIONS FOR FURTHER READING

Allington, R., Johnson, P., & Day, J. (2002). Exemplary fourth-grade teachers. *Language Arts, 79*(6), 462–466.

Burris, C. (2005). A special section on the achievement gap—Closing the achievement gap by detracking. *Phi Delta Kappan, 86,* 594–602.

Hershberg, T. (2005). Value-added assessment and systemic reform: A response to the challenge of human capital development. *Phi Delta Kappan, 87,* 276–284.

McCombs, B. (2001, Spring). What do we know about learners and learning? The learner-centered framework: Bringing the educational system into balance. *Educational Horizons,* pp. 182–193.

CLASSROOMS OF THE FUTURE WEB SITES

Schools for the Future: http://www.teachernet.gov.uk/management/resources financeandbuilding/schoolbuildings/sbschoolsforthefuture/

Classrooms of the Future: http://news.bbc.co.uk/1/hi/education/1749817.stm

Classrooms of the Future: Thinking Out of the Box: http://schoolstudio .engr.wisc.edu/futureclassrooms.html

Glossary

Achievement: Attainments in learning; can be measured by both formal and informal tests

Affective development: The social and emotional aspects of a student's development; positive social and emotional development promotes psychological health and well-being.

Anecdotal records: Informal records of students' progress

ASK to THINK-TEL WHY strategy: A questioning strategy designed to help students ask different types of questions that promote higher-level complex thinking

Attributes: Personal qualities that help identify an individual

Authentic assessment: Measures student learning in a real-life context against specific performance criteria

Case studies: Enable the investigation of particular issues through theories, principles, and practices as they occur in the real world

Child's zone of proximal development: The developmental zone for learning where more competent others can help a child maximize his or her potential to learn; the zone where the child's learning can be extended with the assistance of more competent others

Cognitive coach: An individual who scaffolds another's thinking and learning to progressively higher levels

Cognitive conflict: Opposing answers or solutions that challenge students to reassess the discrepancies they are confronting

Cognitive processes: Thinking strategies

Cognitive roles: Roles adopted by students to provide feedback about specific tasks the group undertook (e.g., the relationships between the predictions and the theories)

Collaboration: A form of cooperation where students work together to help each other but there is no positive goal interdependence

Collaborative strategic reading (CSR): Students dialogue together in small groups to enhance their comprehension of text; students learn to generate questions to help them to predict what the text is about, identify words or concepts they don't understand, recognize the main idea, and reflect on the key questions a good teacher might ask about what they have just read.

Comprehensive school reform programs: Programs that target high-poverty and low-achieving schools to help them implement reforms that are grounded in scientifically based research and effective practices

Computer-supported peer assessment: Assessment occurs in a virtual environment using the computer as the medium to promote interactions and learning.

Concept map: A visual representation of the relationships among different elements in a theme or problem

Cooperative learning: Group members working together to accomplish shared goals

Criterion-referenced assessment: Achievement goals are clearly specified so that students understand what they are expected to accomplish; criteria are usually based on expectations in the different syllabi for students' achievements for specific core learning outcomes and the associated knowledge

Curriculum-based assessment: Assessment based on work in the curriculum

Decenter: This occurs when a child is forced to consider the perspectives of others and accommodate the conflicting information.

Dialogic exchanges: Interactions between individuals

Effective schools: Schools that make a difference in students' learning; also referred to as successful schools

Epistemic script: Specifies and helps sequence knowledge construction activities; designed to guide learners toward specific aspects of the task and toward specific task-orientated activities to help students learn how to elicit information from each other during collaborative learning

Exemplary teachers: Teachers who are regarded as very effective because they know how to motivate students: they create warm, caring environments that encourage students to take risks, think deeply, and challenge abilities, and they set high expectations for their students.

Exploratory talk: Ways in which children can be helped to interact and discuss ideas

Formative assessment: Provides information that informs the ongoing teaching and learning process

Generalize skills: Transfer of skills learned in one setting to another

Generalization: Applying knowledge or skills learned in one situation to a new situation

Generative thought: Individuals actively generate or construct their own ideas and learning based on the information available

Generic: General or common, such as a general list

Group processing: Group members discuss or reflect on how they are managing the learning process.

Guided reciprocal peer questioning: A peer questioning strategy designed to enhance students' comprehension of information learned in class

Heterogeneous groups: Mixed-ability and/or -gender groups

High-stakes testing: Mandatory testing that carries sanctions if students in schools fail to meet required proficiency levels

Ill-structured task: Task that tends to be open or discovery based, requiring students to exchange ideas and information in order to come up with solutions.

Individual accountability: Students understand that each will be held accountable for his or her contributions to the group

Initiation-response-feedback (IRF) exchange: This generally occurs when teachers ask questions to which students already know the answer; it tends to limit the chances for students to engage in an extended exchange

Intellectual reconstruction: A move by the child to accommodate and assimilate new ideas and understandings

Internalization: A process of accommodating an understanding of a situation

Interpersonal and small-group skills: The skills students need to use to communicate effectively with each other: express their ideas, acknowledge the contributions of others, deal with disagreements and manage conflicts, share resources fairly, take turns, and engage in democratic decision making

Inter-psychological level: Between individuals

Intra-psychological level: Within an individual

Learning disabilities: Difficulties with learning owing to a developmental impairment

Means interdependence: Students need to share resources, fulfill different roles, or complete tasks in order to achieve the group's goal.

Mediated-learning behaviors: Behaviors designed to promote thinking and foster learning in students. Such behaviors include prompting, scaffolding, challenging, and asking questions.

Mental schemata: Systems of organizing or structuring information

Meta-analysis: A group of studies that is analyzed to try to determine common trends and outcomes

Metacognitive awareness: Children learn to develop an awareness of their own learning, of how and what they know and need to learn

Metacognitive scaffolding: Questions, prompts, or cues that helps students to think about their thinking. For example, questions such as, "Is there anything else that we need to consider?" are designed to help students reflect on what they have considered and what else they may still need to include.

Metacognitive thinking: High-level complex thinking; students work on problems that require them to evaluate and create solutions.

Mnemonic: A mental technique for making information easier to remember

Multiple intelligences: A theory of intelligence developed by Howard Gardner that proposes that intelligence cannot be reduced to a single construct but rather that individuals have different types of intelligences that they use in different contexts to help them solve problems or create products that are valued by the community

No Child Left Behind (NCLB) Act (2001): An act introduced by President George W. Bush that aims at ensuring that all students, including those who are disadvantaged, achieve academic proficiency.

Outcomes interdependence: Students strive to achieve a goal or reward for their efforts.

Paraphrase: A short restatement of the main point

Pedagogical practices: Teaching strategies that help students learn

Peer assessment: Students assess each other's work, often using set criteria for providing feedback.

Peer tutoring: Students work in pairs with a more-able student or tutor teaching a less-able student or tutee; cross-age tutoring occurs when older students teach younger students; collaborative tutoring occurs when students of equal ability work together to solve a problem.

Person-centered approach: Teaching and learning that focus on the personal and interpersonal relationships, beliefs, and perceptions that are affected or supported by the educational system as a whole. Teachers who adopt person-centered approaches project hope to students, convince them of their worth and ability to succeed, and respect and honor their perspectives.

Personal agency: Children's sense of control as learners

Personal constructivism: A theory of learning proposed by Piaget that emphasizes the intrapersonal dimensions of learning; knowledge is not transmitted directly from one individual to another but is mediated through interacting with others.

Portfolio: Examples of work that reflect learning, often taken from multiple sources; may include different curriculum documents such as lesson plans, units of work, and samples of students' work such as DVDs, CDs, and other multimedia presentations as well as samples of their written work.

Positive interdependence: This involves all members' working together to complete the group's goal, with each member's contribution being indispensable in attaining that goal; each group member has a unique contribution to make to help the group achieve its goal.

Problem-based inquiry: Problem-based inquiries involve students' working together to seek a common solution to the problem they are investigating; also used by teachers to collect both formative and summative information on students' learning and problem-solving skills

Promotive interaction: Students understand that they must actively encourage each other's equal participation in the discussions and promote each other's learning.

Reciprocal teaching: Students work in small groups to generate questions to assist their comprehension of written text.

Reform practices: Student-centered approach to learning; students work in small groups on problem-based activities

Rubric: Checklist for evaluating work

Scaffolding: Modeling problem-solving behaviors; prompting

Scripted cooperation: Students work in pairs where each alternatively acts as the listener or recaller to recount information they have been researching together.

Self-regulated strategy development (SRSD): An approach to helping students improve their writing performance by teaching them specific dialoguing strategies and self-monitoring strategies

Self-talk strategies: Students engage in positive self-talk to promote their self-confidence in managing a task.

Small-group learning: Students are not linked interdependently around a goal but often work individually to achieve their own goals.

Social constructivism: A theory of learning proposed by Vygotsky that emphasizes the interpersonal dimensions of learning; children are introduced to new patterns of thought when they engage in dialogues with others.

Standardized tests: Formal tests that have been norm referenced or standardized on large populations of students so that expectations for proficiency at different ages can be identified

Structured groups: The five key elements of cooperative learning—positive interdependence, promotive interaction, individual accountability, interpersonal and small-group skills, and group processing—are present.

Student-centered learning: Students are actively involved in their own learning, as opposed to traditional learning where students are passively involved because the teacher directs the learning in the classroom.

Success for All: An approach to comprehensive school reform that is based on reforming school reading practices

Summative assessment: Measures what students have learned or have accomplished at the end of a period of instruction

Task-focused behaviors: Students exhibit behaviors that are focused on the task they are working to complete.

Taxonomy: Method of classifying information from simple to complex

Transactive process: Students are equal participants in providing help and assistance to each other as they learn.

Unilateral communication: Teachers talk directly to students, as opposed to bilateral communication where teachers and students interact interchangeably with each other or multilateral communication where several individuals interact with each other.

Well-structured task: Task that involves set answers; student interactions are minimal because they are required only to exchange information and explanations or to request assistance.

Whole-class instruction: Traditional didactic teaching where the teacher stands at the front of the class and directs or instructs the students.

References

About CSR. (2004). Retrieved March 25, 2006, from the U.S. Department of Education Web site: http://www.ed.gov/print/programs/compreform/2pager.html

Abrami, P. (2001). Understanding and promoting complex learning using technology. *Educational Research and Evaluation, 7,* 113–136.

Abrami, P., Chambers, B., Poulsen, C., DeSimone, C., & Howden, J. (1995). *Classroom connections: Understanding and using cooperative learning.* Montreal: Harcourt Brace.

Abrams, L., Pedulla, J., & Madaus, G. (2003). Views from the classroom: Teachers' opinions of statewide testing programs. *Theory Into Practice, 42*(1), 18–29.

Alfassi, M. (1998). Reading for meaning: The efficacy of reciprocal teaching in high school students in remedial reading classes. *American Educational Research Journal, 35,* 309–332.

Allington, R., Johnson, P., & Day, J. (2002). Exemplary fourth-grade teachers. *Language Arts, 79*(6), 462–466.

Almog, T., & Hertz-Lazrowitz, R. (1999). Teachers as peer learners: Professional development in an advanced computer learning environment. In A. O'Donnell & A. King (Eds.), *Cognitive perspectives on peer learning* (pp. 285–311). Mahwah, NJ: Lawrence Erlbaum.

Antil, L., Jenkins, J., Wayne, S., & Vadasy, P. (1998). Cooperative learning: Conceptualizations, and the relation between research and practice. *American Educational Research Journal, 35,* 419–454.

Ayres, P., Sawyer, W., & Dinham, S. (2004). Effective teaching in the context of a grade 12 high-stakes external examination in New South Wales, Australia. *British Educational Research Journal, 30,* 141–165.

Bales, R. (1970). *Personality and interpersonal behavior.* New York: Holt, Rinehart & Winston.

Bandura, A. (2001). Social cognitive theory: An agentic perspective. *Annual Review of Psychology, 52,* 1–26.

Battistich, V., & Watson, M. (2003). Fostering social development in preschool and the early elementary grades through cooperative classroom activities. In R. Gillies & A. Ashman (Eds.), *Cooperative learning: The social and intellectual outcomes of learning in groups* (pp. 19–35). London: RoutledgeFalmer.

Becker, W., & Carnine, D. (1980). Direct instruction: An effective approach to educational intervention with the disadvantaged and low performers. In B. B. Lahey & A. Kazdin (Eds.), *Advances in clinical child psychology* (pp. 429–473). New York: Plenum.

Black, P., Harrison, C., Lee, C., Marshall, B., & Wiliam, D. (2004). Working inside the black box: Assessment for learning in the classroom. *Phi Delta Kappan, 86*(1), 8.

Black, P., & Wiliam, D. (1998a). Assessment and classroom learning. *Assessment in Learning, 5,* 7–74.

Black, P., & Wiliam, D. (1998b). Inside the black box: Raising standards through classroom assessment. *Phi Delta Kappan, 80*(2), 139.

Bloom, B. (Ed.), Kengelhart, M., Furst, E., Hill, W., & Krathwohl, D. (1956). *Taxonomy of educational objectives: The classification of educational goals. Handbook 1: Cognitive domain.* New York: David McKay.

Boekaerts, M., & Corno, L. (2005). Self-regulation in the classroom: A perspective on assessment and intervention. *Applied Psychology: An International Review, 54,* 199–231.

Borman, G., Hewes, G., Overman, L., & Brown, S. (2003). Comprehensive school reform and achievement: A meta-analysis. *Review of Educational Research, 73*(2), 125–230.

Borman, G., & Slavin, R. (2005). Success for all: First-year results from the national randomized field trial. *Educational Evaluation and Policy Analysis, 27,* 1–22.

Borman, G., Slavin, R., Cheung, A., Chamberlain, A., Madden, N., & Chambers, B. (2005). Success for all: First-year results from the national randomized field trial. *Educational Evaluation and Policy Analysis, 27,* 1–22.

Boxtel, C., van der Linden, J., Roelofs, E., & Erkens, G. (2002). Collaborative concept mapping provoking and supporting meaningful discourse. *Theory Into Practice, 41*(1), 40–46.

Brown, A., & Palincsar, A. (1988). Guided, cooperative learning and individual knowledge acquisition. In L. Resnick (Ed.), *Cognition and instruction: Issues and agendas.* Hillsdale, NJ: Lawrence Erlbaum.

Brown, J., Collins, A., & Duguid, P. (1988). Situated cognition and the culture of learning. *Educational Researcher, 18*(1), 32–42.

Brush, T., & Saye, J. (2001). The use of embedded scaffolds with hypermedia-supported student-centered learning. *Journal of Educational Multimedia and Hypermedia, 10,* 333–356.

Bryant, D., Vaughn, S., Linan-Thompson, S., Ugel, N., Hamff, A., & Hougen, M. (2000). *Learning Disability Quarterly, 23*(4), 238–252.

Cazden, D. (1983). Peekaboo as an instructional model: Discourse development at school and at home. In B. Bain (Ed.), *The sociogenesis of language and human conduct: A multidisciplinary book of readings.* New York: Plenum.

Chambers, B., Abrami, P., McWhaw, K., & Therrien, M. (2001). Developing a computer-assisted tutoring program to help children at risk learn to read. *Educational Research and Evaluation, 7,* 223–239.

Chinn, C., O'Donnell, A., & Jinks, T. (2000). The structure of discourse in collaborative learning. *Journal of Experimental Education, 69,* 77–89.

Christensen, C., Aaron, S., & Clark, W. (2005). Can schools improve? *Phi Delta Kappan, 86*(7), 545–553.

Cohen, E. (1994). Restructuring the classroom: Conditions for productive small groups. *Review of Educational Research, 64*, 1–35.

Cohen, E. (1998). Making cooperative learning equitable. *Educational Leadership, 56*, 18–21.

Cohen, E., & Lotan, R. (1995). Producing equal-status interaction in the heterogeneous classroom. *American Educational Research Journal, 32*, 99–120.

Cohen, E., Lotan, R., Abram, P., Scarloss, B., & Schultz, S. (2002). Can groups learn? *Teachers College Record, 104*, 1045–1068.

Cohen, E., Lotan, R., & Catanzarite, L. (1990). Treating status problems in the cooperative classroom. In S. Sharan (Ed.), *Cooperative learning theory and research* (pp. 203–229). New York: Praeger.

Cohen, E., Lotan, R., & Leechor, C. (1989). Can classrooms learn? *Sociology of Education, 62*, 75–94.

Cohen, E., Lotan, R., Scarloss, B., & Arellano, A. (1999). Complex instruction: Equity in cooperative learning classrooms. *Theory Into Practice, 38*, 80–86.

Comer, J. (2005). Child and adolescent development: The critical missing focus in school reform. *Phi Delta Kappan, 86*(10), 757–766.

Comprehensive School Reform Program. (2004). Retrieved March 25, 2006, from the U.S. Department of Education Web Site: http://www.ed.gov/programs/compreform/gtepcomprefom.pdf

Cowie, H., & Berdondini, L. (2001). Children's reactions to cooperative group work: A strategy for enhancing peer relationships among bullies, victims, and bystanders. *Learning and Instruction, 11*, 517–530.

Cuban, L. (2004). Assessing the 20-year impact of multiple intelligences on schooling. *Teachers College Record, 106*, 140–146.

Damon, W. (1984). Peer education: The untapped potential. *Journal of Applied Developmental Psychology, 5*, 331–343.

Damon, W., & Phelps, W. (1989). Critical distinctions among three approaches to peer education. *International Journal of Educational Research, 13*, 9–19.

Darling-Hammond, L., & Snyder, J. (2000). Authentic assessment of teaching in context. *Teaching and Teacher Education, 16*, 525–545.

DeJong, F. (1995). Process-oriented instruction: Some considerations. *European Journal of Psychology of Education, 10*(4), 317–323.

Desoete, A., Roeyers, H., & De Clercq, A. (2003). Can offline metacognition enhance mathematical problem solving? *Journal of Educational Psychology, 95*, 188–200.

Deutsch, M. (1949). A theory of co-operation and competition. *Human Relations, 11*, 129–152.

Doise, W. (1990). The development of individual competencies through social interaction. In H. Foot, M. Morgan, & R. Schute (Eds.), *Children helping children* (pp. 43–64). Chichester, UK: Wiley.

Doise, W., & Mugny, G. (1984). *The social development of the intellect.* Oxford, UK: Pergamon.

Dolezal, S., Welsh, L., Pressley, M., & Vincent, M. (2003). How nine third-grade teachers motivate student engagement. *Elementary School Journal, 103*, 239–267.

Emmer, E., & Gerwels, M. (2002). Cooperative learning in elementary classrooms: Teaching practices and lesson characteristics. *Elementary School Journal, 103,* 75–92.

Engel, M., Pulley, R., & Rybinski, A. (2003). *Authentic assessment: It really works.* Master's action research project, Saint Xavier University and Skylight. (ERIC Document Reproduction Service Number ED 479 959) Available online from: http://eric.ed.gov/ERICDocs/data/ericdocs2/content_storage_01/0000000b/80/23/24/cf.pdf

Executive summary. (2004). Retrieved June 24, 2006, from the U.S. Department of Education Web site: http://www.ed.gov/print/nclb/overview/intro/execsumm.html

The facts about . . . math achievement. (2004). Retrieved January 28, 2006, from the U.S. Department of Education Web Site: http://www.ed.gov/print/nclb/methods/math/math.html

The facts about . . . science achievement. (2004). Retrieved January 28, 2006, from the U.S. Department of Education Web site: http://www.ed.gov/print/nclb/methods/science/science.html

Felner, R., Jackson, A., Kasak, D., & Mulhall, P. (1997). The impact of school reform for the middle years. *Phi Delta Kappan, 78*(7), 528–543.

Foley, K., & O'Donnell, A. (2002). Cooperative learning and visual organisers: Effects on solving mole problems in high school chemistry. *Asia Pacific Journal of Education, 22,* 38–50.

Fuchs, L., Fuchs, D., Hamlett, C., Phillips, N., Karns, K., & Dutka, S. (1997). Enhancing students' helping behavior with conceptual mathematical explanations. *Elementary School Journal, 97,* 223–249.

Fullan, M. (1998). Breaking the bonds of dependency. *Educational Leadership, 55*(7), 6–11.

Gage, N., & Berliner, D. (1998). *Educational psychology* (6th ed.). New York: Houghton Mifflin.

Gardner, H. (1983). *Frames of mind: The theory of multiple intelligences.* New York: Basic Books.

Gardner, H. (1999). *Intelligence reframed: Multiple intelligences for the 21st century.* New York: Basic Books.

Gillespie, C., Ford, K., Gillespie, R., & Leavell, A. (1996). Portfolio assessment. *Journal of Adolescent and Adult Literacy, 39,* 480–491.

Gillies, R. (2003a). The behaviors, interactions, and perceptions of junior high school students during small-group learning. *Journal of Educational Psychology, 95,* 137–147.

Gillies, R. (2003b). Structuring cooperative group work in classrooms. *International Journal of Educational Research, 39,* 35–49.

Gillies, R. (2003c). Structuring cooperative learning experiences in primary school. In R. Gillies & A. Ashman (Eds.), *Cooperative learning: The social and intellectual outcomes of learning in groups* (pp. 36–53). London: RoutledgeFalmer.

Gillies, R. (2004a). The effects of communication training on teachers' and students' verbal behaviours during cooperative learning. *International Journal of Educational Research, 41,* 257–279.

Gillies, R. (2004b). The effects of cooperative learning on junior high school students during small group learning. *Learning and Instruction, 14*, 197–213.

Gillies, R. (2006). Teachers' and students' verbal behaviours during cooperative and small-group learning. *British Journal of Educational Psychology, 76*, 271–287.

Gillies, R., & Ashman, A. (1995). The effects of gender and ability on students' behaviours and interactions in classroom-based work groups. *British Journal of Educational Psychology, 65*, 211–225.

Gillies, R., & Ashman, A. (1996). Teaching collaborative skills to primary school children in classroom-based work groups. *Learning and Instruction, 6*, 187–200.

Gillies, R., & Ashman, A. (1998). Behavior and interactions of children in cooperative groups in lower and middle elementary grades. *Journal of Educational Psychology, 90*, 746–757.

Gillies, R., & Boyle, M. (2005). Teachers' scaffolding behaviours during cooperative learning. *Asia Pacific Journal of Teacher Education, 33*, 243–259.

Gillies, R., & Boyle, M. (2006). Ten Australian elementary teachers' discourse and reported pedagogical practices during cooperative learning. *Elementary Journal, 106*(5), 429–451.

Goddard, R., Hoy, W., & Woolfolk Hoy, A. (2004). Collective efficacy beliefs: Theoretical developments, empirical evidence, and future directions. *Educational Researcher, 33*, 3–14.

Good, T., Burross, H., & Mccaslin, M. (2005). Comprehensive school reform: A longitudinal study of school improvement in one state. *Teachers College Record, 107*(10), 2205–2226.

Graham, S., & Harris, K. (2005). Improving the writing performance of young struggling writers: Theoretical and programmatic research from the Center on Accelerating Student Learning. *Journal of Special Education, 39*, 19–34.

Graham, S., Harris, K., & Mason, L. (2005). Improving the writing performance, knowledge, and self-efficacy of struggling young writers: The effects of self-regulated strategy development. *Contemporary Educational Psychology, 30*, 207–241.

Graves, A., Plasencia-Peinado, J., Deno, S., & Johnson, J. (2005). Formatively evaluating the reading progress of first-grade English learners in multiple-language classrooms. *Remedial and Special Education, 26*, 215–225.

Green, C., & Tanner, R. (2005). Multiple intelligences and online teacher education. *ELT Journal, 59*(4), 312–321.

Gulikers, J., Bastiaens, T., & Kirschner, P. (2004). A five-dimensional framework for authentic assessment. *Education Technology, Research and Development, 52*(3), 67–86.

Guskey, T. (2002). Professional development and teacher change. *Teachers and Teaching: Theory and Perspectives, 8*, 381–391.

Hackmann, D., & Schmitt, D. (1997). Strategies for teaching in a block-of-time schedule. *National Association for Secondary School Principals (NASSP) Bulletin, 81*, 588–596.

Hart, E., & Speece, D. (1998). Reciprocal teaching goes to college: Effects for postsecondary students at risk for academic failure. *Journal of Educational Psychology, 90*, 670–681.

Hartup, W., & Stevens, N. (1997). Friendships and adaptation in the life course. *Psychological Bulletin, 121,* 355–370.

Herrington, J., & Oliver, R. (2000). An instructional design framework for authentic learning environments. *Educational Technology, Research and Development, 48,* 23–48.

Hertz-Lazarowitz, R. (1992). Understanding interactive behaviors: Looking at six mirrors of the classroom. In R. Hertz-Lazarowitz & N. Miller (Eds.), *Interaction in cooperative groups: The theoretical anatomy of group learning* (pp. 71–101). New York: Cambridge University Press.

Hertz-Lazarowitz, R. (2004). Storybook writing in first grade. *Reading and Writing: An Interdisciplinary Journal, 17,* 267–299.

Hertz-Lazarowitz, R., & Shachar, H. (1990). Teachers' verbal behavior in cooperative and whole-class instruction. In S. Sharan (Ed.), *Cooperative learning: Theory and research* (pp. 77–94). New York: Praeger.

Hickey, M. (2004). Can I pick more than one project? Case studies of five teachers who used MI-based instructional planning. *Teachers College Record, 106,* 77–86.

Hmelo-Silver, C. (2004). Problem-based learning: What and how do students learn? *Educational Psychology Review, 16,* 235–266.

Hoerr, T. (2004). How MI informs teaching at New City school. *Teachers College Record, 106,* 40–48.

Hoffman, J., Assaf, L., & Paris, S. (2001). High-stakes testing in reading: Today in Texas, tomorrow? *Reading Teacher, 54*(5), 482–494.

Hunt, P., Staub, D., Alwell, M., & Goetz, L. (1994). Achievement by all students within the context of cooperative learning groups. *Journal of the Association for Persons With Severe Handicaps [JASH], 19,* 290–301.

Hunt, T. (2005). Education reforms: Lessons from history. *Phi Delta Kappan, 87*(1), 84–96.

Ivey, A., & Bradford Ivey, M. (2003). *Intentional interviewing and counselling: Facilitating client development in a multicultural society.* Pacific Grove, CA: Brooks/Cole.

Jenkins, J., Antil, L., Wayne, S., & Vadasy, P. (2003). How cooperative learning works for special education and remedial students. *Exceptional Children, 69,* 279–292.

Johnson, D. (2003). Social interdependence: Interrelationships among theory, research, and practice. *American Psychologist, 58,* 934–945.

Johnson, D., & Johnson, F. (2003). *Joining together: Group theory and group skills* (8th ed.). Boston: Allyn & Bacon.

Johnson, D., & Johnson, R. (1989). *Cooperation and competition: Theory and research.* Edina, MN: Interaction Book Company.

Johnson, D., & Johnson, R. (1990). Cooperative learning and achievement. In S. Sharan (Ed.), *Cooperative learning: Theory and research* (pp. 23–37). New York: Praeger.

Johnson, D., & Johnson, R. (1999). Making cooperative learning work. *Theory Into Practice, 38,* 67–73.

Johnson, D., & Johnson, R. (2000). Cooperative learning, values, and culturally plural classrooms. In M. Leicester, C. Modgil, & S. Modgil (Eds.), *Classroom issues: Practice, pedagogy and curriculum* (pp. 15–28). London: Falmer Press.

Johnson, D., & Johnson, R. (2002). Learning together and alone: Overview and meta-analysis. *Asia Pacific Journal of Education, 22*, 95–105.

Johnson, D., & Johnson, R. (2003). Student motivation in cooperative groups: Social interdependence theory. In R. Gillies & A. Ashman (Eds.), *Cooperative learning: The social and intellectual outcomes of learning in groups* (pp. 136–176). London: RoutledgeFalmer.

Johnson, D., Johnson, R., & Holubec, E. (1990). *Circles of learning* (3rd ed.). Edina, MN: Interaction Book Company.

Johnson, D., Johnson, R., & Stanne, M. (1989). Impact of goal and resource interdependence on problem-solving success. *Journal of Social Psychology, 129*, 621–629.

Johnson, D., Johnson, R., & Stanne, M. (2000). *Cooperative learning methods: A meta-analysis*. Retrieved January 29, 2001, from http:/www.clcrc.com/pages/cl-methods.html

Johnson, D., Johnson, R., Stanne, M., & Garibaldi, A. (1990). Impact of group processing on achievement in cooperative groups. *Journal of Social Psychology, 130*, 507–516.

Jordan, D., & Le Metaias, J. (1997). Social skilling through cooperative learning. *Educational Research, 39*, 3–21.

Kagan, S., & Kagan, M. (1994). The structural approach: Six keys to cooperative learning. In S. Sharan (Ed.), *Handbook of cooperative learning methods* (pp. 115–133). Westport, CT: Guilford.

Kim, J., & Sunderman, G. (2005). Measuring academic proficiency under the No Child Left Behind Act: Implications for educational equity. *Educational Researcher, 34*(8), 3–13.

King, A. (1990). Enhancing peer interaction and learning in the classroom through reciprocal questioning. *American Educational Research Journal, 27*, 664–687.

King, A. (1994). Guided knowledge construction in the classroom: Effects of teaching children how to question and how to explain. *American Educational Research Journal, 31*, 338–368.

King, A. (1997). ASK to THINK-TEL WHY: A model of transactive peer tutoring for scaffolding higher level complex learning. *Educational Psychologist, 32*, 221–235.

King, A. (1999). Discourse patterns for mediating peer learning. In A. O'Donnell & A. King (Eds.), *Cognitive perspectives on peer learning* (pp. 87–116). Mahwah, NJ: Lawrence Erlbaum.

King, A. (2002). Structuring peer interaction to promote high-level cognitive processing. *Theory Into Practice, 41*, 33–40.

Klinger, J., Vaughn, S., Arguelles, M., Hughes, M., & Leftwich, S. (2004). Collaborative strategic reading: Real-world lessons from classroom teachers. *Remedial and Special Education, 25*(5), 291–302.

Kluger, A., & DeNisi, A. (1996). The effects of feedback interventions on performance: A historical review, a meta-analysis, and a preliminary feedback intervention theory. *Psychological Bulletin, 119*, 254–284.

Kock, A., Sleegers, P., & Voeten, M. (2004). New learning and the classification of learning environments in secondary education. *Review of Educational Research, 74*, 141–170.

Kohn, A. (2000). Burnt at the high stakes. *Journal of Teacher Education, 51,* 315–327.

Konings, K., Brand-Gruwel, S., & Merrienboer, J. (2005). Towards more powerful learning environments through combining the perspectives of designers, teachers, and students. *British Journal of Educational Psychology, 75,* 645–660.

Lederer, J. (2000). Reciprocal teaching of social studies in inclusive elementary classrooms. *Journal of Learning Disabilities, 33,* 91–106.

Lisi, R., & Golbeck, S. (1999). Implications of Piagetian theory for peer learning. In A. O'Donnell & A. King (Eds.), *Cognitive perspectives on peer learning* (pp. 3–38). Mahwah, NJ: Lawrence Erlbaum.

Lou, Y., Abrami, P., & d'Apollonia, S. (2001). Small group and individual learning with technology: A meta-analysis. *Review of Educational Research, 71,* 449–521.

Lou, Y., Abrami, P., Spence, J., Poulsen, C., Chambers, B., & d'Apollonia, S. (1996). Within-class grouping: A meta-analysis. *Review of Educational Research, 66,* 423–458.

Lyle, S. (1999). An investigation of pupil perceptions of mixed-ability grouping to enhance literacy in children aged 9–10. *Educational Studies, 25,* 283–297.

Manset-Williamson, G., & Nelson, J. (2005). Balanced strategic reading instruction for upper-elementary and middle school students with reading disabilities: A comparative study of two approaches. *Learning Disability Quarterly, 28,* 59–74.

Mason, L. (2004). Explicit self-regulated strategy development versus reciprocal questioning: Effects on expository reading comprehension among struggling readers. *Journal of Educational Psychology, 96,* 282–296.

McCaffrey, D., Hamilton, L., Stecher, B., Klein, S., Bugliari, D., & Robyn, A. (2001). Interactions among instructional practices, curriculum, and student achievement: The case of standards-based high school mathematics. *Journal of Research in Mathematics Education, 32,* 493–517.

McCombs, B. (2001, Spring). What do we know about learners and learning? The learner-centered framework: Bringing the educational system into balance. *Educational Horizons,* 182–193.

McInerney, D., & McInerney, V. (1998). *Educational psychology: Constructing learning* (4th ed.). Frenchs Forest, N.S.W: Pearson Education.

McInerney, D., & McInerney, V. (2002). *Educational psychology: Constructing learning* (3rd ed.). Sydney: Prentice Hall.

McMaster, K., & Fuchs, D. (2002). Effects of cooperative learning on the academic achievement of students with learning disabilities: An update on Tateyama-Sniezek's review. *Learning Disabilities Research and Practice, 17,* 107–117.

McWhaw, K., Schnackenberg, H., Sclater, J., & Abrami, P. (2003). From cooperation to collaboration: Helping students become collaborative learners. In R. Gillies & A. Ashman (Eds.), *Cooperative learning: The social and intellectual outcomes of learning in groups* (pp. 69–86). London: RoutledgeFalmer.

Meisinger, E., Schwanenflugel, P., Bradley, B., & Stahl, S. (2004). Interaction quality during partner reading. *Journal of Literacy Research, 36,* 111–140.

Meloth, M., & Deering, P. (1999). The role of the teacher in promoting cognitive processing during collaborative learning. In A. O'Donnell & A. King (Eds.), *Cognitive perspectives on peer learning* (pp. 235–255). Mahwah, NJ: Lawrence Erlbaum.

Mercer, N. (1996). The quality of talk in children's collaborative activity in the classroom. *Learning and Instruction, 6,* 359–377.

Mercer, N., Fernandez, M., Dawes, L., Wegerif, R., & Sams, C. (2003). Talk about texts at the computer: Using ICT to develop children's oral and literate abilities. *Reading Literacy and Language, 37,* 81–89.

Mercer, N., Wegerif, R., & Dawes, L. (1999). Children's talk and the development of reasoning in the classroom. *British Educational Research Journal, 25,* 95–111.

Micklo, S. (1997). Math portfolios in the primary grades. *Childhood Education, 73*(4), 194–199.

Miller, N., & Harrington, H. (1990). A situational identity perspective on cultural diversity and teamwork in the classroom. In S. Sharan (Ed.), *Cooperative learning: Theory and research* (pp. 39–75). New York: Praeger.

Mitchell, S., Reilley, R., Bramwell, F., Solnosky, A., & Lilly, F. (2004). Friendship and choosing groupmates: Preferences for teacher-selected vs. student-selected groupings in high school science classes. *Journal of Instructional Psychology, 31,* 20–32.

Mugny, G., & Carugati, F. (1989). *Social representations of intelligence.* Cambridge, UK: Cambridge University Press.

Mugny, G., & Doise, W. (1978). Socio-cognitive conflict and structure of individual and collective performances. *European Journal of Social Psychology, 8,* 181–192.

National Center for Education Statistics. (2005). Retrieved November 2, 2005, from http://nces.ed.gov/programs/coe/2005/charts

National Center for Fair & Open Testing (2005). *The limits of standardized tests for diagnosing and assisting student learning.* Retrieved October 30, 2006, http://www.fairtest.org/facts/Limits%20of%20Tests.html

National trends in mathematics by percentiles. (2005). National Center for Education Statistics. Retrieved January 30, 2006, from the National Center for Education Statistics Web site: http://nces.ed.gov/nationsreportcard/ltt/results2004/nat-math-percentile.asp

National trends in reading by percentiles. (2005). National Center for Education Statistics. Retrieved January 30, 2006, from the National Center for Education Statistics Web site: http://nces.ed.gov/nationsreportcard/ltt/results2004/nat-reading-percentile.asp

Nelson-Le Gall, S., & DeCooke, P. (1987). Same-sex and cross-sex help exchanges in the classroom. *Journal of Educational Psychology, 79,* 67–71.

Newcomb, A., & Bagwell, C. (1995). Children's friendship relations: A meta-analytic review. *Psychological Bulletin, 117,* 306–347.

O'Donnell, A. (1999). Structuring dyadic interaction through scripted cooperation. In A. O'Donnell & A. King (Eds.), *Cognitive perspectives on peer learning* (pp. 179–196). Mahwah, NJ: Lawrence Erlbaum.

O'Donnell, A., & Dansereau, D. (2000). Interactive effects of prior knowledge and material format on cooperative teaching. *Journal of Experimental Education, 68*(2), 101–118.

O'Donnell, A., Dansereau, D., Hall, R., Skaggs, L., Hythecker, V., Peel, J., & Rewey, K. (1990). Learning concrete procedures: Effects of processing strategies and cooperative learning. *Journal of Educational Psychology, 82,* 171–177.

O'Donnell, A., Dansereau, D., & Rocklin, T. (1987). Cognitive, social/affective, and metacognitive outcomes of scripted cooperative learning. *Journal of Educational Psychology, 79*, 431–437.

Palincsar, A. (1998). Keeping the metaphor of scaffolding fresh—A response to C. Addison Stone's "The metaphor of scaffolding: Its utility for the field of learning disabilities." *Journal of Learning Disabilities, 31*, 370–373.

Palincsar, A. (1999). Designing collaborative contexts: Lessons from three research programs. In A. O'Donnell & A. King (Eds.), *Cognitive perspectives on peer learning* (pp. 151–177). Mahwah, NJ: Lawrence Erlbaum.

Palincsar, A., & Herrenkohl, L. (1999). Designing collaborative contexts: Lessons from three research programs. In A. O'Donnell & A. King (Eds.), *Cognitive perspectives on peer learning* (pp. 151–177). Mahwah, NJ: Lawrence Erlbaum.

Palincsar, A., & Herrenkohl, L. (2002). Designing collaborative contexts. *Theory Into Practice, 41*, 26–35.

Paris, S., & Hoffman, J. (2004). Reading assessments in kindergarten through third grade: Findings from the centre for the improvement of early reading achievement. *Elementary School Journal, 105*, 199–217.

Pedersen, S., & Liu, M. (2003). Teachers' beliefs about issues in the implementation of a student-centered learning environment. *Educational Technology, Research and Development, 51*(2), 57–76.

Pedulla, J., Abrams, L., Madaus, G., Russell, M., Ramos, M., & Miao, J. (2003). *Perceived effects of state mandated testing programs on teaching and learning: Finding from a national survey of teachers.* Chestnut Hill, MA: National Board on Educational Testing and the Public Policy.

Pentecost, T., & James, M. (2000). Creating a student-centered physical chemistry class. *Journal of College Science Teaching, 30*, 122–126.

Peterson, K. (2005). *No let up in unrest over Bush school law.* Retrieved January 30, 2006, from http://www.stateline.org/live/ViewPage.action?siteNodeId=137&languageID

Peterson, S., & Miller, J. (2004). Comparing the quality of students' experiences during cooperative learning and large-group instruction. *Journal of Educational Research, 97*, 123–133.

Piaget, J. (1950). *The psychology of intelligence.* London: Routledge & Kegan.

Plata, M., & Trusty, J. (2005). Effects of socioeconomic status on general and at-risk high school boys' willingness to accept same-sex peers with LD. *Adolescence, 40*(157), 47–66.

Posner, D. (2004). What's wrong with teaching to the test? *Phi Delta Kappan, 85*(10), 749.

Prins, F., Sluijsmans, D., Kirschner, P., & Strijbos, J. (2005). Formative peer assessment in a CSCL environment: A case study. *Assessment and Evaluation in Higher Education, 30*, 417–444.

Putnam, J., Markovchick, K., Johnson, D., & Johnson, R. (1996). Cooperative learning and peer acceptance of students with learning disabilities. *Journal of Social Psychology, 136*, 741–752.

Questions and answers on NCLB—Reading. (2003). Retrieved January 28, 2006, from the U.S. Department of Education Web site: http://www.ed.gov/print/nclb/methods/reading/reading.html

Rahm, J. (2004). Multiple-modes of meaning making in a science center. *Science Education, 88,* 223–247.

Rogoff, B. (1990). *Apprenticeship in thinking: Cognitive development in social context.* New York: Oxford University Press.

Rohrbeck, C., Ginsburg-Block, M., Fantuzzo, J., & Miller, T. (2003). Peer-assisted learning interventions with elementary school students: A meta-analytic review. *Journal of Educational Psychology, 95,* 240–257.

Rojas-Drummond, S., & Mercer, N. (2003). Scaffolding the development of effective collaboration and learning. *International Journal of Educational Research, 39,* 99–111.

Roseth, C., Johnson, D., Johnson, R., & Fang, F. (2006, April). *Effects of cooperative learning on middle school students: A meta-analysis.* Paper presented at the annual general meeting of the American Education Research Association, San Francisco.

Ross, J. (1995). Effects of feedback on student behavior in cooperative learning groups in a Grade 7 math class. *Elementary School Journal, 96,* 125–143.

Rutter, M., & Maughn, B. (2002). School effectiveness findings 1979–2002. *Journal of School Psychology, 40,* 451–475.

Ryan, J., Reid, R., & Epstein, M. (2004). Peer-mediated intervention studies on academic achievement for students with EBD. *Remedial and Special Education, 25,* 330–341.

Saenz, L., Fuchs, L., & Fuchs, D. (2005). Peer-assisted learning strategies for English language learners with learning disabilities. *Exceptional Children, 71,* 231–247.

Sahlberg, P., & Berry, J. (2002). One and one is sometimes three in small group mathematics learning. *Asia Pacific Journal of Education, 22,* 82–94.

Sammons, P., Hillman, J., & Mortimore, P. (1995). *Key characteristics of effective schools: A review of school effectiveness research.* London: Office of Standards in Education.

Shachar, H. (1997). Effects of a school change project on teachers' satisfaction with their work and their perceptions of teaching difficulties. *Teaching and Teacher Education, 13,* 799–813.

Shachar, H. (2003). Who gains what from cooperative learning: An overview of eight studies. In R. Gillies & A. Ashman (Eds.), *Cooperative learning: The social and intellectual outcomes of learning in groups* (pp. 103–118). London: RoutledgeFalmer.

Shachar, H., & Sharan, S. (1994). Talking, relating, and achieving: Effects of cooperative learning and whole-class instruction. *Cognition and Instruction, 12,* 313–353.

Sharan, S. (1990). Cooperative learning and helping behaviour in the multi-ethnic classroom. In H. Foot, M. Morgan, & R. Shute (Eds.), *Children helping children* (pp. 151–176). London: Wiley.

Sharan, S., & Shaulov, A. (1990). Cooperative learning, motivation to learn, and academic achievement. In S. Sharan (Ed.), *Cooperative learning: Theory and research* (pp. 173–202). New York: Praeger.

Simons, R., Van der Linden, J., & Duffy, T. (Eds.). (2000). *New learning.* Dordrecht, The Netherlands: Kluwer Academic.

Slavin, R. (1996). Research on cooperative learning and achievement: What we know, what we need to know. *Contemporary Educational Psychology, 21,* 43–69.

Slavin, R. (1999). Comprehensive approaches to cooperative learning. *Theory Into Practice, 38,* 74–79.

Slavin, R. (2004a). Built to last: Long-term maintenance of Success for All. *Remedial and Special Education, 25*(1), 61–66.

Slavin, R. (2004b). Education research can and must address "What works" questions. *Educational Researcher, 33*(1), 27–28.

Slavin, R., & Cooper, R. (1999). Improving intergroup relations: Lessons learned from cooperative programs. *Journal of Special Issues, 55*, 647–663.

Smeets, E., & Mooij, T. (2001). Pupil-centred learning, ICT, and teacher behaviour: Observations in educational practice. *British Journal of Educational Technology, 32*, 403–417.

Sroufe, L., Bennett, C., Engluns, M., Urban, S., & Schulman, S. (1993). The significance of gender boundaries in preadolescence: Contemporary correlates and antecedents of boundary violation and maintenance. *Child Development, 64*, 455–466.

Stevahn, L., Johnson, D., Johnson, R., Green, K., & Laginski, A. (1997). Effects on high school students of conflict resolution training integrated into English literature. *Journal of Social Psychology, 137*, 302–315.

Stevens, R. (2003). Student team reading and writing: A cooperative learning approach to middle school literacy instruction. *Educational Research and Evaluation, 9*, 137–160.

Stevens, R., & Slavin, R. (1995). The cooperative elementary school: Effects on students' achievement, attitudes, and social relations. *American Educational Research Journal, 32*, 321–351.

Stiggins, R. (2002). Assessment crisis: The absence of assessment FOR learning. *Phi Delta Kappan, 83*(10), 758.

Stiggins, R. (2005). From formative assessment to assessment FOR learning: A path to success in standards-based schools. *Phi Delta Kappan, 87*(4), 324–330.

Strough, J., Swenson, L., & Cheng, S. (2001). Friendship, gender, and preadolescents' representations of peer collaboration. *Merrill-Palmer Quarterly, 47*, 475–500.

Taylor, B., Pressley, M., & Pearson, D. (2000). *Effective teachers and schools: Trends across recent studies.* Washington, DC: National Education Association.

Terwel, J. (2003). Cooperative learning in secondary education: A curriculum perspective. In R. Gillies & A. Ashman (Eds.), *Cooperative learning: The social and intellectual outcomes of learning in groups* (pp. 54–68). London: RoutledgeFalmer.

Topping, K. (2005). Trends in peer learning. *Educational Psychology, 25*, 631–645.

Topping, K., & Ehly, S. (2001). Peer assisted learning: A framework for consultation. *Journal of Educational and Psychological Consultation, 12*, 113–132.

Topping, K., Smith, E., Swanson, I., & Elliot, A. (2000). Formative peer assessment of academic writing between postgraduate students. *Assessment and Evaluation in Higher Education, 25*, 149–166.

Tuckman, B. (1965). Developmental sequence in small groups. *Psychological Bulletin, 63*, 384–399.

Turner, J., Midgley, C., Meyer, D., Gheen, M., Anderman, E., Kang, Y., & Patrick, H. (2002). The classroom environment and students' reports of avoidance strategies in mathematics: A multimodal study. *Journal of Educational Psychology, 94*, 88–106.

U.S. Department of Education. (2001). *No Child Left Behind.* Washington, DC: U.S. Department of Education, Office of the Secretary.

Varrella, G. (2000). Science teachers at the top of their game: What is teacher expertise? *Clearing House, 74*(1), 43–45.

Vaughn, S., Klingner, J., & Bryant, D. (2001). Collaborative strategic reading as a means to enhance peer-mediated instruction for reading comprehension and content-area learning. *Remedial and Special Education, 22,* 66–74.

Vermette, P., Harper, L., & DiMillo, S. (2004). Cooperative and collaborative learning . . . with 4–8 year olds: How does research support teachers' practice? *Journal of Instructional Psychology, 31*(2), 130–134.

Vygotsky, L. (1978). *Mind in society: The development of higher psychological processes.* Cambridge, MA: Harvard University Press.

Walker, V. (2000). Valued segregated schools for African American children in the south, 1935–1969: A review of common themes and characteristics. *Review of Educational Research, 70,* 253–285.

Warfield, J., Wood, T., & Lehman, J. (2005). Autonomy, beliefs and learning of elementary mathematics teachers. *Teaching and Teacher Education, 21, 439–456.*

Webb, N. (1984). Sex differences in interaction and achievement in cooperative small groups. *Journal of Educational Psychology, 76,* 33–44.

Webb, N. (1985). Student interaction and learning in small groups: A research summary. In R. Slavin, S. Sharon, S. Kagan, R. Hertz-Lazarowitz, C. Webb, & R. Schmuck (Eds.), *Learning to cooperate, cooperating to learn* (pp. 5–15). New York: Plenum.

Webb, N. (1991). Task-related verbal interaction and mathematics learning in small groups. *Journal for Research in Mathematics Education, 22,* 366–389.

Webb, N. (1992). Testing a theoretical model of student interaction and learning in small groups. In R. Hertz-Lazarowitz & N. Miller (Eds.), *Interaction in cooperative groups* (pp. 102–119). Cambridge, UK: Cambridge University Press.

Webb, N., & Farivar, S. (1994). Promoting helping behavior in cooperative small groups in middle school mathematics. *American Educational Research Journal, 31,* 369–395.

Webb, N., & Farivar, S. (1999). Developing productive group interaction in middle school mathematics. In A. O'Donnell & A. King (Eds.), *Cognitive perspectives on peer learning* (pp. 117–150). Mahwah, NJ: Lawrence Erlbaum.

Webb, N., & Mastergeorge, A. (2003). Promoting effective helping in peer-directed groups. *International Journal of Educational Research, 39,* 73–97.

Webb, N., Nemer, K., Chizhik, A., & Sugrue, B. (1998). Equity issues in collaborative group assessment: Group composition and performance. *American Educational Research Journal, 35,* 607–651.

Webb, N., Nemer, K., Kersting, N., Ing, M., & Forrest, J. (2004). *The effects of teacher discourse on student behavior and learning in peer-directed groups.* Report No. 627, Center for the Study of Evaluation, University of California, Los Angeles.

Webb, N., & Palincsar, A. (1996). Group processes in the classroom. In D. Berliner & R. Calfee (Eds.), *Handbook of educational psychology* (3rd ed., pp. 841–873). New York: Macmillan.

Webb, N., Troper, J., & Fall, R. (1995). Constructive activity and learning in collaborative small groups. *Journal of Educational Psychology, 87,* 406–423.

Weinberger, A., Ertl, B., Fischer, F., & Mandl, H. (2005). Epistemic and social scripts in computer-supported collaborative learning. *Instructional Science, 33,* 1–30.

Weissenburger, J., & Espin, C. (2005). Curriculum-based measures of writing across grade levels. *Journal of School Psychology, 43,* 153–169.

Wertsch, J. (1979). From social interaction to higher psychological processes: A clarification and application of Vygotsky's theory. *Human Development, 22,* 1–22.

Wertsch, J. (1984). The zone of proximal development: Some conceptual issues. In J. Wertsch & B. Rogoff (Eds.), *Children's learning in the zone of proximal development* (pp. 7–18). San Francisco: Jossey-Bass.

Wiggins, G. (1998). *Educative assessment: Designing assessments to inform and improve student performance.* San Francisco: Jossey-Bass.

Wiliam, D., Lee, C., Harrison, C., & Black, P. (2004). Teachers developing assessment for learning: Impact on student achievement. *Assessment in Education, 11,* 49–64.

Wittrock, M. (1990). Generative processes of comprehension. *Educational Psychologist, 24,* 345–376.

Woolfolk, A. (1998). *Educational psychology* (7th ed.). Boston: Allyn & Bacon.

Zimitat, C., & Miflin, C. (2003). Using assessment to induct students and staff into the PBL tutorial process. *Assessment and Evaluation in Higher Education, 28,* 17–32.

Index

Ability groupings, 124–125
Accountability, interdependence and, 39–41
Affective development, cooperative
  learning and, 49–50
Anecdotal records, 163
ASK to THINK-TEL WHY strategy, 8, 24,
  111–113
  five questions of, 204–206
  high order thinking and, 116–117
  points of, 206
  tasks and, 211
Assessing small group learning, 155–190
  authentic assessments, 173–175
  case studies and, 175–176
  computer supported peer assessment,
    161–171
  criterion-referenced, 172–173
  curriculum-based assessments 158–160
  exhibitions of performance 177
  formative assessment, 158
  learning objectives, 155–156
  peer assessment, 160–161
  portfolios, 176–177
  problem-based inquiries, 177–178
  problem-based learning using formative &
    summative assessment, 178–179
  summative, 171–172
  understanding the research, 187–190
  See also Assessment
Assessment:
  authentic, 173–174
  case studies as, 177
  computer-assisted, 161–171

criterion-referenced, 172–173
curriculum based, 158–160
exhibitions of performance as, 177
five-dimensional framework
  for authentic, 174
formative, 158
formative peer, 161
importance of, 189–190
initiation-response-feedback, 189
peer, 160–161
portfolio as, 177
problem-based inquiries as, 177–178
reform practices, 160
standardized testing
  and, 187
summative, 171–172
using authentic in different contexts,
  174–175
See also Assessing small group learning
At-risk readers, analysis of computer assisted
  tutoring program for, 143–144
Attributes of exemplary
  teachers, 194–195
Authentic assessments, 173–174

Bloom's Taxonomy, 77
Bush, George W. (President), 12–13

Case Studies:
  Case of Tom, 2–4
  defined, 175–176
  Developing Criteria for Assessing Grade
    Outcomes in Sixth Grade, 213–216

Discussion Among Students in a Small Group, 71–73

Enhancing Mandy's Low Status in Her Group, 134–137

Example of Cooperative Learning in a First-Grade Classroom, 30–33

Example of Fifth-Grade Students Dialoguing Together Using the ASK to THINK-TEL WHY Questioning Strategies, 111–113

Example of the Four Reciprocal Teaching Strategies, 94–97

Exchange Between an Eleventh-Grade Teacher and a Small Group of Students, 73–75

Exchange Between a Teacher and Small Group in her Fifth-Grade Class, 69–71

Group Discussion Among Eleventh-Grade Students, 76–77

High School Teachers' Experience with Cooperative Learning, 195–19

Middle School Teachers' Experience with a CSR Program, 224–228

Preparing a PowerPoint Presentation on Nicotine, 145–148

Principal's Story, 17–19

Teacher's Dialogue With a Small Group of Students, 62–63

Students' Perceptions of Mixed-Ability Groupings in Classroom, 122–124

Teachers' Reports on How They Assess Small-Group Learning, 156–158

Classrooms of the future, 235–241

Cognitive roles, 162

Collaborative strategic reading, 8, 101–105

Communication skills, training, teachers and, 66

Comprehensive School Reform (CSR), 221–224
effective models for, 223
implications for democratic and learner-centered teaching, 228–229
mandated components of, 222
person-centered approaches to teaching, 228

Computer assisted tutoring programs, 143–144

Computer groupings, ideas for establishing, 148–150

Computer learning:
problem-solving skills and, 234
standardized tests and, 234

Computer-supported peer assessment, 161–171
cognitive roles, 162
epistemic scripts, 162–163

Computer Technology Groupings, 140–144

Concept map, 203

Conducting Formative Assessments of Small-Group Learning, 164–171

Cooperation:
scripted, 24
tasks and, 211–212

Cooperative groups:
establishing successful, 29–58
how long students should work in, 47
structured, 29
unstructured, 29

Cooperative learning, 4–11
affective development and, 49–50
case against testing and, 15–16
classrooms of the future and, 235–240
communication skills and, 65–66, 202–304
creating environment for, 78–82, 198–199
defined, 1, 50–51
helping behaviors for, 208–211
key components of, 33–46, 65
low-ability children and, 49
major benefits of, 1–2
pedagogical practice and, 9, 17–25, 33, 68–60
whole-class versus, 63–64

Cooperative strategic reading, 24

Cooperative tasks, 53

Creating a Cooperative Learning Environment, 198–199

Criterion-Referenced Assessment, 172–173

Curriculum Based Assessments, 158–160

Decenter, 82

Developing Appropriate Helping Behaviors, 208–211

Developing Communications Skills for Group Discussion, 202–204

Dialogic exchanges, 69

Direct Instruction, CSR model, 223

Discussions, small-group, choosing tasks for 211–212

Diverse needs, catering for students with, 125–127

Epistemic scripts, 162–163
Establishing Computer Groupings, ideas for, 148–150
Examples of practice, portfolio as, 177
Exemplary teachers, attributes of 194–195
Exhibitions of Performance, 177

Facts About . . . Math Achievement, The, 13
Facts About . . . Science Achievement, The, 13
Farivar, S., 201–204
Feedback, initiation-response, 189–190
Five-dimensional framework, authentic assessment, 174
Flexible grouping arrangements, reform programs and, 227
Focal elements, of teachers, 10–11
Formative assessment, 158, 178–179
    anecdotal records and, 163
    research on, 163
    small-group learning, 164–171
Formative peer assessment, 161
Friendship groupings, 130–134
Future developments, 219–241

Generalizations, 206
Generative thought process, 117
Group(s):
    cooperative, teacher's role in composition of, 52–53
    developing communications for discussion, 202–204
    inform of expected behaviors, 55
    mixed ability, 125–127
    multiple intelligences, 137–138
    promoting student talk, 144–150
    responsibilities of students to self and group, 55
    same-gender, studies of, 53
    size of, 7
    small, 5, 122–150, 219–241.
        See also Small group
    student interest questionnaire and, 141–142
    students monitor process of, 55–58
    surveying students' interests, 140
    teachers monitor and review students' progress during coop work, 213
    unstructured, 6
Group identity, five stages of, 47

Grouping:
    ability, 124–125
    computer technology, 140–144
    friendship, 130–134
    gender, 127–128
    ideas for establishing computer, 148–150
    interest, 138–140
    teachers' perspective on, 129
Grouping practice, 6–7, 152–153
Group members, positive interdependence and, 4
Group processing, 5–6
    ideas for, 45
    interdependence and, 43–45
Group task, 6
Guided reciprocal peer questioning, 8, 24, 108–110

Help-seeking behaviors, of students, 209–210

Individual accountability, 5
Information computer technology, 233
Intellectual reconstruction, 84
Interdependence:
    accountability, 39–41
    cooperative groups and, 47
    ensuring individual accountability, 39–41
    five stages of group identity, 47
    group processing and, 43–45
    ideas for group processing, 45
    interpersonal and small-group skills, 41–43
    means, 34
    metacognitive thinking and, 44
    outcomes, 34
    outcomes interdependence and, 34
    positive, 33, 35–36
    promoting ways of, 37–39
    promotive, 36–39
    structured groups and, 41
    types of, 34–48
Interest groupings, 138–140
Interest inventory, questionnaire, 141–142
Internalization, 85
Interpersonal and small-group skills, 5, 41–44
Inter-psychological, 116
Intra-psychological, 116
Iowa Scope, Sequence and Coordination Project, 10

Key Points on Summative Assessments and Their Purposes, 179–180
King, A., ASK to THINK-TEL WHY and, 204–206

Learning environment, creating, 78–82
Low-ability children, cooperative learning and, 49
Low-status student, 135–137

Mandatory testing:
    effectiveness of, 16–17
    impact on cooperative learning, 11–12
    impact on teachers, 15
    teachers' perceptions of, 14–15
Mediated learning:
    behaviors of, 64, 206–208
    teacher's role in promoting, 206–208
    types of, 66–67
Mental schemata, 116
Meta-analysis, peer-assisted learning interventions, 53
Metacognitively aware, 117
Metacognitive scaffolds, 199
Metacognitive skills, 204–306
Metacognitive thinking, 44
Mixed ability groups, ideas for establishing, 126–127
Model, Six Mirrors of the Classroom, 236–240
Multiple intelligences, 137–138

National Assessment of Educational Progress, 13
National Board on Educational Testing and Public Policy, 14–15
National Center for Education Statistics, 16–17
National Center for Fair & Open testing, 15–16
Negotiate Expectations for Small-Group Behaviors, 201–202
New American Schools Development Corporation, 223
No Child Left Behind Act, 2, 23, 155, 221
    mandatory testing and, 13–14
    President George W. Bush and, 12–13
    specific requirements of, 12–17
    testing and, 12–14

Paraphrasing, 205
Pedagogical practice, scaffolding as, 68–69
Pedagogy:
    cooperative learning and, 17–25, 229
    practices of, 11, 33, 68–69
    teachers role in, 9
Peer, guided tutoring, ASK to THINK-TEL WHY strategy and, 204–206
Peer assessment, 161–171
Peer assisted learning intervention, meta-analysis and, 53
Peer-mediated strategies, 8–9
Peer questioning, guided reciprocal, 24
Peer tutoring, 7
    ASK to THINK-TEL WHY, 116–117, 204–206
    scripts, 206
Performance, exhibitions of, 177
Personal agency, 51
Personal construction, 82
Portfolios, 176–177
Positive interdependence, 33–34
Problem-based inquiries, 177–178
Problem-based learning, 178–179
Problem-solving skills, computer learning and, 234
Productive small groups, 122–150
    ability groupings, 124–125
    bringing it all together, 150–152
    catering for students with diverse needs, 125–127
    computer technology groupings, 140–144
    friendship groupings, 130–137
    gender groupings, 127–128
    interest groupings, 138–140
    multiple intelligences, 137–178
    promoting student talk, 144–150
    student interest questionnaire, 141–142
    surveying Students' Interests, 140
    teacher's perspective on grouping students, 129
Promoting student discourse, 7–9
    collaborative strategic reading and, 8
    guided reciprocal peer questioning and, 8
    reciprocal teaching and, 8
    scripted cooperation and, 8
Promoting Student Talk, 144–150

Promotive interaction, 4
Promotive interdependence, 36–39
Proximal development, child's zone of, 116

Questionnaire, student interest
    inventory, 141–142

Reciprocal teaching:
    case study of, 94–97
    dialogue script and, 24
    group practice, 7
    strategies of, 8, 93, 97–100
Reconstruction, intellectual, 84
Reconstructivism, social, 84
Reflective journal, 57–58
Reform practices, 160
Research:
    assessing small-group learning, 191–192
    formative assessments, 163
    future development in using small-group
        learning, 241–242
    grouping practices, 152–153
    student's discourse, 118–119
    teachers' cooperative learning suggestions,
        216–217
    teacher's discourse, 87–88
    when cooperative learning works best, 58–59

Same-gender groups, studies of, 53
Scaffolding, 65–66, 205
    as pedagogical practice, 68–69
School Development Program, CSR model, 223
School reform, comprehensive, 22–23
Schools:
    effective, 220–221
    high achievement in high-poverty
        schools, 220
Scripted cooperation, 8, 105–108
    dialogue script and, 24
Segregated schools, 193–195
Self-regulated strategy development,
    five stages of, 114–115
Self-talk strategies, 114–115
Sequence, 206
Six Mirrors of the Classroom model, 236–240
    learning the talk, 237
    physical organization of the classroom, 236

students' academic behaviors, 239
students' social behaviors, 239–240
teacher's communicative
    behavior, 238
teacher's instructional behavior, 237–238
Small group:
    behaviors, negotiate expectations
        for, 201–202
    cooperative learning, versus, 64–65
    discussions, choosing tasks for, 211–212
    interpersonal skills and, 5
    presentations, ideas for establishing audience
        roles during, 100–101
    productive. See Productive small groups,
Social reconstructivism, 84
Social skills training program, 201–202
Specific Metacognitive Skills That Promote
    Discourse, 204–206
Standardized testing, 187
Standardized tests, computer learning and, 234
Strategic reading, cooperative, 24
Strategies:
    ASK to THINK-TEL WHY, 8. See also ASK
        to THINK-TEL WHY strategy
    peer-mediated, 8–9
    student dialogue, reciprocal teaching and, 93
Structured groups, interdependence and, 41
Student-centered learning, 199–200
Student discourse, promoting, 7–9
Student interest questionnaire, 141–142
Student Participation in Negotiating
    Opportunities for Learning, 229–230
Students:
    help-seeking behaviors of, 209–211
    thinking and discourse, cooperative learning
        and, 61–86
Students' Discourse, research on, 118–119
Success for All, CSR model, 223–224
Summative assessment, 171–172,
    178–180
Surveying Students' Interests, 140

Tasks:
    cooperation and, 211–212
    cooperative, 53–54
    ill-structured, 211
    well-structured, 211

Teachers:
    attributes of exemplary, 194–195
    communication skills training and, 66
    determining group's size, ability,
        and gender composition, 52–53
    effective, 9–11, 194–195
    ensuring key components in
        group structures, 51–52
    expert, 9–11
    focal elements of, 10–11
    impact of state-mandatory
        testing and, 15
    learner-centered, 230
    mediated learning behaviors
        used by, 67
    monitor and review progress during
        cooperative group work, 213
    pedagogy and, 9
    perceptions of mandatory testing
        and, 14–15
    perspective on grouping students, 129
    responsibilities in establishing
        cooperative learning, 216
    role in establishing cooperative
        learning, 51–58
    role in promoting mediated learning,
        206–208
    satisfaction with cooperative
        learning and, 20–22

Teaching:
    person-centered approaches to, 228–229
    reciprocal, 24
Technology, small group learning and,
    232–235
Testing:
    case against, 15–16
    high stakes, 11–12
    standardized, 187, 234
Thought process, generative, 117
Three-part social skills training program,
    201–202
Tutoring program, computer assisted,
    analysis of, 143–144

Unilateral communications, 238
Unstructured groups, 6
Using Authentic Assessments in Different
    Contexts, 175–175

*Valued Segregated School for African-American
    Children in the South, 1935–1969: A
    Review of Common Themes and
    Characteristics* (Walker), 193–195

Walker, Vanessa, 193–195
Webb, N., 201–204
Whole-class teaching, cooperative
    learning vs., 63–64

About the Author

Robyn M. Gillies, PhD, is an associate professor in the School of Education at The University of Queensland, Brisbane, Australia. She has worked extensively in elementary, middle, and high schools to help teachers embed cooperative learning pedagogical practices into their classroom curricula and, more recently, has researched teacher and student discourses in the cooperative classroom. Her research has been published in many leading international journals, including *The Journal of Educational Psychology, The Journal of Special Education, The International Journal of Educational Research, Learning and Instruction,* and *The Elementary School Journal.* She is a trained teacher, counselor, and psychologist.